Introduction

Five of us shelter under the pseudonym, 'Fenman'. The chosen name is a reference to the fact that we originally met in the late nineteen fifties while in residence at Cambridge University, where the Railway Club provided a focal point for our activities. In fact the five of us never met all together in those days, and we have probably only done so on about half a dozen occasions since: three of these have been generated by the decision to produce this book.

Through the years which have witnessed the decline of steam motive power on the railways of Britain we have been meeting in smaller groups, sometimes by chance, more often by design, at weekends and on holiday, with the common aim of taking photographs of steam trains before it was too late. Each of us has experienced the thrill of watching steam in action and has gained the satisfaction of obtaining a lasting record of the occasion by means of photography. Friendly rivalry between us has improved our individual techniques, as has membership of the Railway Photographic Society of which each of us has been an active member at one time or another.

Although the book is primarily a collection of photographs, we have ventured to insert brief essays on subjects related to our photographic activities. Accustomed as we are in our individual professional lives to writing such items as reports on metal fatigue, specifications for waterworks, computer programmes or school reports, we have all found essay writing rather hard work, and yet the general subject, steam trains, has been our first love for many years. There is an uncomfortable suspicion

2 'Fenman'

that we might have written better when we were still at school. However, each of the five articles, or essays, embodies more of the individuality of the authors than the photographs, though even there the observant may detect differences of style. Thus we consider that the essays have a place in the book, if only to break up the endless flow of really rather similar photographs. Any reader who considers that it is his misfortune to have read our literary offerings should take comfort in the fact that we did not indulge in verse.

In assembling the pictures for inclusion in this book we have not attempted to provide a balanced, overall representation of the last ten years or so of steam on British railways, nor to conform to any particular theories on railway photography. Rather we have been governed by our own reactions to the material that we had available, and since those reactions have developed along what are now held to be conservative lines, so is the selection we have made. We bring forward the results therefore, not as a tract or a history book, but merely as a collection of pictures which have given us pleasure, and which, we hope, will gladden the eye of many who, like ourselves, find the passing of the steam locomotive an event of lamentable sadness.

John Boyd
John Coiley
Stephen Crook
David Hepburne-Scott
atque Quintus

3   Man of the Fens

IMAGES OF STEAM

Images of Steam

"Fenman"

LONDON

IAN ALLAN LTD

To all those, not in the least interested in railways, who waited patiently by the line-side while some of these pictures were taken.

First published 1968
Second impression 1974

ISBN 0 7110 0056 5

Published by Ian Allan Ltd, Shepperton, Surrey and printed in the United Kingdom by Biddles Ltd, Guildford, Surrey

Down from Cambridge

4   London bound

5   B12 for Liverpool Street

6   J15 at Shelford Junction

7   B17 at Cambridge station

8 Great Northern 0–6–0

9 Great Eastern 2–4–0

10 Clean B1

11 Ex-works A4

R.I.P.
Remaining in Photographs

The last pictures have been taken. The steam train as we have known it for over a hundred years as a means of public transport has gone for good in this country and is fast disappearing elsewhere. There never was, nor will be, anything quite like it. It enjoyed an extraordinary position in engineering and technology; it felt alive both to those fortunate enough to ride at its head or to those hauled in it. This passing is much lamented, even though understood, and the steam locomotive will never be forgotten by those who really knew it.

In view of this special character it is hardly surprising that there has always been unusual interest in the steam locomotive and the train it pulled. From the earliest days the steam train attracted attention from onlookers and became the subject for many artists. It was only logical therefore that when photography started to expand towards the end of the last century, steam trains should be a subject for this new technique. Logical it was, perhaps, but certainly not a subject ideally suited to those early cameras and emulsions. In spite of modern photographic advances it has always remained a challenge to photographers.

Who was it then who tackled such a difficult task? Until latter days they were in the main compounded of the general photographer and the serious student of railways. Undoubtedly both groups included the collector element but only towards the end of the life of the steam locomotive is there much to suggest that the collecting instinct was predominant. Nevertheless, the overall standard of railway photography continued to rise and is still improving even if suitable subjects have become increasingly difficult to find.

From the beginning however, the subject has been formidable, for it is not under the direct control of the photographer. While the train moves in a relatively prescribed manner the details and timing of this movement are not always predictable. Furthermore, the weather in particular has always been an important variable. Even the most popular subject for initial efforts, some kind of shot from the end of a station platform, can be extremely difficult, although when tackled by masters of the subject may yield some of the best of all railway pictures. In fact, the station or shed shot provides a good test of basic photographic technique; careful use of the viewfinder, focussing and estimation of exposure with extremes of illumination. In addition, problems of angle of view, composition, care for backgrounds, all arise and need attention; only the problem of movement is absent and even that may occur unexpectedly—either the subject moves off or other traffic passes the camera. Assuming however that non-stop through trains are not the aim of the photographer at this location, then he can concentrate on overcoming the exacting task already specified. Unless he wishes to photograph a train at the moment of departure, then he probably has the opportunity to take his photograph when the lighting is just right, but not necessarily with bright sun from behind him. Although all this may sound remarkably simple and obvious, experience shows that it doesn't work out that way very often, if at all—other people have a habit of doing the wrong thing at the crucial moment, smoke and steam blow the wrong way or another train obstructs the view. Nevertheless it has usually been worth persevering since the most satisfying pictures could be taken with modest equipment, including a box camera, provided that a large print was not demanded.

Such efforts may however reveal that there is a limit to the simplicity of equipment and for the last thirty or forty years it has usually been accepted that for top quality pictures, of whole plate size or larger, a four element lens was needed in a well made camera with a shutter capable of at least 1/250second for station shots, and faster if more ambitious attempts were to be made. For satisfactorily sharp pictures of trains travelling at speeds in the range 40–90mph a genuine shutter speed of 1/500–1/1000second was needed and even then a slight swinging of the camera with the train might be necessary to secure a really crisp locomotive. Jolts due to rail joints could still cause shake to the front end of the locomotive which even the very best shutters found difficult to conceal.

From before the end of the last century such cameras were available but only as relatively large heavy plate cameras best used with tripods. These cameras have continued in use until the end of steam in Britain, especially the smaller versions. In the last two decades or so with modern emulsions and the latest cleaning and treatment for the old lenses, they have produced some of the finest railway pictures ever taken. In a random collection of railway pictures from the leading railway photographers, prints from older plate cameras stand out for their sharpness and general quality. Latterly, however, their bulk and weight have told against them, and with the advent of well made smaller cameras using 35mm size film in which the hazard of grain has been minimised, plate cameras have only been used by those determined to produce the best, no matter what effort and care was needed.

Having given some thought to starting railway photography and the equipment needed, what is the pattern of progress? Almost inevitably, provided a reasonably suitable camera is available, a suitable location near to a station stop is sought. In this way a shot of a train working hard may be obtained in a site which helps build the picture. While the immediate surroundings of such locations may give the impression of a rural setting, they may in fact simply be cuttings or embankments only yards from an intensely urban environment. Alternatively, the photographer may aim to use the obviously industrial scene as a backcloth which, with skill, may be highly effective. In general, the viewpoint chosen initially will be a three-quarter front view of the train. While this probably remains the most satisfactory viewpoint for recording a particular train on a given line for example, it has become somewhat stereotyped. It is not surprising, therefore, that the last 20 years especially have seen an increasing variety of viewpoints combined with various lighting effects, together with limited use of photographic techniques including short and long focal length lenses and extremely fast emulsions.

If the results of the newer approaches contrast somewhat curiously with the work of earlier railway photographers, it must be remembered that all the conditions have changed. For the photographer of steam trains on British railways, the point of dramatic change came in 1939. In the more leisured atmosphere of the period before that momentous year, not only was the steam train the fastest method of travel available to 90% of the public but its future seemed assured almost indefinitely. In its heyday the steam train nearly always appeared hauled by a clean and often spotless locomotive and the photographer could afford to select his subject, choose his location to suit the time of day and year and wait for the weather of his choosing. Even technical features of the locomotives themselves helped, as steam was less superheated and draughting was such that more smoke was likely to be evident. It was, perhaps, fortunate that the photographer had some assistance as his emulsions were all slow, contrasty and coarse grained compared with those of today. For much of the period lenses were unbloomed and shots against the light were almost impossible.

Immediately after World War II, during which railway photography was extremely restricted, films and plates were almost unobtainable, but for the fortunate few what a feast there was! During the war engines had been moved extensively, new freight engines built and many veterans of all kinds, which would otherwise have been retired, were kept on. For the younger railway enthusiasts to whom railway photography was a new opportunity, the situation was tantalizing. Gradually cameras became available but the older engines were disappearing rapidly and new ones emerging from the works. A crisis in coal supplies brought about the conversion of some locomotives, old and new, to oil burning—even more subjects for photography. Then in 1948 came nationalisation, the locomotive exchanges and prospects of a whole new range of steam locomotives.

12A   Box camera

12B   Folding camera

The winds of change were not however confined to the railways themselves. During the war and immediately afterwards there was a great increase in the number of books and magazines available dealing exclusively with railway matters, especially locomotives. While much of this information had been available many years earlier to members of enthusiast societies, the immensely wider circulation through station bookstalls, together perhaps with the distraction from the war and its aftermath as well as the importance of the railways in the war effort, all helped to stimulate and maintain this increased interest in railways, "spotting" and subsequently photography.

The final stages of the evolution of railway photography were reached with the arrival of good colour transparency emulsions. At the same time suitable cameras for these new films became generally available and while not perhaps meeting all the exacting demands of railway photography, remained reasonably priced. At much the same time it became clear that British Railways were planning for the eventual replacement of all steam engines by electric and diesel traction. Photography of the steam train became therefore even more purposeful and as the intentions became manifest, almost frantic. By now the ever expanding band of railway enthusiasts was armed not only with good cameras, excellent emulsions (both black and white and colour) but with cars, some of them very fast. With skilful driving and intelligent use of 1-inch Ordnance Survey maps, much more could be packed into the daylight hours and on occasions the nights as well. The same train could be photographed many times in the day using cars which might have to average 50mph on circuitous cross country routes to achieve this. Even the remotest branches were invaded by the enthusiasts either in special trains or by cars in an attempt to capture the elusive branch line atmosphere. The paraphernalia multiplied. Cine cameras were to be seen in increasing numbers together with tape recorders. Perhaps, however, for reasons of cost or because these latter gadgets needed even more expert handling with still more equipment, they have never achieved such wide acceptance as single exposure cameras using black and white or colour or two such cameras coupled together so as to obtain simultaneous black and white and colour shots. Had there been more time, who knows what elaborate and costly equipment might have been used to track down and record that famed species, the steam train?

And now here in Britain the last rites have been witnessed and the last steam engines towed ignominiously away. The undoubtedly more efficient diesel and electric locomotives reign alone, but for many British Railways will never be the same again. The fortunate few will doubtless transfer their efforts to Europe and even further afield and pursue steam with even more vigour, wrestling with inferior maps, using bumpy roads to reach breathtaking locations, facing difficulties with the local dialect, trouble with spares for the car, and in some countries even risking prison in pursuit of this curious English pastime. They will however enjoy for several years yet the sight and sound of steam engines of all kinds about their normal work for which some were built many years ago.

Meanwhile in the home of the steam locomotive, there remains still the sight and sound of steam at work where it has always worked; the Festiniog Railway, the Talyllyn, the Ravenglass & Eskdale, the Romney, Hythe & Dymchurch and several others. Fortunately, these delightful lines have been joined by others such as the Bluebell, Keighley and Worth Valley, and Dart Valley, while, for the present at any rate, the main lines are scenes of splendid performances by *Flying Scotsman* and others in a select band of working restored locomotives. They will remain as lines where memories of the age of steam on British railways can be so pleasantly recalled, no matter how fleetingly, for countless railway enthusiasts, photographers among them, for many years to come.

J.A.C.

12C   Hand held

Main Line

13 Dillicar troughs

14 The Great Central at Stoke Mandeville

15 Approaching Wantage Road Station

16   The Waverley Route, near Penton

17   West of England semi-fast

18   "Atlantic Coast Express" from under cover

19   Slipping at Didcot

20   Spying on royalty

21 Fast lady

22 Dignified gentleman

23   "Clan" in summer

24   "Britannia" in winter

25   Morning in Sonning

26   Evening at Fleet

Right of way
at the
Docks

28 Southampton   27 London

West Highland

Surely we've all been to the West Highland, and most of us learnt on our first visit just how wet it can be and how long the rain can last. And the rest of us, for whom the sun shone to start with so that we went back, discovered soon enough that its reputation was not without foundation. Nevertheless, it was a fascinating line, for all its moods, where the timetable was little more than a vague hope, the length of train a constant source of speculation and the number of engines on the front totally unpredictable. It was a line which made heavy demands on the rolling stock, the gradients on the locomotives and the weather on the coaches and wagons. But they were grand the engines that worked the line, picturesque the trains they pulled behind them; set in that magnificent scenery, here are just a few.

29   Off to Glasgow on the main

30 and 31   K2s on the Extension

32   Near Glenfinnan

33 Freight from the Aluminium Works

34 Afternoon passenger to Mallaig

Rural Goods Bedford to Hitchin

38   Hawkhurst branch

39   Northiam

40   Radley to Abingdon

41   Still good for 112mph

42   Lewes

43   Langholm branch

44   Last day for the Westerham branch

45 Fawley branch

46 Approaching Didcot

Relegation

As the displacement of steam by diesel and electric power gained momentum, former express locomotives spent their last active days on less glamorous duties. During this period even the lowest class of main line freight might boast an engine with a name.

47 *Royal Tank Corps* passing Wreay

48 *Herringbone* at Gretna Junction

49 *Blink Bonny* on the Waverley Route

50 *Kenya* pulling out of Penrith

51 South of Penrith

The Folio

Take about two dozen enthusiastic railway photographers, a medium-sized box of brown board reinforced at all corners, some printed forms, postcards, gummed labels and a notebook. Place forms, labels, postcards and notebook in the box, and circulate the resultant concoction to each photographer in turn, with instructions to place two of his own photographs in the box and to criticize the photographs already placed there, to write in the notebook whatever comments he will, and to send on the complete package with the least possible delay to the next on the list. You have now founded a photographic folio.

Take to yourself a title, Secretary or President, and from it gain what consolation you can; you have spawned a monster. Photographers are only human—intractable material to organize: they move house secretly, they fall sick, they leave home unannounced on business or on holiday, and always just before the Post Office attempts to deliver the box to them; the Post Office itself grows slower with age and more expensive, occasionally its employees go on strike, and always the box is so situated as to suffer the maximum of delay. If you have never before believed in that inexorable, and unprintable, Law, that all circumstances always combine to cause the greatest disruption to those least able to take avoiding action, you soon will.

Do not, however, despair; above all, do not give up. Just because some members continually try to show that they have most of the human failings—as though the practice of photography cast doubt upon their nature and so required its continuous proof—by forgetting to enter prints or to remove them, by never finding time to criticize the prints of others or to comment in the notebook, by making bitchy criticisms or complaining that they have suffered them, by the greatest fault of all—retaining the box for more than the permitted time—because of these minor irritations, I say, do not conclude that your efforts are unvalued and ignored. The truth of this observation can easily be proved by a suggestion from you that time is short and affairs are pressing, and a call for a volunteer to take over your self-imposed task. The appreciation of your efforts that members will show, the co-operation by actually obeying the rules of your society, and the modesty in declining the honour of succeeding so altogether a noble fellow as yourself, will all combine to astonish you, until you relent.

But if it is to be a life sentence, is it really worth it? Does your struggle achieve anything apart from an exchange of views that could be made more quickly and with far less effort at a bi-monthly meeting of all members? What is there of peculiar value in the idea of a group of people, who share an enthusiasm while isolated in what may be likened to a series of hermit's cells, as far as effective contact between is concerned, joining in remote criticism of the products of that enthusiasm?

The answer, one may conjecture, lies in that very remoteness of the participants one from another. Thus they are helped to criticize in an impersonal and unbiased manner the photographs that are circulated; they are enabled to give more time to their appreciation of them; the soft-voiced and mild-mannered among the members can exert their full influence. The notebook can be used for the clear expression of considered views, which may be entered with whatever care and at whatever length their author needs for lucidity, without the constraints upon time and style that even a private gathering might impose. Above all, the relative permanence of the written word, compared with the spoken, is a strong encouragement to members to think before expressing an opinion or condemning another's.

Obviously the method has its drawbacks as well. The timeless quality that improves criticisms of members' work, and discussions of matters of principle, has no advantage in the discussion of technical questions. Unfortunately, few can any longer cease from photographic processing when they meet a particularly tricky problem, wait as long as seven or eight months for the folio to arrive, pose their question in the notebook, and then wait a further seven or eight months for the folio to return, hopefully with the collected wisdom of the other members. Such a timescale in these days could easily put a photographer out of action throughout the final reduction of British Rail to the London and Liverpool suburban services.

Well then, even if the folio system has its shortcomings for the solution of technical problems, and is of obviously limited use in the dispensing of news, to what extent is it able to perform its prime function: the encouragement of members to improve the quality of their work, as a result of criticisms levelled at it, and of seeing their photographs side by side with those produced to higher standards by more advanced workers? Clearly there is a risk that an organization with such aims and such methods of working will grow into a mutual admiration society. There is a further risk that some members will adopt an uncritical attitude towards any photograph that can be classed as an "oldie" (a term that seems now to have been stretched to include any shot more than one year old). There is yet another risk that members will play for safety, will submit examples of their conventional work only, since this style has always been found to be acceptable.

On the whole the first of these is an illusory danger, since it requires no more than one member's feeling liverish to shatter any tendency to smugness in all the others (the human element again); in any round of any folio this is practically certain to happen, and its effect as a stimulant on members can hardly be exaggerated.

Both the other two attitudes, it is suggested, are symptoms of a failure to come to grips with current reality. They seem to be based on the theory that no true railway photograph can be taken that does not include a locomotive, that the best angle from which to take a photograph of a steam locomotive is three-quarters front, and that, since post-steam traction units do not respond well to this particular treatment, only photographs of steam locomotives taken in the prescribed manner can possibly be considered as railway photography. Perhaps it might better be described as three-quarter-front-view-of-steam-hauled-train photography.

Another, more "with it", school of thought shuns this reactionary approach. A typical product of one of their members will show a dirty, out-of-focus steam locomotive seen through a thick mist against a background of clumsily placed factory chimneys; this school makes frequent use of techniques to produce heavy grain effects, but rarely to any advantage. The thought behind its pictures seems to be one of despair: it does not matter what you photograph, provided that you make it unrecognizable.

If it can persuade the older members to include only those of their early shots that illustrate a point of photographic technique, and not just those that will produce a strong feeling of nostalgia, if it can persuade the *avant garde* that railway photography should be a combination of pure AND applied, if it can encourage all its members to use their art in the representation of the current scene (whose possibilities are as yet hardly touched), then your folio can be said to be successful. And even if it does not, if it is still flourishing it must at least be supplying its members with one of the more innocent pleasures open to them and helping to keep them off the proverbial street corner. . .   Q.

52

Somerset and Dorset

(The Slow and Dirty)

53   Midford

54 Radstock

55 Cole

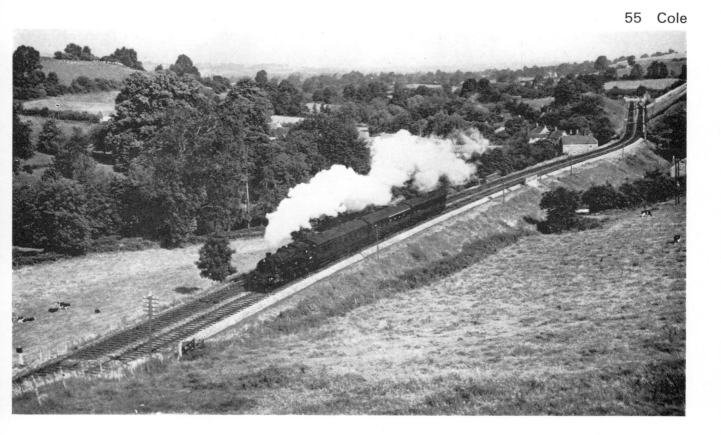

56 Shepton Montague

57 Wellow

58 Masbury

59 Highbridge branch

60   Bath
61   Home with the milk

62 and 63   Rear views

64 and 65   Castlethorpe troughs

Water, Water, Everywhere

66 Prestonpans

67 Horsted Keynes

. . . but not at . . .

68 Stamford Town

MIDLAND RAILWAY

THESE BUCKETS MUST BE KEPT
FULL OF CLEAN WATER, AND USED
ONLY IN CASE OF FIRE.
IN SEVERE FROST THEY MUST
BE EMPTIED AND ARRANGED CLOSE
TO A WATER TAP, UNLESS THEY
CAN BE TEMPORARILY KEPT IN A
CONVENIENT PLACE WHERE THE
WATER WILL NOT FREEZE.
DERBY. JAN. 1909. BY ORDER.

69 *Scott* near Rosyth

70   Slow running with a "Shire"

71   ''Glen'' on the Ballater branch

4-4-0s

72   Fast running with a ''Hunt''

73   The High Road

74   The Low Road

75   Drifting into Cambridge

76   On the banks of the River Spey

77 Fleet

Pullmans

78 Knockholt

Smoke

79 Giggleswick

80　Barmouth

81　Leeds

82 Bradford

Double-heading

83   Holiday traffic in the Mendips

84   Freight in the Pennines

8 Williamthorpe
Colliery, 1967

The Uppingham Branch

The railway to Uppingham was really a branch off a branch: it might almost have been called a twig. It left the Peterborough to Rugby cross-country line at Seaton Junction and was very short. Although the line passed under the North end of Harringworth viaduct which carried the Midland main line, there were no connections with main line trains and any traveller wishing to go further than Stamford, Peterborough or Rugby had a long journey in front of him.

In the late 'fifties the motive power was usually provided by a handsome 4–4–2 tank originating from the London, Tilbury and Southend Railway. Two were assigned to the Midland shed at Peterborough for the duty, but 41975 seemed to take the lion's share. The engine always faced up the hill to Uppingham, ran round its train and pulled it back bunker first. At the junction the bay platform was approached on a gradient and running round was not necessary. After arrival the train reversed on to the main line, the engine uncoupled and moved out of the way, and the guard allowed the single coach to run back into the bay by releasing the brake.

89 Tilbury tank on the branch

90 Victorian Gothic at Stamford Town

Goods Traffic

93 Settle to Lancaster

94 Waverley

95 Lune Valley

100   Far North

101   South from Carlisle

The A4s
Fastest of them all

102   St.Neots

103 Gleneagles

104 Between the tunnels at Welwyn

105 Dunblane

Royal Engine

106   The Royal "Claud"

107 *Royal Sovereign* at work
108 *Royal Sovereign* at home

Nostalgia for . . .

In the evening of their days, the ex-LSWR Drummond 4–4–0s of class T9 withdrew to the far West, as other defeated tribes had done before. In 1959 they left London, in 1960, Wessex; from then till the final disappearance of the class, in the summer of 1961, the survivors were shedded at Exeter to work on the North Cornwall line, which had been a particular haunt of theirs for many years.

Then came the end. And a life hereafter. With an uncharacteristic stroke the Southern Region repainted one of the last survivors in LSWR livery, and used her for two years or so on enthusiasts' specials—a "plastic Greyhound".

. . . "Greyhounds"

110   Leaving Halwill

111   By the Camel Estuary

112 Heading West

113 "Plastic"

114 Eventide

115 St. Pancras

London
by Night

116 Paddington

117 Edgware Road

118 Kings Cross

119 and 120   Euston

On Engines

I was interested to note recently that the driver of a severely derailed diesel multiple unit express, speaking at the public enquiry into the accident, claimed that the diesels ride more roughly than the old steam engines. This is indeed a harsh indictment of modern rail travel, as the ride for the passengers is the same; some of them are in the same coach. With the steam engine the passengers had their own vehicles, designed for their comfort, and the locomotive was designed, not for the comfort of the crew, but so that it stayed on the rails. In fact, riding on a steam engine is very different from travelling in the coaches. There is no sense of 'cushioning', you feel you are right down on the hard, iron road. In the cab you feel the engine swaying to the rhythm of its pulse, and rocking as it fights the changes of direction imposed on it by the track. At speed, on good track, with an engine in good condition you gain a glorious sensation of gracefully bounding along, hardly touching the rails. It is a sensation not easily forgotten.

Of course, as a young man who had no official link with the railways, opportunities to travel on the footplate did not occur frequently, and unofficial cab-riding on expresses was very rare. One of my colleagues was rather more forward than I would ever have been, but met his match when he clambered through the corridor of the A4 hauling the Elizabethan one day and was curtly told to go back the way he had come. My first invitation to travel on the engine was unusual in three respects: I mounted the engine while it was in motion, it greeted me by stalling half a mile further on, and finally I drove it back to where I wanted to get off. It was one of the last surviving 0–6–0s of the Furness Railway which I had spotted about to take a goods train from Whitehaven up the hill to Cleator. As it laboured up the gradient towards me I took a very inadequate photograph, much too soon, but with clouds of smoke, and started to put the camera away. As she came past the driver made unmistakeable signs of invitation. I ran alongside and climbed up. "She's not steaming. Bit of the brick arch fell in this morning," said the driver. Five minutes later we were sitting under a bridge raising steam for the final assault. We made it in the end, and duly deposited our train in the Cleator sidings. The crew had been expecting to go on to Workington but, rather to my relief, we were sent back light the way we had come. As it was getting dark I was anxious to be home, and after asking if I could be dropped off near where I had left the car, I was shown the brake and told to stop the engine where I wanted to. I did, stepped down, thanked them and said goodnight.

In the Railway Club at Cambridge we had official 'instruction' in engine driving once a year. In 1956 the Station Master at Cambridge one day rather challengingly remarked that our predecessors in the Club before the War had hired a train and spent a day driving it under instruction up and down a quiet branch line. With his encouragement and the willing co-operation of the Operating Department an outing was duly arranged for a day in November. A handsome, clean "Claud Hamilton" 4–4–0 was turned out, complete with a single mainline coach for those who were not on the footplate, and we spent a happy day trundling backwards and forwards along a stretch of the line to Colchester and Marks Tey. The engine was decked out with a crude headboard, a "Special" headcode, and L-plates. Unfortunately it was as gloomy a November day as one can imagine and the photographers were poorly rewarded. The next occasion was arranged for a better time of year and a most enjoyable outing was enjoyed by all concerned on April 27, 1958. The last E4 2–4–0, No. 62785, was turned out complete with a two coach train of Great Eastern origin to match. Looking now at the photographs taken on that occasion with the ancient 2–4–0 polished specially and the two antique coaches still in LNER varnish, it is difficult to believe that all the vehicles concerned were still in general service. The finishing touch was given by the provision of a cast locomotive headboard, bearing a discreet 'C.U.R.C.', which some member of the club had managed to have specially

121A   CURC Special at Haverhill

made. Engine 62785 behaved very well and responded with spirit to all the demands
made on her by her unaccustomed handlers. Subsequently she survived the scrapyard
and has been at the Clapham Museum of Transport, restored to the glorious royal
blue of the Great Eastern Railway who built her.

Engine driving activities at Cambridge have continued until recently, but in
1967 the locomotive concerned had to come from as far afield as Crewe, and it must
be doubtful if the practice will continue into 1968. This will be the last year in which
it will be possible to enjoy such an occasion with a steam locomotive in general
service on British Rail, and I suspect that there may well be sufficient enthusiasm to
track down an engine in one of its last haunts.

Concentrating on photography the opportunities for riding on the engine
usually cropped up only on the remoter branch lines and were only indulged in when
weather conditions rendered photography an unsatisfactory pastime. The T9s which
used to run alongside the Camel estuary from Wadebridge to Padstow made lovely
pictures in the sunshine, but waiting in the rain in that area was not fun; far better
to be experiencing the final fling of the South Western "Greyhounds" from the
comparative comfort of their narrow cabs. Some engines indeed seemed almost to
issue their own invitation. Such a type was the 4–4–2 tank which originated from the
London, Tilbury and Southend, and ended its life working the branch line to
Uppingham in the South Midlands. A handsome machine, as most tank engines of
this wheel arrangement tended to be, the LTS tank seemed the essence of friendliness,
with its rounded features and perfect proportions. No wonder then that the crew
was correspondingly friendly and seemed to take it as a matter of course that a
passenger would want to travel back to Seaton Junction on the engine, as photographers were wont to do because in this direction the engine was usually pointing
its less elegant end at the camera.

One summer Saturday I caught an early morning train from London down to
Kent, in the days when steam trains still ran that way and branch lines wound their
way through the hop fields. It was a very early train, soon after six o'clock departure;
I caught it on a sudden whim after arriving back after a party which had gone on

rather late. The driver of the "West Country" class pacific must have been somewhat surprised to find a passenger whose automatic action before the train left was to go and see the engine and talk to the driver. This resulted in an invitation to join him in the cab at Orpington. (It might have been tactless at Charing Cross.) The journey thence to Tonbridge was brief but thrilling. The sensation gained with a modern engine working a mainline train to a tight schedule is very different from that with an old engine spending its last days pulling a coach or two up a country branch. The fire roars, and its appetite for coal has to be matched by sustained effort by the fireman. The whole machine is alive with effort; it wants to burst with the power being generated. My recollection is of continual acceleration up the gradient to the Downs, finally storming into the tunnel at the top, with the exhaust battering the tunnel roof, and of the rapidly quickening tempo as the gradient eased and we commenced the descent into the Weald of Kent with the regulator wide open. At Tonbridge I was very torn between continuing with the engine along the dead flat and dead straight 'racing stretch' to Ashford, and my original plan for photography in the Tonbridge area. At the time financial discretion prevailed, and the galloping pacific left me to a gloomy morning and a very weary mid-day return to London.

121B

Finally, a story of the Great North of Scotland, or, more correctly, that part of Scotland in which the railway of that name used to operate. Two of us were seeking out the last of the GNoS 4–4–0s, *Gordon Highlander*, still in service from Keith shed in the spring of 1957. We had borrowed a 'bubble car' for the expedition, rather a novelty in those days, particularly in the remoter parts. After a day's photography in the district of Craigellachie and Glenlivet, where whisky distilleries are tucked into the folds in the Speyside hills, we found the Highlander about to work a Saturday morning pick-up goods to Buckie and back.   It was a day of low cloud and drizzle and cameras were firmly in their cases: we decided to follow the train, in the hope that the weather would be better at the coast. The road closely followed the line and a rendez-vous between car and train was kept at each station. Soon one of us was on the engine while the other drove the bubble car, and each section became a race. The train would usually be ahead out of the town as the car found its way back to the main road. The engine driver was most intrigued. He had never seen a bubble car before, and must have wished he could have had his turn in the car. He was always looking for it after leaving the stations and was amazed by its ability to catch up. It was a most enjoyable morning. The next time I was up in those parts *Gordon Highlander* had been restored to Great North of Scotland livery and was working a Scottish Tour special with the restored 4–6–0 of the Highland Railway. Escaped museum pieces as they were, the two gleaming engines looked magnificent in the brilliant summer sunshine, but it was not quite the real thing. It never will be.   J.L.B.

121C   Undergraduate at the regulator

Branch Lines

122   Lyme Regis

124   Teign Valley train at
        Longdown

123   Paddling in the Looe

125   Mary Tavy

129 Hayling Island

130 Hawkhurst

131   Off to Silloth

132   Longwood viaduct

133 and 134   Killin

135   Henley-on-Thames

136   Gloucester to Chalford local train

137   West Pennard

138   Lambourn branch

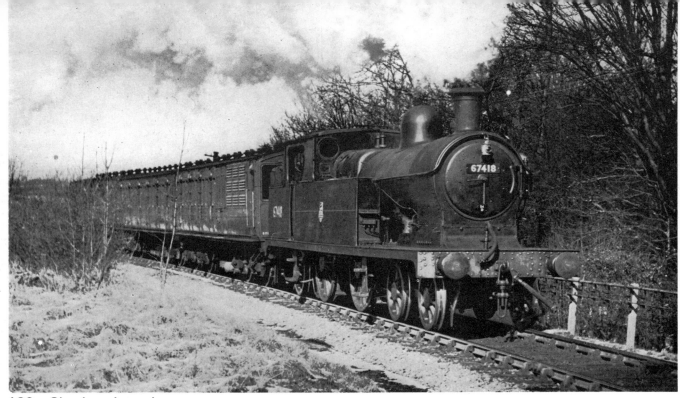

139 Chesham branch

140 Durham

141 Ballachulish

142 Marlborough

143   Bere Alston—Callington

144   Three Bridges—East Grinstead

145 Redhill

Scenes on Shed

146 Basingstoke

147   In Eastleigh MPD

148   Far North–Helmsdale

149   Down South–Tonbridge

150   Stilton Fen

151   Castlethorpe Troughs

152 Sonning Cutting

Trains

153 Whitchurch, Hants

156 Up "Bristolian"

158   The last up "Cambrian Coast Express"

Snow

159 Mad Dogs and . . .

160 Compton

161 Bourne End

63   Near Wantage
      Road

Scotland

164   Near Newcastleton

165   Car carrier in Glenfarg

166   West Coast Postal leaving Aberdeen

167   School train in Glen Ogl

168   The Garve pilo

169   "The Grampian" leaving Perth

170   Evening in Perth Yard

171 Dalbeattie

172 Foreigner on the G&SW, Annan

173 North British excursion, near Inverkeithing

Tricks of the Trade

I collect engine numbers. No, I do not mean that I spend my leisure hours on the end of station platforms, and in the evening underline the results of my observations in my 'ABC Combine'. I simply mean that I collect in transfer or replica form the numerals displayed on our locomotives before nationalisation.

The fact is that to my mind with the inception of British Railways in 1948 the appearance of all British locomotives suffered a major setback, quite apart from the colour of the paint they were later to wear. From the day that the attractive and distinctive numerals and lettering of the four former companies were painted over for the last time—to be replaced, on the tender, by a cartoon of a crest, and on the cab by the diminutive gill sans figures (which must surely be the least impressive numerals ever designed)—each engine had undergone a personality change that was definitely for the worse. The final indignity was the fitting to the smoke-box door of a plate featuring these unattractive characters, thus disfiguring what for me has always been the face of the locomotive.

In the summer of 1950 I was just starting photography; moreover my activities at this time were limited to taking engines at rest. Locomotives retaining pre-nationalisation livery were given absolute priority as choice of subject, and during my school holidays I scoured northern Britain in search of the few remaining examples. But by the following summer these had finally disappeared. As my aesthetic susceptibilities would still not permit me to register on locomotives sporting the new degrading symbols, only one course of action remained. I should have to restore the engines to their former glory by my own efforts. This meant having numbers of my own which could be applied to the engine when required.

My attentions were to be directed mainly to former LNER engines as I considered that the disappearance of their beautiful yellow and red block numerals was the greatest loss of all. By writing round to various works and transfer manufacturers I finally managed to get transfers of all the LNER numerals and letters. From these I was able to make copies that were completely accurate down to the last 'twiddly bit' in the shading, until I finally had a complete do-it-yourself renumbering outfit for buffer-beam, cabside and tender. These I then stuck to the engine with flour and water paste, which enabled them to be removed easily enough when the photographic session was over. Dirty engines were the most suitable to work on in that parts of the BR number, crest, or lining were less likely to show through—any that did were usually smeared over with the engine's own grease.

174A   Forgery—Carlisle 1955

174B   ...polished up the knocker on the big front door

This particular perversion kept me happy until 1959, when I was inspired by the work of others to start photographing moving trains. Obviously the sticking on of numbers was now no longer practicable. I suppose it could fairly be said that this aspect of my activities was replaced by cleaning all or part of the engine concerned whenever convenient. Latterly this has been common practice with many of the younger photographers; but when back in 1961 I made a modest start at sprucing up my subjects, I was considered by some to be either excessively keen, remarkably daring, or simply somewhat odd. I must admit I had a few qualms when, on a perfect summer's day at Bodmin Road Station in June 1961, I stepped straight off the platform on to the running-plate of the grimy GW 2-6-2 tank waiting to take her train over the hill to Bodmin General, and, equipped with a rag specially prepared by the driver, proceeded to massage her smoke-box with loving care and paraffin oil.

By the end of 1962 I had laid hands on the paintwork of many engines, and in particular the "Princess Royals", which, against all the odds, had been granted a new lease of life at Kingmoor. Quite apart from the highly beneficial effect any cleaning had on the anticipated photograph, it was a thoroughly enjoyable activity in itself, even if the subsequent state of my clothes and person did not always increase my popularity at home.

The other step that the photographer can take in his quest for the perfect picture is to turn his charm full on in the presence of the engine crew in an attempt to secure an impressive smoke-effect at some prearranged location. I can certainly claim no originality whatever for this practice—I merely confirm from one or two results I have had it is definitely worth trying!   s.c.c.

174C   Clean by endeavour–smoke by arrangement

Season Ticket

175 'Commuting', Gresley style

E 86242 E

Midland Four Coupled

4–4–0s of Midland Railway design became a familiar sight over most of the system of the London, Midland and Scottish Railway, which continued to build to the pre-grouping designs for several years. Long after nationalisation 2Ps were still spread over much of the country on lighter passenger work and double-heading heavy expresses. Several were at work in Scotland in the early 'sixties, both in the South-West and, more surprisingly, in the North-East, where they rubbed shoulders with 4–4–0s of Caledonian and Great North of Scotland origin. The Compounds, by way of contrast, tended to return home and the last few were to be seen on the lines for which the class was designed.

176   Inspection saloon

177 Compound at St Pancras

178 Derby, 1959

Museum
Pieces

183   Maryport and Carlisle

184   Leighton Buzzard to Dunstable

185   Milk empties at Latchmere Junction

oods

186   Barnstaple line

190   Large roundhouse

Swindon

191   On test

192   Narrow gauge too !

193   Last of the line

196 Old before t
     days

195 Tempus fug

197 Final attent

Scottish Rail Tour

In June, 1962, the Railway Correspondence and Travel Society and the Stephenson Locomotive Society organized a tour of Scotland making use of the preserved locomotives of the Scottish pre-grouping companies as motive power. Besides the Highland Railway 4–6–0 and *Gordon Highlander* pictured here, *Glen Douglas* of the North British Railway and the Caledonian 'Single' No. 123 also took part.

198   Rogart

199 Confrontation !

200 Dalnaspidal

Bluebell Railway

201

202

203

Permanent Way Trains

205 and 206   A Great Eastern J15, temporarily named *Lottie,* assisting with the removal of the track from the Cambridge to Kettering line

Over . . .

207 Ouse Valley

209 Walkham

210 Canningt•

208 Langston

211 and 212 Great Eastern
Line Suburban

213 Lifton

214   West Hoathly

215   Potters Bar

216 Glenfield

Through . . .

217 Old Warden

218 Stratton
St Margaret

219 Cambridge

. . . and off

220 Propped

221 Hoisted

Southern 4-4-0s

222 Two heads are better than one

223 Pin head

224 Big head

227 and 228   English veterans eking out their time

Banking

Back end on
Beattock

Broadside on
Shap

232

233

234

235

Scottish Goods Lines

236 Charlestown branch

237 South Queensferry

238 Bound for Balerno

239 Last day of steam at Brechin

Wadebridge to Wenford Bridge

Just look
at that !

247 Cambridge

248 . . . South End

Portrait
of the E4

249 Shelford

252   Near Blackwater

Redhill

253   Downhill into Reading

254   Passing Earley

255   Leaving Reading Southern

256 Crowthorne

257 Ash Junction

258 Feltham freight

259 Interchange working

Isle of Wight

260   Pierhead

261   Ryde St. John's

Smallbrook

264   Shanklin

265   Line's end

266A   Alnwick branch, 1957

With the end of steam on British metals now an accomplished fact, and the tendency abroad indicating that a similar situation will exist everywhere before long, to start the last decade of this country arbitrarily round about 1957 is possibly stretching it just a little, but nevertheless, we hope that it will not seem too large or unacceptable an extension. May we begin at Alnwick, latterly one of the largest stations at the end of one of the shortest branches, tucked away in the remoter regions of Northumberland, where Wilson Worsdell's class Rs (LNER class D 20) were still hauling two coach trains down to the junction at Alnmouth, and even making more ambitious expeditions to the metropolis of Newcastle? These indeed were graceful machines, their enormous driving wheels and vast splashers contrasting delicately with their slender boilers, and at the same time conferring on them a lady-like dignity in their secluded and humble retirement. At that time, everything on that disregarded off-shoot had an atmosphere of grandeur and permanence; not only did the station itself cover a huge area, but its roof was a solid symmetrical structure, in a style symbolic of stateliness, and the signal box that stood next to it was a magnificent monument towering majestically above it. And there was also the gantry, a kind of gateway to the station: together with the empty spaciousness of the trains those important-looking signals silently but resolutely implied from their airy loftiness that admittance was only for the very privileged. The turn-table worked, and was used too, though the need for it probably disappeared in 1930, when the passenger service to Coldstream

Decade

266B C12s at Stamford

ceased to operate. Yes, this was the last example of truly grandiose solidarity where no economic argument could possibly support it, but it still looked as if it would last for ever.

But there were other places to be, and similar trains to worship and photograph. The C12s still ran between Stamford and Essendine, though recently dislodged from their lair at the East station, and forced to use the Midland one, Stamford Town, instead; and on the London Transport system that incredible combination of rolling-stock, an Atlantic tank and de-electrified carriages, still plied back and forth between Chalfont & Latimer and Chesham, while at the eastern extremity, 2–4–2 tanks of Great Eastern origin made the weary plod up the hill from Ongar, before drifting with a great pant of relief down into Epping, to connect with the more modern, more comfortable and more universally appreciated—though not with the dis-crimination of the artist—electric Underground. In Scotland, as well, steam founda-tions were yet solid, though possibly less so, as people had heard of diesel railcars, some in fact used them, and this great sparsely-populated expanse seemed to be an obvious region in which to try them out on a grand scale. But, up till now, this hadn't happened; nor was it evident, except to the most perspicacious speculators, that it ever would. Nevertheless, traffic was dwindling, and this was having its effect on some of the older locomotives that were still to be found in odd corners on hum-drum duties, while even the not-so-old varieties were beginning to see that the day

266C   F5s at Epping

when they, too, would be threatened was no longer very far off. The Speyside Branch
now only very occasionally saw a Great North of Scotland 4–4–0, although Keith
depot was the home of 62277 *Gordon Highlander*, but in Fife "Scotts" and "Glens"
and also Scottish "Directors" were still putting up a good stand on the ubiquitous
stopping trains, together with the newer B1s. This, however, was the territory that
the Multiple Unit was soon to conquer.

In the West Country, Dainton was as it always was, and the doubling of the
"Kings'" chimneys proved beyond doubt that steam had longer to live. Cornwall, too,
was as yet virtually untouched, green tank engines being the most recent change,
and this again was interpreted as a manifestation of faith in the future of steam.
Indeed, looking back, those were good days, and though the end was inevitable,
and the form that it would take perfectly clear, it wasn't seriously considered to
be in sight.

If, the year before, the paint was beginning to peel of the structure of steam
haulage, it was in 1958 that cracks definitely appeared in the foundations. There was
talk of complete dieselisation west of Exeter in the very near future, and for those
who couldn't or wouldn't believe it, Norwich trains out of Liverpool Street had
already partially succumbed to the threat, and in the late summer, the 1735hrs
Newcastle to King's Cross express was regularly entrusted to an English Electric
Type 4 for a trial period. As it rumbled through Durham shortly before six o'clock
in the still of the early evening, it presented a truly hideous sight, a really revolting

smell and an almost intolerable noise; was this really progress? The second fissure in the system, destined to crumble away eventually, was the total elimination of the 2–4–0 wheel arrangement, which disappeared with the withdrawal of E4s from regular operation on the Mildenhall branch. These were quaint machines, and the even quainter coaches they hauled, fitted with moveable steps for use at those remote wayside halts with platforms barely raised above ground level. It was these little peculiarities which gave the railways so much of their interest, and enriched their appeal beyond pure attraction for the locomotive. Inevitably such refinements meant the journey took a little longer, but there is no intrinsic merit in speed, and the other advantages are usually no more than an attitude of mind.

As 1958 gave way to 1959, further locomotives, once commonplace, became scarce, and it was no longer always possible to see interesting specimens without travelling a considerable distance. But there were still surprises: who could have

266D   Worlington Golf Links Halt

foreseen the drafting of genuine Midland 7ft 2Ps to Kentish Town and their still giving a helping hand on heavy expresses out of St. Pancras? And who predicted the use of LTS 4–4–2Ts on the little line from Seaton Junction to Uppingham—a Tilbury locomotive allocated to a Midland shed (Peterborough, Spital Bridge) on a North Western branch? Yes, anomalies still existed, but most of us will remember that year for its glorious weather, when it was possible to visit even Blea Moor or Talerddig with a reasonable chance of sunshine, and when expeditions to Corrour and Attadale weren't doomed to frustration. Indeed that was the year for mountainous routes, when pairs of engines were the order of the day on heavy trains, on some lines with the weaker one on the front, on others with it marshalled next the leading coach. Whichever way round, there was always something romantic about a double-header; if a single locomotive wasn't going to be enough then it was the customary remedy just to add another, sometimes at the last minute. What a truly flexible policy, and how gloriously inefficient! Twice the man-power, and one-and-a-half times the coal consumption of a single, but larger locomotive; but for the aesthete, efficiency is never much of a consideration. Today, whether for reasons of greater productivity, or otherwise, the railways are possibly too preoccupied by the need to pay their way and to eliminate economic waste, and this may explain why they have degenerated into an uninspiring institution of unparalleled drabness.

If the sun shone bright and long in 1959, it was possibly for the last time; never after that was steam virtually supreme on all lines. Of course, there were minor

266E   Double heading on the Midland

266F   Highland Line

266G   Oban Line

266H   East Coast finale

exceptions—dwellers on the Cockermouth, Keswick and Penrith had almost forgotten what a regular steam service was like, nor did they mind forgetting—but when
the Highland line north of Perth capitulated, this was no minor incursion by the
diesel into a tiny insignificant region; a main line through a vast area of Scotland
was this time the victim of inevitable progress. It didn't happen overnight, but the
inexorable tendency was clear throughout 1960, and by the spring of 1961 only the
Kyle line of the Highland system was not completely dominated by the green box.
Worse still, the cancer was spreading to the West Highland as well, and the Callander
and Oban was undoubtedly to be the next candidate.

Other outposts, too, were changing their character: T9s were banished from
the North Cornwall line, those amazing contraptions with outside frames no longer
wound their way through the Welsh passes nor round the coast to Barmouth and
Pwllheli. On the Callington branch, there were at last locomotives that were big
enough, but to look at they were no improvement on the diminutive O2s. At this
time, a certain plainness was falling on the land, and East Anglia was very barren
indeed.

With the virtual passing of the branch line as a steam attraction—there were
still, of course, isolated and well-worn examples such as Highbridge and Lyme Regis
—attention naturally became focussed on main routes. Large pacific locomotives
could still regularly be seen at three London termini in the way that they had been
for a couple of decades, and, what is more, they were usually fairly clean, sometimes
even spotless. If the "Elizabethan" ceased to run after 1961, Leeds and Newcastle
trains frequently boasted engines in comparable condition, whilst on the rival line,
46207, the pride of Camden, really was something; gleaming red and often rostered
to the 1205 hrs departure from Euston to Liverpool, the "Red Rose", topping the
1 in 77 at the end of that formidable climb from the platform end, here indeed was
the personification of power, mighty, yet controlled, determined, but not out of hand.
But 1962 saw the end of these dignified ladies, and they gave way to fatter, more
portly matrons, an improvement mechanically, but scarcely a match in the eyes of
those particular about outline. But in spite of the "Duchess'" hunched-up appearance
from the front, produced largely by those huge smoke deflectors and squat chimney,
from the side they were basically well proportioned, and when on the move, only in

2661   West Coast transition

dire stress did they make much fuss. To the uninitiated, however, it seems peculiar that comparable engines on the other side of the Channel, also with high temperature superheat, an adequate boiler and the refinement of a double chimney, manage both to get trains on the move and to drag them up hills with practically no noise at all. Ah, the savants will say, it's a question of compounding; but then we had compounds, and nobody could have called them quiet. Oh, it's the size of the boiler that counts; but our 9F 2–10–0s which were lavishly equipped to supply steam, made few concessions to the aurally sensitive and some had double chimneys. But in this context, is silence a virtue? If so, we must show considerable enthusiasm for electrics— and they're clean as well.

Sandwiched between these two historically famous routes lay the system which has claimed devotees out of all proportion to its success or necessity, the company which originated in the industrial north and attacked London by a pincer movement on shared metals, the erstwhile Great Central. In its heyday obviously an ambitious concern, but in the early 'sixties half-way down an irrevocable decline. Services cut, locomotives filthy and coaches so unutterably shabby as to be an insult to those who were unfortunate enough to have to use them. Later on it degenerated further, till it reached the stage when a small boy was almost overcome with excitement as he saw a red engine at the head of one of those abysmal semi-fasts out of Marylebone to Nottingham, when in fact it was just tinted with rust. It was a long drawn-out, painful death and the end, when it came, was a relief from incomparable misery. But on another front, things were looking up in a way which was completely contrary to the countrywide trend. Possibly the re-introduction of 3-hour expresses, all named, between Aberdeen and Glasgow was the last improvement which steam, in its own right, was able to effect. Admittedly the Gresley A4s were locomotives which had, on many an occasion in their youth, put up performances twice as spectacular, but they were now reaching respected old age, and once more they were being deliberately called upon to speed up existing trains. And how they did! That racing stretch between Perth and Forfar certainly provided ample opportunity for a sprint, but the distance was invariably covered start to stop, and in the up direction, the environs of Perth had to be threaded, paying at least lip service to the demands of caution and safety over the network of points, while in the down there was that frightful hill

266J   Effortless in France

soon after the start. In view of this, even with only seven coaches, timings of just over 27 minutes for the 33 miles were certainly exciting, and as the engines were usually clean, the whole performance was thoroughly excellent; there were clearly a few people who still had a pride in their job.

But as time wore on, the rot of both kinds was getting a progressively firmer hold and nowhere was this more obvious than at Alnwick. In 1966, what a dreary spectacle this station presented! The whole branch had been technically reduced to the level of a single-line siding, the terminus end being operated by remote control from Alnmouth. The graceful gantry had gone, the signal box stood abandoned and pillaged, half the track had been ripped up and in its place either weeds had spread unabated, or it had become the trampled desert of the unofficial foot-path. The building itself had deteriorated into a sepulchre of gloom where smoke from the engines hung constantly, and through the murky darkness could be heard a steady drip on to the platform from the now only half covered roof. Instead of the graceful D20s, which had skipped so light-footedly, were K1s which merely made a vulgar clank, and seemed somehow to resent the effort of moving at all. And as the last train at night left Alnmouth, screeched round the corner as if in excruciating agony, chugged laboriously with its two ageing coaches up the hill, and finally creaked to a halt in that cavernous haven under the three arches, shrieking a last plaintive whistle

266K   English and inefficient

which faded into the night as one solitary passenger stepped on to the platform, and soon afterwards those feeble lights were finally extinguished altogether, it seemed that life itself had ebbed away, and solitary darkness reigned supreme.

And what about the final phase—those Southern pacifics, eventually restricted to the line between Waterloo and Weymouth, with periodic if not daily trips to Salisbury? O misery! What wrecks! The living embodiment of decrepitude! What principle, what moral could justify the continued existence of these neglected hulks, staggering up and down the line on schedules which were nothing but a deliberate insult, until they got entangled in the net which was calculated to catch them, single line working in the New Forest? The fact that these locomotives carried on at all is probably the greatest unintentional tribute that could have been paid to steam; to see these monsters shuffling along, encrusted with grime, dripping with dirt, leaking steam from wherever it was possible to leak steam, and sometimes other places as well, was a sight that could do little else but disgust the onlooker, and evoke in sympathetic breasts an emotion of heroic admiration. To the visitor from overseas, newly arrived at Southampton Docks, the state of these engines was the greatest indictment of the British way of life, what it stands for and what it believes in, that there has yet been. It was both pathetic and tragic.

But this, thank goodness, wasn't the concluding chapter. At the very end, for the last few months, there was an improvement; not just a return to an uninspired

266L   Alnwick, 1966

266M   Indian Summer

normal but something better, something with spice and dash in it. Although shorn
of their nameplates, the engines were cleaned up as much as their blistered paint
would allow, and before their final extinction, drivers and firemen seemed keen to
show, as a last fling, what steam could still do. Slowings due to the final stages in the
electrification sometimes delayed trains in the early part of their journey, but after
that a ghost of the old determination to arrive on time came back, and the best of
those performances made one reflect on whether electrics were really going to be
faster after all. It was very exciting, and a magnificent last bow.

And in the same summer, the "Jubilees"—those two trusty survivors of a once
numerous class—were shedded at Holbeck and each rostered to make a weekly outing,
on Saturdays, over the line they knew so well, the Settle and Carlisle. This pair seemed
to epitomize the past, slogging their way through the mountains with their distinctive
three-cylinder beat, the distant hills echoing their laboured assault on those grades
up to the summit at Ais Gill. As we watch the end of the rear coach disappear into
the cutting, and the plume of exhaust evaporate into the still air, we know, with the
feeling of sadness often engendered by the realization of the truth, that apart from
artificially organized tours we shall not see them or their like again.   D.M.C.H-S.

267   Baron Wood

British Rail–

268   Birkett Tunnel

269 Armathwaite

The Last Act

270 Curtain Falls — Diss

Let Us Now Adjourn

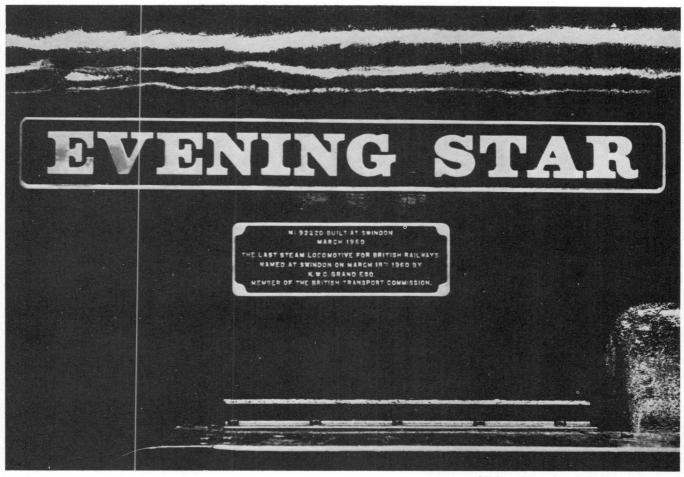

272   Observed and preserved

273   Full stop

274 S.C.C. poses with last K2 to work on West Highland

275 J.L.B. and J.A.C. learning to drive

Rogues' Gallery —An afterthought

276 D.M.C.H-S. in action

List of Photographs

47. Unrebuilt "Patriot" No. 45507 *Royal Tank Corps* passing the disused station at Wreay, Cumberland, in August, 1961.   [SCC

48. A2 No. 60524 *Herringbone* passing Gretna Green on the Glasgow and South Western main line with the 12.30 (Sundays) Carlisle to Glasgow parcels train in April, 1964.   [SCC

49. A3 No. 60051 *Blink Bonny* near Riddings Junction on the Waverley Route with the 11.15 Carlisle to Millerhill freight in August, 1964.   [SCC

50. "Jubilee" No. 45613 *Kenya* passing Penrith with an up freight in June, 1963.   [SCC

51. Scene at Eamont Junction, Penrith, in June, 1963. "Royal Scot" No. 46136 waits in the down loop, while "Patriot" No. 45529 passes with an up freight.   [SCC

52A. Photographers photographed at Rolvenden on the occasion of a special working on the Kent and East Sussex line in June, 1961.   [JAC

53. In April 1960, 4F No. 44557 restarts across the viaduct from Midford with the 16.35 Bath—Templecombe stopping train.   [AQ

54. 4—4—0 No. 40696 entering Radstock with a southbound stopping train (23/8/58).   [JAC

55. A BR standard 4MT 2—6—4T passes Pitcombe, south of Cole, with the 08.15 Bath—Templecombe stopping train (17/7/65).   [AQ

56. Collett 0—6—0 No. 2204 near Shepton Montague with a train from Highbridge in August, 1962.   [JLB

57. 2P No. 40564 and No. 34043 *Combe Martin* climb the valley between Midford and Wellow with a train from the Midlands to the South Coast (5/8/61).   [AQ

58. S&DJ 2—8—0 No. 53806 piloted by a Great Western 0—6—0 tops Masbury summit with an Exmouth—Cleethorpes train on an August Saturday in 1961.   [JLB

59. Midland 0—6—0 No. 43216 approaching Glastonbury & Street with a Highbridge to Evercreech train in May, 1960.
                                                                   [DMCH–S

60. One of the Derby-built S&DJ 2—8—0s climbing Devonshire bank out of Bath with the 14.00 goods; 12/9/62.   [JLB

61. Two 3F 0—6—0s heading the evening milk train on the Highbridge branch near Evercreech Junction en route to Templecombe and London (Vauxhall); 17/6/60.   [JAC

62. Templecombe shed in the Spring of 1961.   [JAC

63. 7F 2—8—0 No. 53808 poses for JAC at Evercreech Junction while waiting to work an enthusiasts' excursion on to Bath (30/9/62).   [AQ

64. A down Blackpool express behind rebuilt "Patriot" No. 45535 *Sir Herbert Walker, KCB*.   [DMCH–S

65. "Jubilee" No. 45631 *Tanganyika* at the head of an up troop special on Castlethorpe troughs (7/5/55).   [DMCH–S

66. A North British Railway drinking fountain on the platform at Prestonpans, near Edinburgh, photographed on 27/9/56.
                                                                          [JLB

67. Warning notice displayed on the water column at Horsted Keynes in 1957. Extravagant use was liable to affect the supply to the station house.   [AQ

68. A warning in the toilet at Stamford Town.   [AQ

69. Stopping train from Inverkeithing to Thornton via Dunfermline with NB "Scott" class 4—4—0 *Black Duncan* (16/6/58).
                                                                   [DMCH–S

70. D49 No. 62712 *Morayshire* near Stobs with the 12.25 (SO) stopping train from Hawick to Carlisle on 8/4/61.   [SCC

71. Small-wheeled 4—4—0 *Glen Mamie* working the daily goods on the Ballater branch near Cambus-o-May in September, 1958, shortly after being displaced from the West Highland line.
                                                                   [DMCH–S

72. "Hunt" No. 62738 *The Zetland* leaving Harrogate with a Leeds train in August, 1959.   [SCC

73. Scottish "Director" *Maid of Lorn* with a southbound train climbing to the Forth Bridge from Inverkeithing (3/7/54).
                                                                   [DMCH–S

74. The last active Scottish "Director" No. 62677 *Edie Ochiltree* at the head of a workmen's train from Rosyth passing under Jamestown Viaduct which carries the main line between Inverkeithing and the Forth Bridge; 15/8/59.   [JLB

75. D16/3 4—4—0 No. 62618 passing Barnwell Junction, Cambridge, with a stopping train from March on 4/4/59.   [JAC

76. GNoS 4—4—0 No. 62271 with a train from Craigellachie to Boat of Garten near Advie on 27/5/55.   [DMCH–S

77. The down "Bournemouth Belle" near Fleet in May 1954, with an unrebuilt "Merchant Navy" pacific in charge.   [DMCH–S

78. "West Country" class No. 34091 *Weymouth* climbing the North Downs at Knockholt in August 1958, with the down "Golden Arrow".   [JAC

79. A 9F pounding up the bank from Giggleswick with a westbound tanks train in June, 1967.   [SCC

80. A BR standard 4MT 2—6—4T climbs away from Fairbourne with the 09.10 (Saturdays only) Barmouth—Paddington (20/6/64).   [AQ

81. 4—4—0 No. 40581 piloting "Jubilee" No. 45600 *Bermuda* out of Leeds City with a Newcastle to Liverpool express (13/4/57).
                                                                          [JAC

82. With a Class 5 banking at the rear of the train, "Jubilee" No. 45565 *Victoria* climbs the steep gradient out of Bradford with a day excursion to Blackpool on Whit Monday, 1966.   [SCC

83. A Somerset and Dorset 2—8—0 piloted by a BR standard 2—6—0 near Binegar with the Saturday Cleethorpes to Exmouth train in August, 1962.   [JLB

84. A class 5 assisting a standard 9F between Clapham and Giggleswick with a train of tanks in June, 1967.   [SCC

85. "Hunt" No. 62738 *The Zetland* and A3 No. 60086 *Gainsborough* on Ripon Viaduct in August, 1959, with the 16.13 Newcastle—Liverpool.   [SCC

86. J69 No. 68499 and J17 No. 65577 leaving King's Lynn with a sand train for Middleton Towers in September, 1960
                                                                          [SCC

87. A J15 piloting a J17 out of March with a rake of wagons for Whittlesey in December, 1960.   [SCC

88. Last job for the "Jinties"—Nos. 47629 and 47289 prepare to take a load of coal from the sidings at Williamthorpe Colliery (Near Chesterfield) up to the main line in September, 1967.
                                                                          [SCC

89. Seaton Junction to Uppingham train halfway along the branch in May, 1959.   [DMCH–S

90. No. 41975 at Stamford Town station with an afternoon train from Uppingham to Peterborough on 23/5/59.   [JLB

91. The Tilbury tank waits on the main line by the water column while the single coach of the Uppingham branch train drifts down the slope into the bay platform at Seaton Junction; (30/5/59).   [JLB

92. Midland "Jinty" 0—6—0 No. 47250 in charge of the Seaton Junction to Uppingham train in October, 1959, instead of the usual Tilbury tank.   [SCC

93. Class 5 No. 45211 passing Giggleswick with a westbound freight in May, 1967.   [SCC

94. "Hunt" No. 62747 *The Percy* passing Harker station at unusual speed with a Hawick—Carlisle bonus goods working in December, 1958.   [SCC

95. "Black Five" No. 45373 approaches Lowgill with a down goods on the ex-LNW main line. The viaduct in the background formerly carried the branch from Clapham Junction via Ingleton; (30/7/66).   [AQ

145.   An overall view of Redhill shed in July, 1960, with a rich Southern assortment visible. No. 30331 (last surviving rebuilt Drummond H15 4–6–0), LBSC C2X 0–6–0 No. 32451, SR Q class 0–6–0 No. 30549 (with stove-pipe chimney), a Q1 0–6–0, an S15 4–6–0 and various SR 2–6–0s.   [AQ

146.   S15 4–6–0 No. 30512, *Lord Nelson* and "West Country" pacific *Wilton* lurk behind Basingstoke shed (March, 1961).
                                                                                              [AQ

147.   B4 0–4–0T 30096 under the tripod at Eastleigh shed in March, 1961.   [AQ

148.   Helmsdale shed in August, 1960.   [DMCH–S

149.   Spring evening at Tonbridge; 20/4/57.   [JAC

150.   The "Flying Scotsman" near Holme in May, 1957.
                                                                                         [DMCH–S

151.   The "Royal Scot" on Castlethorpe troughs in May, 1955.
                                                                                         [DMCH–S

152.   *King Henry VIII* in Sonning Cutting with the down "Cornish Riviera Express" on 19/7/58.   [JAC

153.   The down "Atlantic Coast Express" near Whitchurch in January, 1962.   [JLB

154.   N 2–6–0 No. 31836 between Tavistock and Bere Alston with the Plymouth portion of the down "Atlantic Coast Express" (18/4/63).

155.   No. 42699 passing Thrimby Grange in August, 1964, with the up Keswick portion of "The Lakes Express".   [SCC

156.   The up "Bristolian" near Wantage Road in 1958.   [JAC

157.   The "Bristolian" waiting to leave Bristol Temple Meads for Paddington behind 4–6–0 No. 5090 *Neath Abbey*. In the background the northbound Cornishman prepares to depart for Birmingham; 3/6/59.   [JAC

158.   BR standard 4MT 4–6–0 No. 75033 approaches Talerddig Summit with the last up "Cambrian Coast Express" on 4/3/67.
                                                                                              [AQ

159.   Watched by a solitary dog the branch train from Marlow enters Bourne End on a wintry January afternoon in 1962. [JLB

160.   The restored *City of Truro* leaving Compton for Newbury and Southampton with the 12.42 from Didcot on 22/1/58. [JAC

161.   Almost the only object not completely blanketed in newly fallen snow on the first day of 1962, an up stopping train for Euston is hauled near Berkhamsted by Class 5 No. 45391.   [JLB

162.   9F No. 92044 restarting a long freight south of Hatfield on the wintry New Year's Day of 1962.   [JLB

163.   A Great Western 2–8–0 approaching Wantage Road with a ballast train from the West of England : 4/1/59.   [JAC

164.   A1 No. 60161 *North British* crosses a Border river with a Waverley route stopping train in September, 1961.   [JLB

165.   A3 *Felstead* at the head of an Anglo-Scottish Car-Carrier soon after leaving Perth on 26/7/60.   [DMCH–S

166.   The West Coast Postal departs from Aberdeen Joint Station behind Peppercorn A2 No. 60528 *Tudor Minstrel* on 29/7/60.   [DMCH–S

167.   The school train in Glen Ogle; an unadvertised daily working from Callender involving the locomotive from the Killin branch (31/8/61).   [DMCH–S

168.   The 10.40 Inverness to Kyle of Lochalsh was often piloted between Dingwall and Achanalt in the summer season. It is here seen near Garve in August, 1960.   [DMCH–S

169.   A2 No. 60532 *Blue Peter* leaving Perth with the up "Grampian" on 2/8/66.   [SCC

170.   A Caprotti standard 5MT No. 73152 heads out of Perth with an evening train for Glasgow and passes B1 No. 61081 which is waiting to back on to a train to Edinburgh; 15/8/59.
                                                                                              [AQ

171.   A Stanier Class 5 and a standard 4MT 2–6–0 cross the Urr Viaduct, North of Dalbeattie, with the 08.07 Dumfries to Kirkcudbright and Stranraer on 21/4/65.   [AQ

172.   During their brief time at Polmadie, the A2s often worked stopping trains over the G&SW main line. Here No. 60535 *Hornet's Beauty* is leaving Annan with the 11.00 Carlisle to St Enoch in August, 1964.   [SCC

173.   An excursion train drifts down from the Forth Bridge towards Inverkeithing in July, 1954.   [DMCH–S

174A.   J36 No. (6)5312 at Carlisle Canal shed in 1955, sporting home-made paper numerals pasted on to the engine.   [SCC

174B.   Bearing evidence of some unofficial cleaning, No. 5553 climbs away from Bodmin Road station with the 18.15 to Padstow in June, 1961.   [SCC

174C.   After being thoroughly cleaned at Carlisle by the photographer and two friends, Jubilee No. 45584 *North West Frontier* climbs up to Wreay with the Sunday 16.30 stopping train to Manchester on 26/7/64.   [SCC

175.   A broadside view of a Great Northern main line evening commuter train composed of the Gresley articulated stock (1/5/62).   [JLB

176.   2P No. 40622 with the Inspection Saloon near Bucksburn, north of Aberdeen on the GNoS main line (30/6/54). [DMCH–S

177.   Compound 4–4–0 No. 41181 leaving St Pancras with the 15.20 semi-fast to Kettering on 16/2/57.   [JAC

178.   No. 41157 was the last Midland compound to go through works (apart from the restored No. 1000), and is seen here shortly afterwards leaving Derby for Birmingham with a parcels train in May, 1959.   [SCC

179.   The restored Great Northern J52 0–6–0ST. No. 1247 now privately preserved at the Keighley and Worth Valley Railway.
                                                                                              [JLB

180.   Caledonian Railway No. 123 and London and South Western No. 120 are admired at Horsted Keynes before working the return leg of an excursion to the Bluebell Railway, from Haywards Heath to Victoria (15/9/63).   [AQ

181.   Restored "Star" class 4–6–0 *Lode Star* about to enter Swindon Museum on 29/4/62.   [JAC

182.   Great Western 4–4–0 *City of Truro*, reputedly the first steam locomotive to attain 100mph, in regular service near Hermitage on the Didcot–Newbury line in January, 1958, after a long spell in the York Railway Museum.   [JLB

183.   4F No. 44125 approaching Cummersdale on the Maryport & Carlisle line with a freight for West Cumberland in August, 1964.   [SCC

184.   London and North Western 0–8–0 No. 49094 climbing up to Dunstable with the afternoon goods from Leighton Buzzard (29/9/61).   [JLB

185.   01 0–6–0 No. 31370 passes Latchmere Junction (WLER) with milk empties for Kensington Olympia on 11/7/59.   [AQ

186.   A Southern mogul No. 31848 with a Barnstaple line goods on 14/4/62.   [DMCH–S

187.   J25 No. 65727 climbing away from Rothbury on 22/10/59, with the return working of the pick-up goods from Blyth (T,Th,F only).   [SCC

188.   Not quite the job for which it was designed; an ageing T9 ambles through the New Forest with a goods train (30/5/54).
                                                                                         [DMCH–S

189.   C class 0–6–0 No. 31695 on a Tonbridge to Tunbridge Wells goods in 1960.   [DMCH–S

190.   Inside the large roundhouse at Swindon in December, 1961.   [JAC

191.   *Manorbier Castle* running on the Swindon test plant on 4/3/58.   [JAC

192.   Vale of Rheidol 2–6–2 tank *Prince of Wales* under repair at Swindon works on 6/3/60.   [AQ

193. BR standard 9F No. 92220 after completion at Swindon Works, but before her official naming as *Evening Star* to mark the end of steam construction for British Railways, photographed on the same date as *Prince of Wales*   [AQ

194. GWR 2–8–0 No. 4701 and BR standard pacific No. 70022 *Tornado* in the yard at Swindon in September, 1960.   [AQ

195. All now withdrawn, steam and diesel alike—replica of *North Star* as built in 1837, driving wheels from the broad gauge 2–2–2 *Lord of the Isles* and one of the first Western Region main line diesels, "Active" class No. D601, inside 'A' shop in November, 1959.   [JAC

196. Withdrawn locomotives outside 'C' shop in February, 1960.   [JAC

197. "Dukedog" No. 9005 being cut up in 'C' shop on 27/9/59.   [JAC

198. Returning from the furthest North the "Jones Goods" has sole charge of the Scottish Rail Tour near Rogart (15/6/62).   [JLB

199. Photographed in pouring rain from the main road, the Scottish Rail Tour meets a regular service train hauled by two diesel locomotives on one of the few lengths of the Perth–Inverness line which is double track (14/6/62).   [JLB

200. Great North of Scotland 4–4–0 *Gordon Highlander* and Highland Railway 4–6–0 No. 103 climb towards Dalnaspidal with the Scottish Rail Tour of June, 1962.   [JLB

201. LSW 4–4–2 tank No. 488 heads the *Wealden Rambler* on the Bluebell line near Freshfield on 23/5/65.   [AQ

202. The North London tank leaving Horsted Keynes on the Bluebell Railway (28/5/67).   [DMCH–S

203. GWR 4–4–0 3217 *Earl of Dartmouth* approaches Freshfield with the 13.55 Sheffield Park–Horsted Keynes on 13/6/65.   [AQ

204. Between the tunnels at Ganwick before the widening of the line between Hadley Wood and Potters Bar. J6 0–6–0 No. 64223 on 16/5/55.   [DMCH–S

205 and 206. Great Eastern 0–6–0 No. 65420 at Huntingdon on 1/8/61 during the removal of the track from the Cambridge–Kettering line.   [JLB

207. One of the ornamental pavilions on the Ouse Valley Viaduct (2/10/58).   [AQ

208. A *Terrier* and its train are silhouetted against the setting sun as they cross Langston Viaduct with the Hayling Island branch train in April, 1962.   [JLB

209. 2–6–2T No. 5564 crosses the Walkham viaduct with the 08.45 Tavistock North to Plymouth on 28/4/62.   [AQ

210. 0415 class 4–4–2T crossing Cannington Viaduct with a Lyme Regis to Axminster train in April, 1960.   [AQ

211. "Britannia" pacific No. 70017 *Arrow* passing Shenfield and Hutton with the 10.30 Liverpool Street to Norwich in February 1961.   [AQ

212. Work on the installation of equipment for the overhead electrification, seen here from the window of a "Britannia"-hauled train nearing Chelmsford in February, 1961.   [AQ

213. 2–6–2T No. 4591 leaving Lifton for Launceston with train from Plymouth on 19/4/60.   [JAC

214. BR standard 4MT 2–6–4T No. 80154 (the last locomotive built at Brighton Works) approaching West Hoathly tunnel with the 14.28 East Grinstead–Lewes, on the second closing day of the Bluebell Line; 16/3/58.   [AQ

215. An A1 pacific emerges from the South end of Potters Bar tunnel with an up express for Kings Cross in the summer of 1962.   [JLB

216. Midland 2F 0–6–0 No. 58148 clearing Glenfield Tunnel on her way from Leicester to Coalville with a freight in March, 1963.   [SCC

217. 3F 0–6–0 No. 43565 leaving Warden Tunnel with the morning Bedford to Hitchin goods in April, 1962.   [JLB

218. Derailed 4700 class 2–8–0 at Stratton Green Bridge, Swindon, on 12/11/58 after a mishap while working a newspaper train the previous night.   [JAC

219. The fire being extinguished on O1 2–8–0 No. 63890 derailed outside Cambridge station (31/8/57).   [JAC

220. British Railways' standard 4MT 2–6–0 No. 76026 derailed in the sand drag at Whitchurch North (Hants) while working a southbound freight, and seen supported on edge of embankment by ropes and trees; 20/2/60.   [JAC

221. London Midland Region casualty at Cambridge (3/6/57).   [JAC

222. Southern 4–4–0s Nos. 31739 and 31067 climbing Grosvenor Bank out of Victoria station with a Ramblers' Excursion for Hawkhurst on 28/5/61.   [DMCH–S

223. London (Charing Cross) to Hastings train in April 1957, soon after leaving Tunbridge Wells Central. The locomotive is No. 30913 *Christ's Hospital*.   [JAC

224. Large chimney Schools class No. 30918 *Hurstpierpoint* approaching Vauxhall on the 12.54 semi-fast to Basingstoke and beyond in March, 1961.   [JLB

225. L class No. 31766 entering Selling with a stopping train from Faversham to Dover Priory via Canterbury East (16/5/59).   [JAC

226. No. 31779 starting a down stopping train from Chatham in June, 1959.   [AQ

227. The often photographed 07.24 London Bridge to Ramsgate approaching Ramsgate in May, 1961. This was the last regular working for a 4–4–0 out of London in the South Eastern division and came to an end in June of that year.   [JLB

228. T9 No. 30717 heads a mixed train for Padstow beside the Camel estuary in April, 1961.   [JLB

229. Standard No. 73107 on Beattock, with an LMS mogul giving rear end assistance; 28/5/66.   [SCC

230. Caledonian Railway 0–4–4T at the rear of a northbound train ascending Beattock Bank in April, 1962.   [DMCH–S

231. Double-chimney standard class 4 No. 75026 banking a heavy freight train up Shap on 22/7/67.   [SCC

232. Round the coast from Barmouth to Machynlleth with No. 7801 *Anthony Manor* in charge on 18/4/63.   [DMCH–S

233. 8F 2–8–0 No. 48150 heads an up goods train East of Bangor on 3/7/65.   [AQ

234. GWR mogul No. 7306 heads south for Carmarthen out of Aberystwyth; 5/4/62.   [DMCH–S

235. No. 7802 *Bradley Manor* heads the up *Cambrian Coast Express* through Afon Dyfi (8/9/64).   [AQ

236. On the northern shores of the Forth J35 No. 64525 hauls the Charlestown branch goods over weed-strewn track (13/6/62).   [JLB

237. Almost under the southern approach to the Forth Bridge a diminutive J36 0–6–0 has charge of the South Queensferry goods on 13/6/62.   [JLB

238. One of the LMS dock tanks No. 47163 at the head of a train for the Balerno branch near Slateford, Edinburgh, in September, 1959.   [JLB

239. J37 No. 64611 trundles up to Brechin with the branch freight from Montrose on 31/3/67, the last day that this turn was worked by a steam engine.   [SCC

240. Deep in the Cornish woods on 24/4/61 the Wenford Bridge branch train approaches the watering place on the climb from Wadebridge.   [JLB

241. No. 30587 at Boscarne Junction in April, 1961.   [JLB

242. In the shed at Wadebridge stand two of the very old well tanks, Nos. 30585 and 30586, maintained specially for duty on the Wenford Bridge branch (13/4/60).   [JAC

243. Recalling hair raising pictures of the turn of the century, one of the crew of a Bluebell Railway *Terrier* makes an inspection *en route* in the summer of 1962.   [*JLB*

244. A diverting spectacle was provided on the platform of Freshfield Halt on the Bluebell line on the occasion of a full dress outing of an historical society.   [*JLB*

245. A1 0—6—0T No. 72 *Fenchurch* approaches Sheffield Park with the 14.25 from Horsted Keynes; 'P' 0—6—0T *Bluebell* waits at the platform to help marshal and work the next train (17/9/67).
[*AQ*

246. *Douglas* at Abergynolwyn awaits the signal to depart with the last train of the day to Towyn; 17/7/66.   [*AQ*

247. A portrait of E4 No. 62797 at the South end of Cambridge station; 5/7/57.   [*JAC*

248. No. 62785 approaches with a train from Marks Tey as No. 62797 waits at the platform end at Cambridge; 5/7/57.   [*JAC*

249. No. 62789 near Shelford with the 13.34 from Cambridge to Colchester on 12/3/57.   [*DMCH—S*

250. The Mildenhall branch train on 13/10/56, complete with the usual E4 and the former Great Eastern stock, one compartment of which was fitted with steps for the convenience of passengers at the halts which did not have platforms.   [*DMCH—S*

251. No. 62785 at Barnwell Junction with a train for Mildenhall on 28/11/59.   [*JAC*

252. A "Schools" class 4—4—0 near Blackwater with a train from Reading on a windy March day in 1962.   [*JLB*

253. A train from Redhill coasts into Reading South station behind SECR class D No. 31496 on 16/4/55.   [*DMCH—S*

254. An M7 0—4—4 tank near Earley with an afternoon train to Guildford; 20/4/56.   [*DMCH—S*

255. LSWR T9 4—4—0 No. 30705 leaving Reading South with the 12.47 train to Guildford on 30/11/57.   [*JAC*

256. Mogul No. 31873 near Crowthorne; 14/5/64.   [*DMCH—S*

257. N class No. 31852 with a Guildford—Reading train at Ash Junction on 24/3/63.   [*DMCH—S*

258. S15 No. 30510 passes Earley with a freight for Feltham in September, 1961.   [*DMCH—S*

259. Western Region working on the Reading—Redhill line on 1/7/64. No. 7813 *Freshford Manor* near Gomshall & Shere on the westbound run.   [*DMCH—S*

260. Ryde pierhead from above.   [*DMCH—S*

261. Isle of Wight 02 No. W29 *Alverstone* near Ryde St Johns with a train for Newport on 14/4/62.   [*JLB*

262. Scene at Ryde shed in April, 1962.   [*JLB*

263. A Newport train hauled by *Ventnor* on 14/4/62, shortly after leaving Smallbrook Junction.   [*JLB*

264. *Seaview*, with the 09.25 Ryde to Ventnor, and *Ventnor*, with the 09.42 Ventnor to Ryde, meet at Shanklin on 16/9/61.
[*AQ*

265. A general view of Ventnor station looking south from over the tunnel mouth in August 1958.   [*JAC*

266A. A North Eastern D20 4—4—0 hauling the Alnwick branch train in the early spring of 1957.   [*DMCH—S*

266B. A pair of C12 4—4—2 tanks at Stamford in May 1958.
[*JAC*

266C. Epping—Ongar trains worked by F5 2—4—2 tanks passing at North Weald (2/8/57).   [*JAC*

266D. Passengers both human and canine using the special steps provided on the Cambridge to Mildenhall train at Worlington Golf Links Halt on 21/4/56.   [*JLB*

266E. A Midland 2P 4—4—0 piloting a St Pancras express at Sharnbrook on 22/5/58.   [*DMCH—S*

266F. A Stanier class 5 on the Highland main line; 7/4/61.
[*DMCH—S*

266G. A class 5 on the Oban line; near Tyndrum with a heavy freight (2/8/61).   [*DMCH—S*

266H. A spotless A4 pacific climbing out of London with a down Leeds express at Belle Isle on 23/5/62.   [*DMCH—S*

266I. A "Duchess" pacific still takes an express up Camden bank but a diesel glides down the hill for empty carriage working; October, 1961.   [*DMCH—S*

266J. A PLM pacific on Caffiers Bank near Calais.   [*DMCH—S*

266K. Poor quality coal, slack firing technique and a following wind all contributed to the monumental smoke column towering over a 9F 2—10—0 on the Midland main line North of Luton in May, 1962.   [*JLB*

266L. K1 No. 62021 leaving Alnwick station with the branch train to Alnmouth in May, 1966.   [*SCC*

266M. One of the last express passenger locomotives to remain in service on British rail, "Jubilee" No. 45593 *Kolhapur* crossing Ribblehead Viaduct with the relief to the down "Thames—Clyde Express" on 5/8/67.   [*SCC*

267. No. 70013 *Oliver Cromwell* passing Baron Wood Siding with BR's last steam excursion — Northbound for Carlisle (11/8/68).   [*SCC*

268. Nos. 44871 and 44781 south of Birkett Tunnel with the return working of BR's final fling.   [*AQ*

269. Another shot of the "End of Steam" return from Carlisle on the same date, this time south of Armathwaite.   [*SCC*

270. Preparations being made in Diss Yard for the loading of 70013 *Oliver Cromwell* on to a road transporter *en route* to the museum at Bressingham Gardens; 17/8/68.   [*AQ*

271. Remembered in stone, a head on view of a handsome locomotive decorates a plaque on the Railway Tavern at Silvertown in East London. (4/3/61).   [*JLB*

272. The nameplate of *Evening Star*, the last steam locomotive to be built for British Railways.   [*JAC*

273. The big gantry at Newcastle, all signals at stop.   [*AQ*

274. S. C. Crook poses on Fort William shed with the last "K2" to work over the West Highland line. The locomotive is a genuine "K2", and not a disguised "K1". (August 1960).   [*DMCH—S*

275. J. A. Coiley and J. L. Boyd are prevented by the driver and an inspector from making off with "E4" 62785. (27/4/58).   [*AQ*

276. D. M. C. Hepburn-Scott (incognito) steals a shot of 30861 on an up Bournemouth train, by Beaulieu Road station, in 1960.
[*JAC*

Footnote: Quintus wishes to apologise for his mechanical colleagues, who, faced with even a dash of Latin, were thrown into confusion and, by the addition of an unnecessary initial in the list of photographs, gave him a conjunction for a first name. Vivat Alma Mater !

CONTENTS

7. Channel
Frontispiece.
8. Research Development
Following five years of analogue to digital transition,
the Neville Brody Studio has embarked on a new
direction and identity, *Research Development*.

INTRODUCTION

In 1994, we are at the crux of a social revolution in communications. The transition from analogue to digital technology and the advent of the personal computer are innovations whose effect will be as profound as Gutenberg's movable type. This has already become a commonplace analogy as people become more aware of the power of digital communication. We cannot let this obscure the depth of the revolution that is taking place, since so much of it is being presented to us on the surface, in the world of entertainment with its sanctified amnesia. This makes it even more difficult to pin down.

Our Western civilization is markedly different from a world dominated by religious and royal authority. Materials were in scarce supply and it took hundreds of years before the implementation of new print technology was accepted as commonplace. Only in recent times has access to the printing press been relatively straightforward.

Past leaders were quick to recognise the threat posed by the free exchange of printed information. Until the Licensing Act was revoked in 1695, every printer and typefounder in England was controlled by the ruling class. Censorship of the printed word was widespread across Europe; in 1543 Cardinal Carafa decreed that no book could be printed or sold without the permission of the Papal Inquisition – offenders were burnt at the stake. To avoid incrimination, the origin of publication was concealed – computer hacking in reverse. Today's use of passwords harks back to the cover-up colophons of the past: Dutch printers in the 16th century, for example, marked their publications 'Printed in Utopia' (such was the popularity of Thomas More's book). Censorship was not lifted in Germany until 1848 and, despite the Revolution, France did not definitively legislate to remove controls until 1872.

The development of the written word in the West, from symbol and pictogram to alphabet and book, took place over thousands of years. The computer has the power to reverse this process in less than thirty. Because the personal computer has so quickly changed the *modus operandi* in almost every area of communication in the space of only five years, we tend to believe that the digital revolution is over and done with. Nothing could be further from the truth. According to Goethe, "The second part of the history of the world begins with the invention of printing." We have just entered the third phase. The Electronic Revolution is upon us.

"A language is an implement quite as much as an implement of stone or steel; its use involves social consequences; it does things to you just as a metal or a machine does things to you. It makes new precision and also new errors possible."
HG Wells, *In Search of Hot Water*, c.1898, quoted in Frederick Bodmer, *The Loom of Language*, 1943.

"We cannot prohibit that which we cannot name."
George Steiner, "The Language Animal", in *Extraterratorial*, Faber and Faber 1972.

9. Business cards for Digitalogue, Tokyo 1993
Opposite:
10. Font for Digitalogue, 1993
Digitalogue is the world's first "digital gallery", since branching out to become a CD-ROM publisher. Started by Akira Gomi and Naomi Enami, whom Brody had met whilst working with Propeller Art Works, Digitalogue is a rare example of Anglo-Japanese collaboration. The computer processed typeface is used to contrast the digital clarity of the original font, different characters being selected to publicise different events.

11–14. Background images for the *Floriade* stamps, PTT, The Netherlands 1991
The introduction of the image-manipulation programme for the Macintosh, Adobe Photoshop, enabled Brody to continue to pursue the idea of "painting through technology", an approach that he had first followed with the use of the PMT camera at the LCP, and in his designs for *Fetish*, *Touch* and the "Hitting Town" poster shown in the first book. Discovering Photoshop's potential involved climbing through a steep learning curve and, as a fulfilment of an original ambition, it was a regeneration.

Previous revolutions prove that technology changes language. The printing press made mass distribution of information possible, encouraging the steady erosion of oral traditions like storytelling, based on myth and individual recall, but it facilitated the spread of knowledge that led to the Renaissance in the arts and the establishment of an education system. The invention of the camera challenged the perception of the distance between recorded experience and reality, depriving Fine Art of its traditional representational role, forcing artists to look for a new and more expressive language to redefine their realm. A context was created for painters like Cézanne to experiment with colour and light. Kandinsky and Klee pushed the limits of shape and symbolism even further. The quest for a pure language of visual abstraction will continue beyond the work of Jackson Pollock and Mark Rothko. Photography made an impact on Fine Art just as the computer has undermined the design industry. But the time-frame is far more compressed in the rapidly changing environment of digital design.

We do not yet fully appreciate how other technologies like cinema affect our perceptions, or what the long-term effects of television might be. The impact and widespread application of the telephone provides another rarely considered precedent to the computer. What will happen next to the printed word? Language and information are not stable commodities. Our interpretation of information and thereby our behaviour when we come to act upon it is always defined by its presentation, whether consciously acknowledged or otherwise. This difficulty is compounded by the computer's ability to combine and relocate all the internal, invisible language structures and processes of previous information technologies.

One factor that differentiates the computer from previous inventions is its long period of gestation. The common man was not prepared for printing, for photography, for film; the element of "Eureka!" remained intact, so that upon first exposure, readers, viewers and audiences were usually enraptured, excited by their gain and quickly overlooked what they might have lost in the process. Secondly, before the PC, it was never assumed that these readers would swiftly become writers, the viewers photographers and every member of the audience a film director. Through popular culture and the Science Fiction genre, however, we have been prepared for the computer revolution for nigh on one hundred years. As a result, we have a conditioned set of responses to new technology – the most basic is to become passive subjects of its endless development.

As Steiner and Wells insist, any new conditions affecting the way we use language will inevitably have social and psychological consequences. As well as looking back to specific inventions for clues that help us to understand how computer technology will shape the future, we should also compare the Industrial Revolution to the present. For the great majority, the first machine age came as a massive shock to the conventional way of life. Against the backdrop of the French Revolution, urbanisation and the imposition of the factory system catalysed the most turbulent period in modern British history; any outbreaks of civil disorder and machine breaking quickly met with a draconian response from government who, in the days before a police force was established, freely deployed the army to quell disturbances.

With technological change come demands for social reform. The Luddite uprising... The Peterloo massacre[1]. In 1984, the introduction of computers was used as a pretext to destroy the power of the print trades unions in Britain, again a deliberate policy that, alongside rising unemployment, has sent working peoples' hard-won advances into recession. The current climate is not brightened by the prospect of imminent reforms, but clouded by the fight for survival and the "inevitability" of technological takeover.

For much of this century, we have been living out future predictions – artificial intelligence, fast food, faster transport systems, videophones, space travel, urban breakdown, hi-tech warfare. We have been well briefed by popular culture for one set of eventualities. However, it has not turned out as envisaged. We are neither liberated nor controlled by robots. If anything, those in employment work longer hours and harder than ever. The machine age has not simply acted as an external force upon humankind. Instead, the revolution operates on our sense of inner space. The great changes will take place on a linguistic and biological level. We have subjected our physical reality to technology, and now we are in the process of mutating our mental reality. What new names will our new minds come up with to define the impending chaos? In digital terms, a rose is not a rose is not a rose.

Computer games are popular because they impose a sense of order. They give a glimpse of the intensified perceptual fields of the digital, whose worlds approximate the chaotic contours of an LSD trip, yet the drug is interrupted by the message "Game Over". In reality, there is no dry land from which to observe and quantify the full effects of the computer. The new technology has set us off on a limitless conversation with the limitations of our own brains.

Today, we have no idea what the future will look like. The previous ground we walked upon has been levelled out by digital technology, leaving us in a state of uncertainty. Society and its institutions have changed so dramatically since the Second World War due to other mass-applied technologies and forms of distribution (principally television and advertising) that society seems in a poor state to accommodate further transformations. "The Shock of the New" has been downgraded by the dull repetition of marketing slogans trying to fire our enthusiasm for the lastest update.

There is an urgent need for us to challenge the currently perceived central role of computers – as control machines in a brave new world of surveillance and escapism. The prime drawback is the present lack of any language of optimism. The new possibilities the personal computer might offer are seldom seen as potential benefits.

FOR THE PAST FIVE YEARS, Neville Brody and his studio have embraced the computer as a new medium that allows the artist to explore and create a completely new set of activities and codes in visual language. This has involved a series of translation processes – from publicity to invisibility, solo to studio, analogue to digital. The work in the first volume of *The Graphic Language of Neville Brody* was based around the categories of BOOKS/MAGAZINES/RECORD COVERS. The content of this second book is more chaotic, with fewer fixed statements. The new categories have yet to be set, and may never be; nor does the client format fit so easily to an obvious and immediate function. This is because the computer gives new meaning to the process of publishing – in digital form, any software is not a consumer durable but increasingly a professional and consumer bendable. Digital design is like painting, except the paint never dries. It is like a clay sculpture that is always being twisted into new shapes without ever being fired."

Digital technology also accelerates and intensifies the publishing process, promising us the power to send or access information instantaneously. We are already building personalised networks for this; corporations are constructing information superhighways that can send data at the speed of light, yet it is still far from clear exactly what the traffic will consist of, or even what it will look like. Telecom companies have formed consortiums with the manufacturers of technological hardware, pledging their futures to the potentially massive revenues of this traffic.

Inevitably, our lives will be played out from our living rooms. Digital distribution will further compound the process of domestication initiated by television, rising crime and the loss of public space. Home shopping has already been established in the USA by the cable TV channel QVC. As a contrast to this calculated commerce, will networks be used to provide a wealth of specialised knowledge that could form the basis of a new education system? Or will an endless flow of weather reports, news updates, and electronic quiz-shows punctuate a fattening diet of escapist entertainment that tries to compete with the sensational possibilities of another imminent technology, virtual reality? It will be difficult for any methodical, tutorial ambitions to compete with the 'fresh horizons' of cyberspace, a computerised yet playful version of reality that anyone can, theoretically, design for themselves and then take refuge in.

Clearly, in the very near future our relationship to institutions and to the organisation of the outside world will be fixed to and by the screen. However, this clearly defined endpoint of focus does not hide the lack of any coherent planning. We have no idea how the data banks will be organised, nor how the options will be displayed. We take it for granted that the networks and superhighways will be patrolled by some form of Traffic Police, but how and by whom remains a mystery.

The design world is disintegrating thanks to the power of the PC, and is failing to take the initiative. The once steady relationship between client, designer and general public is being dissolved by the ease of access that any disseminator of information now has to the current tool of the trade. The wall of protectionist professional practice has been blown open. There is no longer the same need for specialist designers and precious presentations. Companies are increasingly taking care of their needs in-house.

Design as we knew it is dead. Split between established practices and the guerilla deviations of younger designers, its function of making invisible ideas tangible has been eroded by the computer's tendency to turn tangible forms into ether. Design's new state as a formless medium brings opportunities for the research and development of new ways of communicating. Just as the camera challenged artists to develop new forms of abstraction, so the breakdown of the designer's traditional role allows for the birth of a new visual language.

THE IDEA TO START A STUDIO came about in 1985. I was working on a new edition of *Touch*, the audio-visual magazine I had edited since 1982: the theme was media ritual. Brody had contributed to *Touch* since its first edition and was working on a new design, *The Death of Typography*, which was also to be the title of a lecture he had been asked to give to coincide with *The Face* magazine's "First Five Years" exhibition at the Watershed Gallery in Bristol. Apprehensive, nervous, Brody suggested we do the talk together. On the train to Bristol, we talked about his plans to start a studio which would act as a point of focus for other freelance designers wishing to pursue a collective but also independent vision. The structure was linked to the same concept as *Touch*, which brought together and encouraged new combinations between musicians, artists, writers and designers.

The first Neville Brody Studio was a small second floor office in Tottenham Court Road, opposite the YMCA, sandwiched between hi-fi stores, record shops and fast food out-

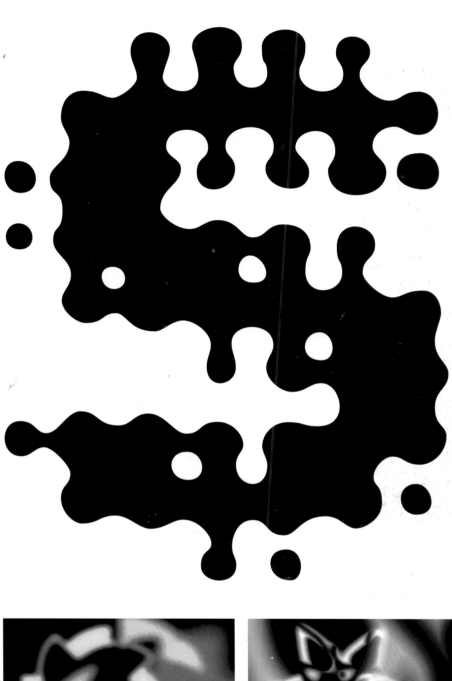

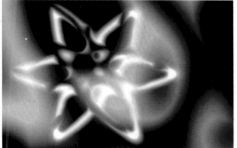

Below:
15. Cover for *Sex Money Freaks*, Cabaret Voltaire, Parlophone Records 1988
Brody's first use of computer-generated type. Before the development of the PostScript standard by Adobe, type could only be output from the Mac at "bitmap" resolution, and until ATM (Adobe Type Manager) arrived, output was always printer-dependent. The type for this 12'' single was printed out on an ImageWriter, then retouched and PMTed for artwork.

Opposite:
18–22. College briefs, 1978/79
The crossword and photomontage bottom right show the influence of Punk and Dadaism on Brody's college work. *British Writers and the Sea* rejects the landscape photography tradition of the travel book in favour of a more turbulent design. The background for the book cover at the top of the page indicates that Brody's approach to image processing has remained consistent – only the means of execution has changed. Sand-papered details from a map were photographed, scratched out again and then recoloured with felt-tip pens.

16, 17. Illustrations for *Graphics World* and LetraStudio software package, London 1988
Designs which are not so good and a reminder to beware the first steps when using new technology... Brody's early work on a colour Mac cannot escape the obvious computer tricks, which seem impressive at first, making these illustrations now look like something out of a manual.

lets. Initially, Grant Gilbert helped out with the administration. Fwa Richards made up the team, using her organisation skills as studio manager which she remains to this day. It was March 1987. The first major project was to write, design and artwork volume one of *The Graphic Language*: before that could happen, the three of us had to collate and edit ten years' work. During the day, jobs were followed through as usual: after dark, record covers, letterheads, posters and magazine spreads quickly covered every table-top as the rough layouts for the book took shape.

It was an on/off routine strangely mirrored by the activity outside. Many of the retailers, banks and services that straddled nearby Oxford Street were chopping and changing their logos, their signage systems and their advertising strategies in a frantic attempt to appear 'youthful', such had been the success of *The Face* magazine and its contemporaries. Design agencies fell over themselves to become financial institutions, hoping to regulate the distribution of the new look. Because we had been so thoroughly prepared for it, less glaringly obvious was the way in which the hi-fi stores were gradually taking their turntables from window displays and replacing them with compact disc players. An increasing number of computer stores were starting up along the street. A more fundamental revolution had filtered down to the consumer market, following decades of development by military and industrial concerns – the conversion from analogue to digital methods of information storage.

Apple's first home computer became available in 1984, around the same time as compact discs arrived in the shops. The change was highlighted in terms of the enhanced sound and everlasting quality of the compact disc (both these improvements have since been called into question), as if the digital conversion were little more than a change of formats in the entertainment business. With CD-ROM, it has since become apparent that the format is a far more effective carrier of text and image rather than music.

This was a turning-point that would lead to a long period of transition. Britain and the rest of the world was already experiencing great upheaval. The social and political disintegration caused by the stylish redecoration undertaken by the Conservative government was packaged to look like an urgent economic objective – this in itself brought confusion and disbelief. The feverish pursuit of new trading images gave the impression of dynamic change, yet this cosmetic front was in fact a classic case of strategic deception. State-owned industries and welfare services were progressively being taken apart and sold off to the private sector. Each change was presented as an evolutionary improvement.

The essential kit used to produce the work for the first *Graphic Language* book was as follows: paints, paintbrushes, sketchbook, Rotring pen, straight edge, blue pencil, graph pad, compass, casting-off rule, typesetters' catalogues, Letraset, felt-tip pens, Tippex, photocopier, scalpel, Electro-Stik waxer, art board, Stanley knife, Ronsonol lighter fuel, PMT machine[2], drawing board, tracing paper, cover paper, clay, plaster, chicken wire... and an intuitive sense of how to apply ideas laterally.

Once made public, the ideas, let alone the simple techniques that were used to give form to them, were often smothered by the success of the style culture in England with which Brody had been associated. Here, style is used as an ointment to seal in any 'difficult' material that might interfere with the gloss finish. The principal ideas behind Brody's work are to encourage an understanding of the way language affects our lives and to demonstrate how technological

processes affect language – to question the growing power of the media, to promote a dialogue on the techniques that corporations use to present information – as Brody said of his earliest college work in 1976, "following the idea of design to reveal, not to conceal".

The essential kit for the greater part of this second volume is the personal computer – namely, Apple Macintosh, scanners and laser printers. The ideas have had to be matched to the new technology and its effects – late-night sessions spent fathoming the computer's less obvious possibilities, hours of research in a quest to get behind its defaults, its index of fixed linguistic styles and standardised commands, like cracking a safe.

"Photography implies that we know about the world if we accept it as the camera records it. But this is the opposite of understanding, which starts from *not* accepting the world as it looks."
Susan Sontag, *On Photography*, Penguin Books 1978.

BORN IN 1957, Brody grew up in Southgate, North London. From an early age he set his sights on being an artist and chose to enrol on a Fine Art foundation course at Hornsey College of Art in 1975. He felt the Fine Art world to be elitist, however, and switched his attention to graphic design: "I wanted to communicate to as many people as possible, but also to make a popular form of art that was more personal and less manipulative." So went the theory. Brody began a three-year degree course at the London College of Printing, but found its atmosphere and the attitude of most of his tutors dull and inhibiting. They, in turn, branded his work "uncommercial" and failed him.

Underpinning all Brody's work is his belief in the possibilities that come from adopting a painterly approach to design, whether analogue or digital. This comes through clearly in his cover designs for Fetish Records, and rings equally true in his most recent computer-generated work for *Fuse* and *Graphic Arts Message* (see p.26 and p.15).

Brody felt strongly that his three years at college should be used to push ideas as far as possible, to experiment and take risks that it would be more difficult to find time for in a commercial context. In spite of its hard technical background, the LCP was more interested in turning out traditional art directors for the traditional design and advertising industries. This narrow educational ambition is still with us, despite the decline in new jobs in the design industry. Coupled to their dwindling resources, most design colleges offer only the most rudimentary exposure to the implications of new technology, or indeed, enough time spent using it.

Luckily, in 1977 Brody was able to take his inspiration from the Punk movement which gave him the confidence he needed and spearheaded a new graphic vitality which connected with Brody's interest in Dadaism and Pop Art, which had formed the subject of his first-year thesis. Brody was also exposed to the work of William Burroughs and Brion Gysin, who in 1959 had invented the "cut-up" technique – dividing a text into strips or sections that could be rearranged to create new meanings – a device that could also be applied to visual media, extending Eisenstein's cinematic use of montage and the Dadaist development of photomontage (notably by artists such as John Heartfield and Hannah Höch). Gysin's innovation grew into a long-term collaboration with Burroughs which they called *The Third Mind*.

Other important influences for Brody were the poetic photographers of the 1920s, Man Ray and László Moholy-Nagy, whose 'paintings with light' supported his own belief in transmedia commercial art; none more so than the Soviet designer Alexander Rodchenko, who subverted the whole notion of artist as specialist by experimenting across a variety of media, questioning the boundaries between them.

"The record shop was just as valid a showcase as the framed environment of art galleries...I thought this area was the only one that would offer any chance of experimentation." On leaving college, Brody spent the best part of two years working first for Rocking Russian, a design company run by Al McDowell, whose work he had greatly admired – "a time of absolute poverty, living in a squat in Covent Garden, washing dishes in the evening at Peppermint Park" – and subsequently for Stiff, who introduced him to the seamier side of the music business. Luckily he had met 23 Skidoo, and through them, Rod Pearce, who was setting up the independent label, Fetish Records. The group would be one of Fetish's first signings. In 1981, Brody became the label's art director.

"Fetish gave me total freedom, within the obvious limitations of its budget. A lot of the work represents a reaction to the commercial marketplace where the human form has become plastic. The sleeves all revolve around my intention to reintroduce human markings into commercial art – putting man back into the picture." Brody was able to use this freedom – numerous cover designs for Clock DVA (*Thirst*...), 8 Eyed Spy, the Bongos, 23 Skidoo and Z'EV combine ritualistic paintings, clay sculptures and macabre shapes with vivid exploitations of the two-colour printing process.

Process was the overriding concern of another major collaboration in which he had become involved. The Sheffield-based group Cabaret Voltaire worked with Brody on ten records between 1979 and 1987. Brody's dominant theme was: "The loss of human identity that results from communication being transmitted through machines that condition, not serve, human interaction." The group were among the first exponents of video experiments; stills would be passed on to Brody for adaptation to the print medium. Here he had the opportunity to develop typographic structures. The cover and inner sleeve for the 1983 release *The Crackdown* include circular type formations executed entirely with Letraset – hours of work that today's computer programmes can achieve in a few minutes. For *2X45* (1982), *Microphonies* (1984) and *Dont Argue* (1987) Brody chose to use specially hand-drawn type. By this time he had become art director for *The Face*.

"I never in my wildest dreams intended working on magazines. I'd always dealt with images. I found myself out of necessity having to get the same emotive impetus from the way I used type. I hated type. It was out of frustration, because I was falling into the trap of treating type in the same way as everybody else. I thought typography was boring, overladen with traditions that would repel change."

ACCESS TO BASIC EQUIPMENT like a drawing board or PMT machine with which to transform designs into camera-ready artwork for printing was not always easy. Conventional typesetting was expensive. In the UK typesetting was craftily contained within an occult language and a trades union closed shop, forcing typographers and designers to "mark-up" copy. Instructions had to be specified in em measures, picas, point sizes and leading, using "casting off" rulers and tables, just as accountants once used adding machines, slide rules and log' books before pocket calculators took the toil out of square roots and long division. Letraset was by no means cheap and quickly ran out.

Conventional type did not always supply the language designers wanted to use. This is one reason why Brody's

early work revolves around image-making, closer to painting and illustration than graphic design – an apprenticeship to the approach Brody brings to his later typographic work.

Brody showed Nick Logan his portfolio when Logan was editor of *Smash Hits*, Britain's biggest-selling pop magazine. Seeking a fresh challenge, Logan set up *The Face* in 1980 on a miniscule budget of £7000, and, remembering Brody's work, invited him to become art director 18 months later. In spite of (or because of) his initial typographic ignorance, Brody made a great impact by combining existing typefaces but was even more influential later, designing his own typefaces and intercepting the imminent outcome of digital type design. During his five years there, Brody revolutionised magazine design and developed a new graphic language which was applied to any outlet or item of packaging that wished to appear *ahead*. Shop fronts, restaurants, advertisements for British Rail... it made no difference.

The new magazine became the uniform of a culture on the never-never. The more successful *The Face* became, the more it was looked upon as a 'Style Bible', which provided a monthly graphics phrase book that enabled imitators to make the right visual noises. Such was the business demand for 'style culture' to exploit new patterns of consumer behaviour, few took the time to reflect or even care whether or not they were getting the genuine article.

"I wanted people to challenge *The Face*. The argument was this – how can design bring a greater dynamism to the content, now that we live in a predominantly visual age? In many ways, *The Face*'s commercial success took the impetus out of this and forced people into a corner where the easiest choice was to adopt the style. People had no option but to ignore what was really happening because the information was being presented to them second-hand." Design was used as camouflage. "I was pointing out the means to a way of thinking and a way of working, not the solution. But you can see the same misconceptions being applied today to David Carson's *RayGun* magazine."

In the divisive social climate of the mid-80s, you were either "in" or "out". Such was the hunger for certainties that any subtlety or nuance was swiftly glossed over. As it is with television, the more mass the media, the more generalised

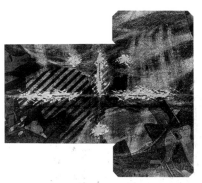

the audience, the more irony, satire and paradox tend to evaporate as the ink dries on the page.

One irony has survived. The most successful of these typefaces – the hand-drawn *Typeface 3*, now known as *Industria* – is commonly used in computer advertising and to package 'techno' products. "The geometric quality of the type was authoritarian, drawing a parallel between the social climate of the 1930s and 1980s." Carefully outlined with a Rotring and then laboriously filled in with a felt-tip, the masters that Brody drew up for monthly use in *The Face* had to be completed so fast that blemishes were touched up with Tippex, if there was time: because the letters were drawn large enough, once they been reduced by a PMT camera the print process disguised any defects. *Typeface 6* was adapted by CNN for the logotype used for their Gulf War coverage in 1991. The contextual leaps from magazine to High Street to warfare went unquestioned.

Towards the end of his time at *The Face*, Brody reacted to his own experimentation and tried to refine it into a more interwoven structure of image and text. The design of *Arena* aimed to get expressive results out of a much tighter range of devices. His starting-point was the straightforward language of information design, intentionally boring, and never intended to carry a strong personality – "I wanted to suggest that some of the hysteria should be taken out of contemporary design."

In effect, the simple and elegant structure of *Arena* was even easier to appropriate and copy. Lowercase-only *Helvetica Black* was soon everywhere. Gradually, the kerning of headlines was reduced and words began to burst in on themselves, one of the first "new looks" of Mac-generated typesetting. The compressed shape of a word was taken to signify fashionable information, usually liberated from any content... Once again, this typographic style gave the impression of a bold, dynamic culture, aware of change but still in command of its future. Not according to many: the Green issue was taking centre stage.

THE FIRST VOLUME of *The Graphic Language* was ready to go into production at the end of September 1987. Shortly after this, Brody was approached by The Body Shop to design their annual report. The Body Shop brochure was all determinedly analogue-produced. Brody refused to go anywhere near a computer, feeling that if any work could be done by hand, then it should be done by hand. The brief required a double-page spread of a Body Shop interior; conveniently, Ian McKinnell, who specialised in architecture and product photography, rented studio space just upstairs. It turned out that McKinnell had purchased one of the first Mac Plus computers in the country, which he finally persuaded Brody to borrow and play around with.

Typographically this early model was best suited to low resolution 'bitmaps'. The coarse edges of early computer-generated typefaces were so obviously illustrations of the machine's limitations; nevertheless, they found their champion thanks to an independently produced magazine from California, *Emigre*, which quickly recognised that computers would revolutionise the way type could be used. The magazine became a quarterly advertisement of this fact and from this *Emigre* became the first independent type label.

For the cover of *Sex Money Freaks*, a 12" single by Cabaret Voltaire, Brody used a computer-bitmapped type design for the first time. The Paris fashion company, Repetto, and their artistic director Elisabeth Djian commissioned him to design an A3 brochure, which combined freestyle computer-generated typography with a freestyle setting of *Franklin Gothic Heavy*, similar to the way that type was being stag-gered in *Arena*. The studio had not yet reached the stage of directly outputting from disk to bromide or film. Dot matrix print-outs from an ImageWriter were still being PMTed, retouched and cut to size for artwork.

The removal of union constraints and the alignment of design and print media to the broader church of 'Service Industry' during 1987 and 1988 did however encourage the emergence of numerous typesetting agencies in central London. Increased competition meant a greater choice of fonts but Brody and his studio never relied upon traditional typesetting techniques. If a hand-drawn headline was thought unsuitable, then individual letters would be photocopied large from an old hot-metal typesetter's catalogue, pasted together one by one onto a graph pad, retouched, and then reduced to size under a PMT machine. 3D letters were sculpted and then photographed. An IBM golf-ball or Canon Typestar typewriter was often used. At this point, the computer could not compete with the flexibility and range of these techniques. Nevertheless, Brody was always keen to control as many stages of the process from design to print as possible and it was clear that computers would soon allow designers to do this more easily. Brody had to buy a Mac and got an SE, a small but then relatively powerful black-and-white machine whose hard disk capacity was a meagre 20 megabytes.

Before he could disappear behind a screen, a great deal of preparation was necessary for an exhibition of his work at London's Victoria and Albert Museum, planned to coincide with the publication of the *Graphic Language* book. March, April and May 1988 were crazy months. An increasing amount of work was commissioned from abroad. Brody had stopped designing covers for *City Limits* and was now art director for the Milan-based Condé Nast magazines *Per Lui* and *Lei*. He had also worked for the New York department store, Bloomingdales, and had just completed designs for his first Japanese client, Mens Bigi.

Work from Japan had come thanks to the efforts of Grant Gilbert, who was Brody's agent in Tokyo for the next five years. In London, the studio had quickly expanded from a nucleus of three, and had employed Jon Crossland, a student from St Martin's, and Mark Mattock, Robin Derrick's assistant at *The Face*. In the summer of 1987 Cornel Windlin arrived from Switzerland having decided to work as a designer rather than pursue his other option to become a professional footballer. David Davies and Tony Cooper joined the studio at the end of '87. Ian Swift, designer at *The Face* and *Arena*, helped out and soon became a full-time employee. Simon Staines, still at the London College of Printing, arrived on a student placement in good time to help organise the work for the exhibition and joined the studio six months later.

The V & A exhibition featured a massive type-mosaic mounted on the floor of the new 20th Century Gallery, type designs screen-printed onto plexiglass "windows", *The Death of Typography* printed onto a huge canvas, and a soundtrack played through a hidden sound system. It was attended by nearly 40,000 people. However, the consequences of the show and the book's publication were not totally positive. Work from British clients soon dried up for the now familiar reason – it was thought to be much easier and cheaper to imitate Brody's design, rather than commission it direct. In any event, Brody was seen to be over-exposed and too successful for his own good. The gap between public perception and personal reality was wider than ever. Because of the amount of preparatory work that had gone into the book and exhibition, the studio was struggling to break even. New commissions were few and far between. A year later, it narrowly escaped going bankrupt.

23. Advert for Plein Sud, Paris 1988
This design for a French fashion company was never printed. The film work was incorrectly processed by a London printing company, and the Brody Studio left in a financial limbo that nearly resulted in its bankrupcy.

DESIGNED WITH TONY COOPER

24. Advert for Prato Expo, Milan 1987
Brody linked the type design he had drawn for *The Face* to a more experimental use of imagery for Prato Expo, an Italian fashion company.

DESIGNED WITH JAMIE MORGAN / BUFFALO

In July the exhibition moved to the Fruitmarket Gallery as part of the Edinburgh Festival. Shortly after this Brody was approached by Greenpeace to design a new image for their *Breakthrough* project in the Soviet Union. Later in the year Brody received a timely commission from the Haus der Kulturen der Welt, an arts institution similar to London's Commonwealth Institute, based at the Kongresshalle in Germany – a building that had been donated to the Berlin people by the United States in 1945. HdKdW wanted the Brody Studio to design a new identity and to art-direct a series of posters that promoted their exhibitions and events. This meant regular work that could be organised alongside a design for the German magazine *Tempo,* which Brody completed with Cornel Windlin at the end of 1989. Visits to Berlin also allowed regular contact with MetaDesign, whose chief designer, Erik Spiekermann, Brody had met at the "Type '87" conference in New York. Spiekermann and his partner, Joan, had set up the first FontShop, a mail-order digital type distributor with whom Brody would later become centrally involved.

BY THE SUMMER OF '88 the Tottenham Court Road studio had become so cramped that another move was essential – to an old Victorian furniture warehouse in East Road, near the Old Street roundabout – a strange environment in which to learn how to use the computer, situated in an area of London bombed in the Second World War and still half-derelict. One by one, everyone did learn the Macintosh. David Davies, Mark Mattock and Jon Crossland no longer worked at the studio. Patrick Glover, Giles Dunn and John Critchley joined soon after moving to East Road. Two Japanese students, Yuki Miyake and Nana Shiomi, helped bridge the gap. Dawn Clenton and Simon Emery arrived in 1991 after Windlin, Swift and Cooper had gone freelance. Paula Nessick worked on TV graphics. Simon Staines and Fwa Richards ran the studio. Brody was increasingly abroad.

25, 26. The installation of *The Graphic Language of Neville Brody*, **20th Century Gallery, Victoria & Albert Museum, London 1988**
The first photo shows the wall of logos, and on both can be seen the large letterforms produced in lino and fastened to the floor.
27, 28. Poster and Bookmark for *The Graphic Language of Neville*

Brody, **20th Century Gallery, Victoria & Albert Museum 1988**
Mont Blanc, the sponsors of the V & A exhibition, commissioned Brody to come up with a special item to commemorate its opening. The bookmark was produced in brass, and its shape combined with the type used for the front cover of the first book to produce the promotional poster.

29. Poster for *Signals*, **Channel 4 TV, London 1988**
One of Brody's first designs using Adobe FreeHand 1.0.
30. Poster for *Die Zeichensprache des Neville Brody*, **Kongresshalle, Berlin 1988**
Using both digitally output and photocopied type against a background created by PMTing a clay sculpture, the poster was supplied as flat artwork. The German printers completely misinterpreted the mark-up; this time, the mistakes were a vast improvement on Brody's original specifications.
31. Poster and logo for Gioblitz, Asics Corporation, Japan 1991
Gioblitz was a new shoe and sportswear range introduced by Asics. The logo, based on a wing, was developed after a long list of image "projections" had been supplied by the client.

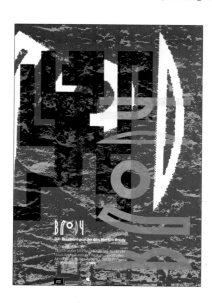

After producing an illustration and software review for *Graphics World*, Brody was able to get Apple Computers to loan him a colour Macintosh II, a black-and-white scanner and a laserprinter (all still in use). Much discussion went into the choice of a name for the new studio. "Concrete" was a favourite and the laserprinter was initialised as such, but the idea got lost in the workload and never went any further.

In November, Brody was offered the opportunity to design the front page of the *Guardian Review*. In 1980, the total advertising expenditure in England was £2815 million: by 1988 it had risen to £7309 million. The *Guardian* article was a critique of the design industry's greedy collusion in this massive increase, largely the result of the Government's reliance on advertising to press through its policies. At this time, 9 of the world's 10 biggest design groups were based in London. This large agency form of design was being presented as a key to national salvation. The *Guardian* received a big response and felt bound to publish a full-page riposte. The original article was later developed with Stuart Ewan for the US *Print* magazine in December 1988.

"Design consultancy Fitch RS have produced a grim reaper lookalike for Southern Electric. The hollow eye sockets and the dynamic horizontal bars clearly mean 'Business or Death' and God help anybody who ignores a Final Reminder. Going further, the John Michael logo for the London Electricity Board's Power Stores omits the human touch altogether and offers a variant on the SS insignia. If this logo fails to invite customers into the shop, it may at least be depended upon to deter shoplifters."
Graham Vickers, 'Design: signs of the times', *The Sunday Correspondent*, 17 September 1989.

THE *GUARDIAN* ARTICLE marked the end of an era for Brody and the studio. Increasingly isolated from the design industry, for the next four years the studio embarked on an exploration of the computer's wider possibilities and Brody looked to make links with companies who shared a global vision. He decided to work with few clients but on a long-term basis, preferably on a one-to-one collaboration where 'service' could be replaced by an new emphasis on evolutionary process. Rather than design more logos, he wanted to create a language and system for each company that would enable them improve the content of their communications and control their design in-house, working as a consultant with clients receptive to this intention – almost none were based in Britain.

Alongside the Photographers' Gallery, Vitsoe and Pilcher Hershmann, one of the studio's few remaining London-based supporters in 1989 was Mike Collins, who ran a management company representing, amongst others, the German group Propaganda, composer Steve Martland and long-time associates Wire, for all of whom Brody's studio created designs.

A chief ambassador at this time was Brody's exhibition, which travelled to Berlin, Frankfurt and Hamburg. In London, Brody made plans with FontShop to broaden its international scope. Following FontShop Canada, by April 1990 a London-based outlet was registered, having had to change its name for copyright reasons to FontWorks UK. Sited downstairs from the East Road studio, it opened in June on a shoestring budget and now stocks over 9000 fonts. In 1990 to buy one involved a wait of between four and fourteen days. In 1994 a font can be delivered in central London within an hour.

For the Brody studio, understanding how to use the Macintosh was a slow struggle. The studio had also leased a photocopier that could produce brilliant results by pushing its halftone, reverse-out and contrast functions. Different paper stocks were always being experimented with. The fax machine could produce some startling visual effects. When work was slow, everybody would take turns playing the computer game Crystal Quest, which for a few months became an addiction. You had to be quick to avoid the pacmen, mines and crawlers, but the game not only provided a lesson in how to use the mouse and keyboard at speed – it served as an example of the need to battle with the computer, and then to call a halt. Working on the Mac, it is easy to come up with infinite variations of a single design, and then lose sight of any qualitative differences.

As a complete contrast to *The Face* and *Arena*, Brody worked for a year as art director of the French magazine *Actuel*, giving it a new masthead and altering the editorial sequence. At *The Face*, everything was done quickly and discreetly. At *Actuel*, night-long discussions, debates and dialectic were the order of the day... plus the last-minute panic to meet the printer's deadline.

Following the job for Nike and a series of one-off UK commissions, in 1990 Brody finally got the chance to delve deeper into television graphics with a commission from a new Hamburg-based cable TV company, Premiere. He then completed his first totally digital design work for print during the summer – a calendar for the Tokyo department store, Parco. The commission gave Brody the chance to redefine his computer experimentations. Emphasising an interplay and tension between organic and inorganic shapes, the Parco Calendar also utilised recycled paper for fluorescent printing inks. Its production coincided with the Tokyo "UK90" Festival. In its latest and best-arranged incarnation, the *Graphic Language* exhibition was displayed in the largest available space on the top floor of Parco's store in Shibuya.

This collaboration with Parco entailed extended visits to Tokyo which further underlined the need to embrace and transform new technologies. Brody and Gilbert's agent in Tokyo, Junko Wong, arranged commissions from Asics and Gioblitz. It was clear that while Japan was highly advanced in developing hardware, the opportunity to create new software to exploit this was still wide open. An attempt was made to set up an Anglo-Japanese multimedia foundation, Global Force. Plans were also developed for a new digital publishing project, *Fuse*, which FontShop International would produce and distribute. *Fuse* would be a 'magazine' that promoted a dialogue on the state of digital typography and its effect on language by contrasting print and digital media, with a copyright waiver that encouraged purchasers to adapt and abuse the given typefaces.

The then-new Macintosh programme, Adobe Photoshop, enabled designers to distress image and type, manipulating shape, density, detail – and letters as if they were photographs, or more accurately, dabs of digital paint. Programmes like Altsys Fontographer and Letraset FontStudio allow anyone to draw typefaces, but this is often electronic graffiti, not necessarily type design. With Photoshop or Adobe Illustrator, anyone can mess up the existing typefaces, turning typography into performance art.

32. Catalogue cover for *Bienal Internacional de São Paulo*, The British Council 1989
Order.
DESIGNED WITH SIMON STAINES
33. Proposed Image poster, Schauspielhaus, Hamburg 1992
Chaos.

34. Signations for *Bodystyles*, Channel 4 TV, London 1989
For this series of four programmes on how clothes express cultural ideas, Brody projected slides of hand-drawn type onto moving bodies.
DESIGNED WITH FWA RICHARDS

Programmes like QuarkXPress and PageMaker were developed as extensions of the printing press. Macromind Director and Adobe Premiere are extensions of the very different media of film, photography, video and television rolled into one. Design for the screen insists upon different precepts to design for print. Clarity and legibility are to the page as impact and metamorphosis are to the screen.

The traditional pillars of design language – typographic specifications, legibility, the grid – have quickly been forgotten. The typesetter, once central to the early stages of any design work, has become the output bureau, the last port of call before printing. In the main, a service that was once interpretive, requiring a high degree of professional skill, has become increasingly mechanical – a question of checking the settings and pressing the appropriate buttons. Using a desktop publishing programme, a scanner and a printer, a magazine can be designed from the comfort of your own home; the disks can then be sent direct to the printer. Like service bureaux, printers are struggling to catch up with the demands of new technology. Technical Support Services and Software Clinics set up to cure malfunctions are often as much in the dark as their confused clients. High quality digital scans are only now managing to compete with conventional hi-end repro. This situation will improve, but so far, the burden has fallen on designers to direct the pre-press process. Computers have cut out the typesetter middle-man but they have not been a labour-saving device for designers.

While it is now possible to produce the best quality highest resolution typesetting since the invention of printing, distressed letterforms appear everywhere – on billboards and flyposters, in magazines, no doubt soon in annual reports. The development from the Daguerrotype, the first photographic image, to the abstraction of Picasso's *Demoiselles d'Avignon* took seventy years. Digital typography has passed through its Cubist phase in just three years. This demonstrates how type users have been empowered by the computer but it also suggests that language is out of control – we may need to come up with a new definition of 'Anarchy'.

We now have the opportunity to develop Freeform designs. Not only can elements of language be sampled like drum sounds off a record and manipulated in any direction – the dislocation of the written word from its traditions and the global range of communication networks insist upon new ways of using language. More than ever before, the assumptions we make about our mother tongues are challenged by their continual contact with different linguistic concepts. The picture language of Chinese and Japanese Kanji characters embrace the spiritual dimension of human expresssion, highlighted by the movement of the brush-stroke. We now have the chance to move towards a language which is more intuitive than the linear mould of Western contructions.

Fuse is both a forum wherein such present concerns can be raised, and a language laboratory for the future. The editorial and promotional posters that come with *Fuse* are used to push the limits of digital processing. Combining complicated Photoshop images with both standard and experimental typefaces in QuarkXPress is a sure recipe to make the computer crash: getting them to print is a major headache. "All along we've been challenging the machine, trying to force it to do things it really wasn't supposed to do."

Brody designed a new type family in 1991, *Blur*, reflecting the present transitional period. A frequently-used technique had been to create softer edges on 'classic' typefaces by experimenting with the focus and exposure settings on the PMT camera. This was unpredictable and time-consuming, but often produced brilliant results. It also made headlines

35. Page for *Vagabond*, *Touch*, London 1991
The début of *Blur*... the quotation taken from Benjamin's 1936 essay "The Work of Art in the Age of Mechanical Reproduction". The typeface *Blur* is an analogue-digital collision, a mechanised version of previous practice whereby type was shot out of focus using the PMT camera, and the visual voice of a new language emerging from the keyboard.

Vagabond updated the idea of the almanac – Kandinsky's *Blue Rider* is an example – and pursued a similar hybrid, combining criticism, short stories, interviews, photographs and poetry with specially commissioned pages that took design processes to the limit. The main motive was to give a voice to ideas that fell outside the narrow mainstream agenda.

36. Cover for Photo-CD
by Akira Gomi, Digitalogue, Tokyo 1993
Originally drawn for *Fuse 9* (see p.33 and p.173), *Autosuggestion* is based on the negative space of *Blur*.

13

37. Postcard for *Touch*, 1994
The blurred and exaggerated chaos of com-
muters moving across the main hall at New
York's Grand Central Station embodies the
sense of alienation, contained within the
rush of a shared direction.

**38, 39. Proposed covers for *Life –
The Observer Magazine*, London 1994**
Following the recent history of manic section-
building amongst newspapers, Brody's new
design for *The Observer Magazine* reintro-
duced a modernist spirit. Having completed
a dummy issue, the design was taken over
by *The Observer*'s in-house team.

40. Personal business card, 1990
Repeatedly photocopied, the motif of a bull's
head was originally devel-
oped for a Canadian calendar for the month
of April, but never published. The recycled
image was eventually used for a business
card printed on recycled Kraft board.

41. Poster for Graphic Arts Message, .Too Corporation, Tokyo 1992

appear more fluent after the harsher geometry of *Industria*
and *Helvetica*. *Blur* emulates a physical process. In this
sense, it is undesigned, a sign of digital technology starting to
dictate its own language. Other font designs – *Pop, Gothic,
Harlem* – continue to question the relationship between the
printed word and digital language. For Brody, this is an obsession. As well as working with *Fuse* and FontShop International, Brody frequently collaborates with the Boston-based
Font Bureau in the United States.

Having experimented with Photoshop (and by now in pos-
session of a faster Macintosh, the IICI) the first full-colour
designs that Brody created using the programme were for the
Dutch telecom company PTT, a special edition of stamps to
commemorate the *Floriade*. The electronic colours produced
on the screen were ahead of the computer's ability to translate them accurately to film. At that time, the Macintosh had
no colour management system. Following numerous proofs
which revealed wild colour variations, Brody used water-based
Iris ink-jet prints (processed direct from disk) which were then
scanned for film-making. First commandment of the colour
monitor: what you see on screen, never expect in print. But
this too is changing.

Brody has recently completed a signage and print system
for the Kunst und Austellungshalle, a new arts complex in
Bonn. He set up a Austria-German company, DMC, working
with Hubert Schillhuber and Oliver Kartak to develop television
design systems. He has created and is still working on the
station identity and screen graphics for the Austrian state
broadcasting company, ORF.

In Japan, Brody now works closely with Naomi Enami of
Propeller Artworks and the new CD-ROM company Digitalogue,
who also run a "digital gallery" in Tokyo. Overseas travel has
exposed Brody to different working practices and cultures but
also to long hours in departure lounges and hotel rooms.

In the summer of 1992, the studio moved from East Road
to a larger space in Islington. After its erratic years of development at East Road, the studio personnel settled down to the
hard core of Richards, Staines, Critchley, Dunn and Emery.
Ian Wright, who had rented a studio space at East Road, still
occupied his corner. Tony Cooper oscillated wildly in and out
of the studio, doing his freelance work. His death in October
1993 came as a great shock.

NEW TECHNOLOGY IS NOT A PANACEA. But unless we create an
open context to embrace its possibilities and investigate
ourselves, its darker potential of control and surveillance
might easily take hold. There needs to be an alternative to
the predictable scenario.

The "freeform" approach is at an early stage. The *Virtual*
type design for *Fuse 5* and the poster and font for Digitalogue
poses the question, is the alphabet at its most expressive
point of development, or is the written word more or less
redundant? The posters for GAM and for the Rio Earth
Summit in Brazil highlight the liquid language of digital technology, layered, out-of-focus, seemingly chaotic shapes, burst-
ing for change.

The *Fuse* posters highlight how letterforms might once
again become objects of beauty and inspiration rather than

commerce. Upgrades like Apple's QuickDraw GX and the
PowerPC further bias typography to the screen, and because
of the new range of activities that these faster processing
capabilities induce – different patterns of behaviour from the
ones we use for printing – our relationship to and perception
of information is inevitably transformed. Soon we will be able
to customise software programmes to suit our own individual
interests and activities.

"Unless we are prepared to claim special attributes for the
poet – the attributes of vision – and unless we are prepared
to admit the work of the artist (that is to say the function of
the 'imagination') as an essential part of the modern world,
there is no reason for continuing to bother with any of the arts
anymore, or with any imaginary activity. No reasons except
money, snobbery, propaganda or escapism."
Humphrey Jennings and Charles Madge, Introduction to
*Pandæmonium – The Coming of the Machine Age as Seen by
Contemporary Observers*, André Deutsch 1985.

Language is the last line of security. Every communication
is based on a contract, a consensus that binds its participants to basic terms and conditions. Digital technology
throws such arrangements out of the window. It changes the
DNA of language. If the history of communication is a continual quest to refine the means of communication, it is clear
that the more we try and refine it, the more we strive to communicate. And the more money we spend in the process.

The old rules have been thrown out and the new principles have yet to be established. For Brody, the last five years
have been a period of exploration and risk-taking, a tense,
exciting time whose outcome is far more important than that
of the previous decade. The decisions taken in the next few
years are crucial. The new world of computer-generated
images has, for the first time, absolutely no precedent in the
natural world. What are the limits to the powers we are able
to exert on this planet? We must take full responsibility for
whatever we create. We should see it as a fantastic privilege
that we have such an opportunity.

1. The Luddites were not simply impetuous, backward-looking machine breakers as
most history books would have them, but a well-organised if diffuse utopian workers'
movement. Luddite activists would break into factories and damage only those
machines that did not match the quality of finish that could be achieved by hand.
They received the full support of local communities, and those whose endeavours
were not ended on the scaffold continued to be involved in the political and social
movements that followed.
Demands for electoral reform and better working conditions – including a minimum wage – culminated in a peaceful gathering of thousands of textile workers and
their families at St Peter's Field in Manchester in 1819 to listen to Henry 'Orator'
Hunt, a gentleman-farmer turned political reformist who had become their spokes-
man. Fearing an uprising, local magistrates sent in the yeomanry to arrest him and
when this proved unsuccessful, they called in the cavalry to disperse the crowd. A
bitter struggle ensued in which 11 people were killed and over 400 wounded.
The Peterloo massacre caused a national outcry but it did not catalyse the revolution which many "respectable citizens" had feared. Economic conditions improved,
granting Lord Liverpool's Tory government a brief respite before signs of popular agi-
tation re-emerged in 1825.
For a full account of this period and one of the very few that covers the Luddite
uprising in any detail, see E.P. Thompson, *The Making of the English Working Class*,
Victor Gollancz 1963.

2. PMT = photomechanical transfer – in the US, better known as a 'stat' machine.

GRAPHIC
ARTS
MESSAGE

EXHIBITION SEMINAR WORKSHOP

'92

THANKS FOR 73 YEARS CAMPAIGN

TOKYO

**42, 43. Logos for Graphic Arts Message,
.Too Corporation, Tokyo and Osaka 1992**

**44, 45. Posters for Graphic Arts Message,
.Too Corporation, Tokyo, Osaka and Sapporo 1992**

The importance of this work is on a number of levels, representing a crossroads in Brody's confidence in working with digitally-generated images. First of all, every element was created and processed entirely by using Adobe Photoshop, resulting in an image that is both organic and entirely synthetic. The design for the Tokyo poster was completed more or less in one go, overnight, digitally transmitted to Japan and printed the following day.

For each application, Brody took the cold language of logos and transformed it into something more fluent and emotive. The layering of typographic shapes and colours in Photoshop can be likened to the use of multitracking in sound recording. By using up to 32 alpha channels in the programme, individually processed layers can be stored as a series of masks that can be called up at any time. Unlike sound recording, these masks can be used as "stencil resists" so that only a section becomes visible through another. Brody used separate channels to place the GAM logo in different positions, one interacting with the other as a stencil. The backgrounds were produced by treating and enlarging a section from the final typographic combination.

Having begun to master the details and defaults of computer image making, digital painting ceased to be a metaphor or an aspiration, but became the most accurate way of naming both the activity and the result. The computer could be used as an electronic palette.

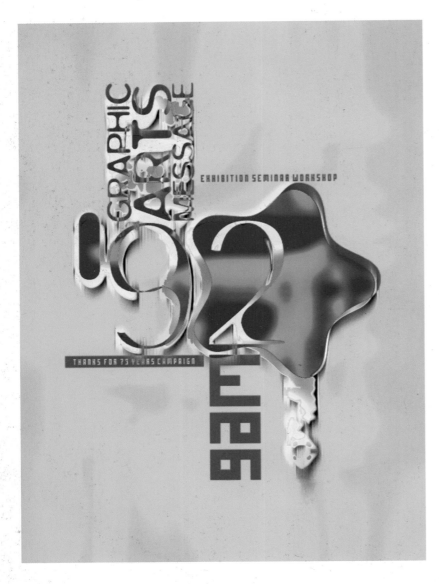

maclab

**47. Page for *Interview*,
New York 1989**
Brody was asked by art director
Fabien Baron to come up with
a page design for a feature in
Interview based on an ecological
theme. Echoing his approach to the
record cover for Z'EV shown in book
one, and following the work for the
Guardian Review (see p.131), Brody
highlighted the relationship between
urban pollution and the degradation
of language.

Environmentalists tell us we have
thirty years in which to save the
planet, but we have barely started
to address the damage caused by
mental pollution – and what effect
the great investment into an electromagnetic lifestyle will have. This
was an attempt to push the Green
issue in this direction.

**48. Proposed phonecard for BT,
London 1991**
49. Page for Gilbert Papers, USA 1991
The phonecard design was never used by BT
due to administrative delays.

Digital to Paper... Co-ordinated by the
design studio Thirst, Brody was one of seven
who took part in an exercise of "Chinese
whispers" based on the Surrealist game
"Exquisite Corpse", a process of building
unusual associations – one player writes a
phrase on a piece of paper, folds it over,
and passes it on for the next person to add a
few words. In this case, the seven designers
used computers and fax machines. Gilbert
Papers sponsored the production of a beautifully printed booklet in an unusual format –
380 x 135mm – as for the outcome, this is
where it started...

When roads and canals were constructed
at the start of the Industrial Revolution in
Britain in the 1790s, they were paid for and
charged for by private enterprise – as a result
many were of inferior quality and badly
planned. Just like the later development of
the rail network, these new methods of travel
and transportation attracted investors seeking quick profits, who paid heed to the infrastructure only insomuch as it might effect
their finances. Eventually, the government
was forced to intervene to standardise the
chaos that this forerunner of the "Free
Market" had caused.

With the exception of a new initiative by
Clinton and Gore's administration in the USA,
the same is being sanctioned by govern-
ments who decline to finance and co-ordinate
the construction of information superhighways. Monopoly holds disguised by a general
free-for-all turn out costly in the long run.

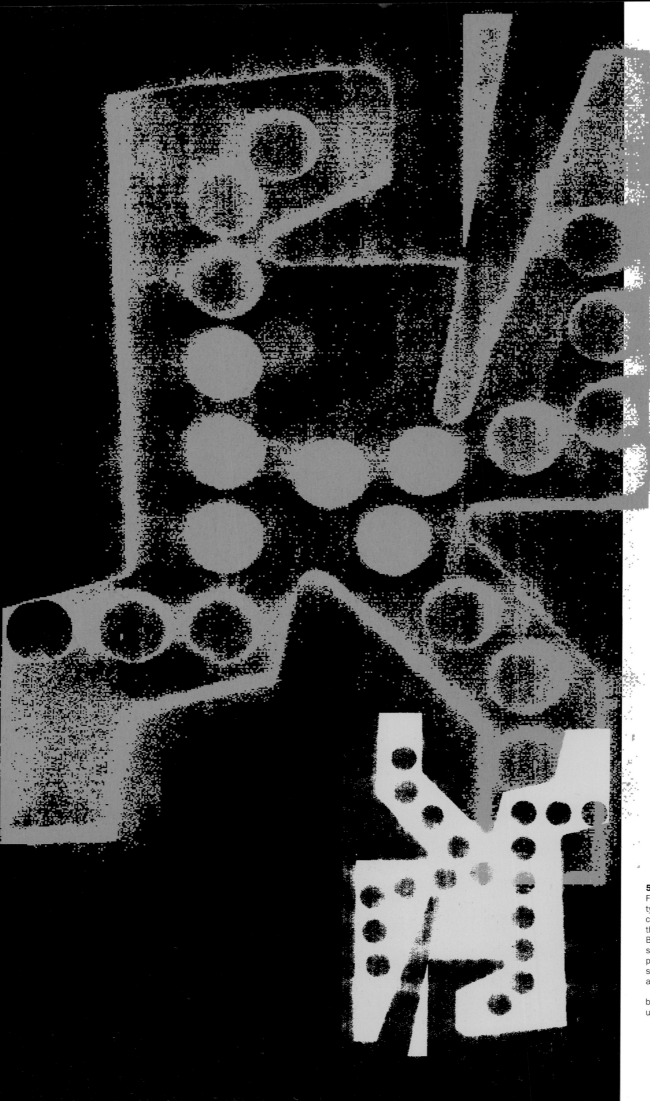

50. Page for *Emigre 13*, USA 1989
For the issue "Redesigning Stereotypes", designers were invited to create new, updated versions of their national symbols. Brody's British lion is also based on the studio's logo, used only as a trumpet blast for special occasions – such as invoices, project proposals and compliment slips.

Emigre restricted the design to black and white. It was also printed upside down!

30 POSTERS ON ENVIRONMENT AND DEVELOPMENT

CLEARRELEASEFLOWGROWOPENINTEGRATEILLUMINATE

51. Poster for the UN Earth Summit, Rio de Janeiro 1992
Thirty international designers were invited by Fellipe Taborda to design a poster on the theme of "Environment and Development" to mark the Rio Earth Summit.

The image is both a plea and a provocation. The fish – now cast as a man-made object – is being pushed from the water, seemingly inanimate, yet potentially freed from its man-made fate. The fish – no more than a skeleton on the surface – is also clasped by the hand that seeks to hide the reality. A clue to this visual paradox lies in the structure of the fish, its centre suggesting the contours of the globe. The double image is further underlined by the white to black sequence of words, whose meanings are in opposition to the accompanying image and project an underlying optimism.

52–56. CD Posters, Cover, Label and LP cover for *Manscape*, Mute Records, London 1990

On their first LP *Pink Flag*, Wire proposed that if you explore an idea once, why repeat it? Their policy has been an inspiration ever since.

Manscape was the last LP cover Brody was directly involved with. The design was done over two months at the end of 1989 – our intention was to create artworks that not only indicated the scale of Wire's new work and its title, but extended the limited parameters of the compact disc packaging format. Everything had gone to CD, its badly-designed jewel case and basic booklet (at the outset, often no more than a thin double-sided card) seen as secondary to "better quality" sound.

Touch had already released two alternatives to this format, and for Wire we carried this forward, supported by their record company, *Mute*. LP, CD and cassette each featured a different treatment of an image provided by the group, a scratched-out postcard of the main roads leading to a colonnade in Lisbon's city centre. This we turned into an absurd UFO-like object: a mode of transport to who knows where... the decay of science reality, not the dream of science fiction.

Different sets of information were processed by either computer, photocopier or fax. Brody used FreeHand 1.0 to design one side of the CD poster; I laid out the other and worked on the print production. The collaboration reflected the collision of analogue and digital thinking, new and old techniques – and how in practice they could be combined. Different paper stocks, rough and smooth, were used for each element of the CD package – Kraft board for the outer case, wrapping paper for the poster and coated cartridge for the booklet. The record cover was printed on matt art board using different Pantone colours to the CD, including a slate grey that gave the scratched-out lines of the processed postcard the texture of blackboard and chalk.

wire
man
scape

Life in the Manscape Stampede Patterns of Behaviour Other Moments Small Black Reptile Torch It Morning Bell Where's the Deputation? What Do You See? Goodbye Ploy Sixth Sense Children of Groceries You Hung Your Lights in the Trees/A Craftsman's Touch

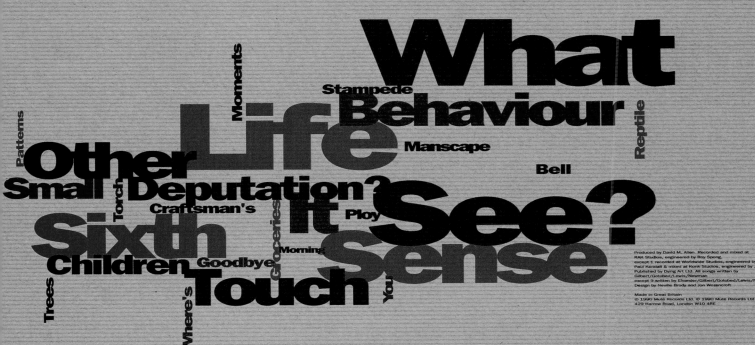

Produced by David M. Allen. Recorded and mixed at RAK Studios, engineered by Roy Spong, except 1 recorded at Worldwide Studios, engineered by Paul Kendall & mixed at Konk Studios, engineered by Joe Gibb Published by Dying Art Ltd. All songs written by Gilbert/Gotobed/Lewis/Newman except 9 written by Elvander/Gilbert/Gotobed/Lewis/Newman Design by Neville Brody and Jon Wozencroft.
Made in Great Britain
℗ 1990 Mute Records Ltd. © 1990 Mute Records Ltd.
429 Harrow Road, London W10 4RE

57. *Life in the Manscape*,
Mute Records, Unreleased

Erase then cut and paste, from here to another place. The lyrics to "Patterns of Behaviour" reflected Wire's own transition from analogue to digital recording processes, which they contrasted with songs about the storming of the Berlin Wall ("Stampede"), social breakdown in Britain ("Children of Groceries") and personal catharsis ("Torch It!"). Technology, society and the individual collide at the centre.

Life in the Manscape was an all-formats single to be released concurrently, but it was shelved by *Mute* and only appeared in the USA as a CD. The cover image selected by the group's guitarist, Bruce Gilbert, was digitised using the studio's recently acquired black-and-white scanner.

DESIGNED WITH JON WOZENCROFT

58. TV commercial for Nike, Weiden and
Kennedy, Los Angeles 1988
Using just *Franklin Gothic*, the differences
in typographic scale were combined with a
powerful yet playful positioning of the letterforms to convey an emotive dynamic through
a sense of continual motion. Individual characters are used as onomatopoeic shapes, a
kind of 2D animation.

59. **T-Shirt for Nike, 1988**
60. **Magazine advert for Nike, 1988**
61–63. **Logos for Nike, 1988**
Brody was supplied with a series of phrases and developed combinations of them; these were then storyboarded as 2D movements and distortions using the expressive typographic structures that he had been experimenting with for *Arena* magazine. The final choice for TV advertising was produced and directed by Propaganda Films in LA and then made into a press campaign. Nike wanted to target a young audience and applied the design to various items of merchandise, a blitz of baseball caps, beach towels, and T-shirts.

DESIGNED WITH CORNEL WINDLIN

FUSE1

FUSE is a new venture in type design, containing
four experimental fonts digitised for Macintosh.
The fuse disc is Accompanied by four A2 posters
showing each typeface in creative application.

Issue One features four British designers :
PHIL BAINES
NEVILLE BRODY
MALCOLM GARRETT
IAN SWIFT

Produced by Fontshop International and distributed exclusively through the Fontshop network

Opposite:
64. Poster for *Fuse 1*, FontShop International 1991
Below:
65–67. Posters for *Fuse 2*, *3*, *4*, FontShop International 1991–2.
Fuse 1, *Invention*, questioned the occult traditions of typography, protectionist practices and the impossible pursuit of the "classic" typeface. This has been reflected by the emphasis upon reviving and digitising hot-metal letterforms, created for a different age with different preconditions, instead of designing type for the present environment. *Fuse 2* was an investigation into the magical origins of language, focusing on *Runes* and the idea of "secret", intuitive information, its presence in the synapse between feeling and thought, proposing that we take full responsibility for the elements we use to create new linguistic models. At the opposite end of the history of writing, the theme for *Fuse 3* was *Disinformation*, a playful turn on hi-tech design and its role in fixing the grid of controlled climates like airports and shopping malls. The designers for the first three issues have been, respectively, English, Dutch and German. The theme for the US *Fuse 4* was *Exuberance*, extolling the virtues of ornamental type and giving birth to the "Dirty Face" – Barry Deck's *Caustic Biomorph*.

FUSE

In the last 500 years of typographic history, the most significant changes have taken place in the last five years. Given that the digital conversion affects all spheres of human activity, it is remarkable that there should be such limited attention in the mainstream media to how this change might be visually represented. The *Fuse* project was set up by the Brody studio in October 1990 not as a strictly commercial venture but as a necessity. Published through the FontShop network as a new medium to highlight the creative possibilities of digital typography, *Fuse* creates an outlet that allows type designers to challenge conventional thinking about the form and function of typography. Producers and purchasers are urged to experiment with digital language in a context liberated from client/commercial constraints – contributors are briefed to push the boundaries of both the printed word and its fusing into electronic language so that typography's professional representation in graphic design is revolutionised, and digital type can be seen as a common feature of everyday life and not something that happens in confinement.

68. *Fuse* format, *Fuse 1*, FontShop International 1991
The Fuse box is made out of corrugated card with the logo screen-printed in a different colour for each issue. A sticker seals the contents – comprising five two-colour posters and a disk loaded with at least five experimental typefaces.

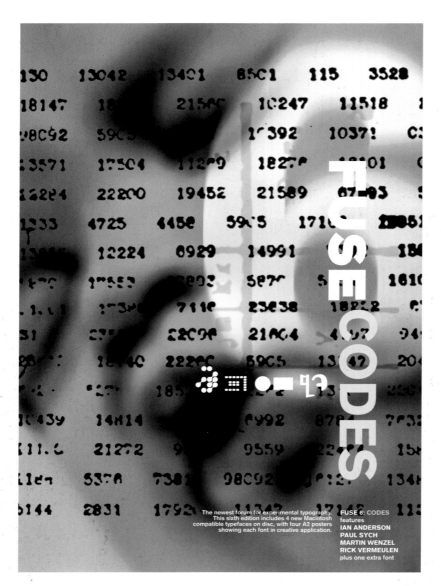

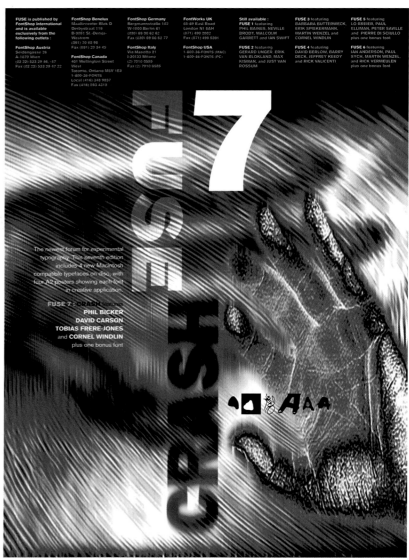

Access to digital typography empowers more people with the tools to question and develop alternative forms of visual language. By adapting old typefaces and drawing up new fonts, users are able to remodel the basic vehicles we use to construct written language. New forms and new visual codes have quickly emerged.

Fuse is a language research project. Designers are commissioned to develop an experimental typeface that follows through a thought process on the state of the visual word, and on an accompanying A2 poster they imply its creative potential. An editorial booklet or poster outlines the theme and focus of each quarterly issue. Brody designs a promotional poster for each release, and since *Fuse 5* he has designed a "hidden" font to accompany the set of four. The digital format of computer disk is packaged with five posters in a corrugated card case, reflecting the hybrid state between print and screen. The contrast between the two methods of storage and display is used as a platform to promote a dialogue on the extent to which the digital code alters communication.

**69–70. Poster for *Fuse 6* and *7*,
FontShop International 1993**
Fuse 6 covered the codes of language, and the devices used to protect information from being deciphered. *Crash*, *Fuse 7*, underlined the fragility of our language system, probing the connection between violent imagery and physical violence, drawing a parallel between this form of information overload and the possible collapse of the systems we depend on to communicate.

Opposite:
**71. *F Code*, *Fuse 6*,
FontShop International 1993**
New technology recodifies language. The transmission of information *seems* to be a smoother and "more efficient" process, when in fact the shock of the new creates a temporary state of confusion and anxiety, the pain of (re)birth, until such time as the new codes are, once again, completely taken for granted. Codification – the most basic form of packaging – thus easily corrupts the message being transported.

"It's clear that the greatest damage yet done to reading and writing is that contemporary readers have now generally become incapable of forming mental images on the basis of the written word. They're in the habit of having images that replace interpretation. These images stun you like a blinding light, so they have damaged people's ability to create mental images, to make their own cinema in their heads."
Interview with Paul Virilio by Jerôme Sans, *Flash Art* No.138, 1988.

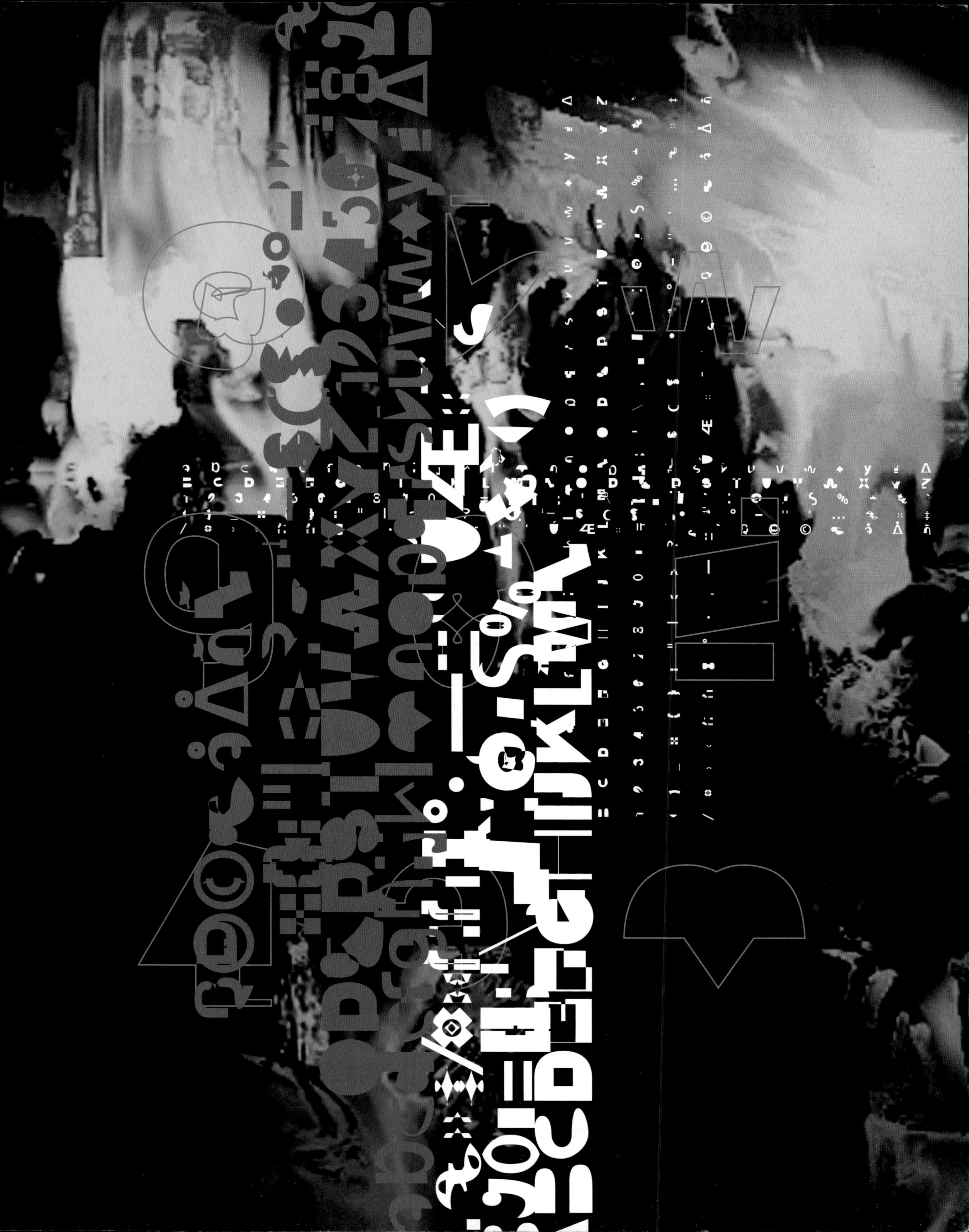

**72. Poster for *Virtual Fuse*, *Fuse 5*,
FontShop International 1992**
Virtual Fuse questioned the possibility that
written language might be outmoded by the
fantasy worlds of VR technology. The computer becomes a dangerous force when,
like an eclipse, its apparent ability to replace
a physical process or reality obscures its
power to transform mental realities.

***F State*, *Fuse 1*,
FontShop International 1991**

The *Fuse* medium is also an attempt to set a standard for
the idea of "interactive". *Fuse* typefaces do not come with the
usual copyright restrictions and users are encouraged to play
around with the designs, to re-interpret what is presented on
disk to see if the ideas can be taken any further. This breaks
down the guarded past and precious image of typography.

"Never is an arrangement-combination technological, indeed it
is always the contrary. The tool always presupposes the
machine, and the machine is always social before it is technical. There is always a social machine which selects or assigns
the technical elements used."
Gilles Deleuze and Claire Parnet, *Dialogues*, Flammarion
1977, quoted in Jean–Louis Comolli, *Machines of the Visible*,
Macmillan Press 1980.

While it's been called "the magazine of the future", *Fuse*
does not fit into an existing category. Strangely, the possibilities of digital publishing have so far been fixed to compact
discs and computer games: other uses of the format have
been few and far between. This is also reflected by the distance between computer performance and the limitations of
the various programmes, since hardware outpaces software in
its development. Walter Benjamin wrote that the new repro-
visual technology of cinema created a state of shock and distress in viewers' perceptions. Electronic type does the same.

Fuse works on a polemical and educational level. Its most
active audience is students – this year, a series of design colleges will take part in *StudentFuse* projects and *Fuse* exhibitions will be held. At present, *Fuse* commissions both
Mac-aware typographers and designers who have had scant
experience of working on a computer, thereby pushing them
into new working processes with often unpredictable results.
The Roman alphabet, once typeset and printed, is regarded as
information "set in stone" but its status on the screen is
entirely different. Any message can be manipulated, and it
soon becomes apparent that the stone is more like clay that
can easily be transformed. Concurrent with its traditional
status is the more recent proposition from semiotics and
structuralism that the alphabet is no more than a code that
needs to be challenged.

Fuse tries to bring a sense of vitality and danger to the
current chaos of communication and provokes an expressive
response. The starting point need not be the alphabet. The
keyboard can be seen and played like a musical instrument,
allowing type design to reach the range of any other form of
composition. Post-war composers like John Cage and
Stockhausen took the precedent of earlier dissonant music
and reconfronted the limits of atonality, LaMonte Young the
drone of religious music. Beuys made new worlds of the art
gallery – Beckett cut through literature. We have been conditioned to recognise words at high speed by television and
advertising. Shape and outline become increasingly more
important than the fine detail of a serif.

73. Poster for *F State*, *Fuse 1*, FontShop International 1991
Using the overlapping shapes and negative space of letter-forms, the *State* font was further abstracted for the *Fuse* poster in Adobe Illustrator. "A line through the chaos of communi-cation", the block of type at the bottom of the poster reads "SIGNAL PROCESS MERGER".

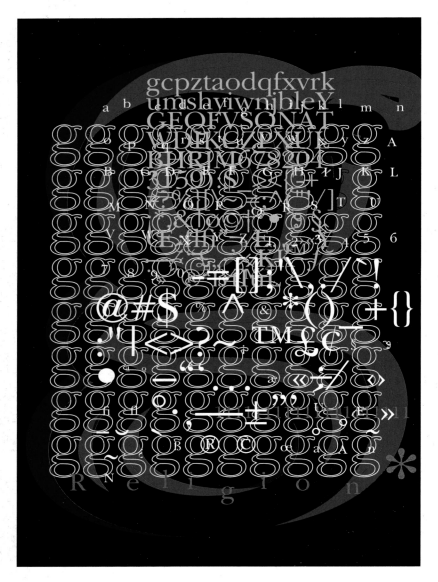

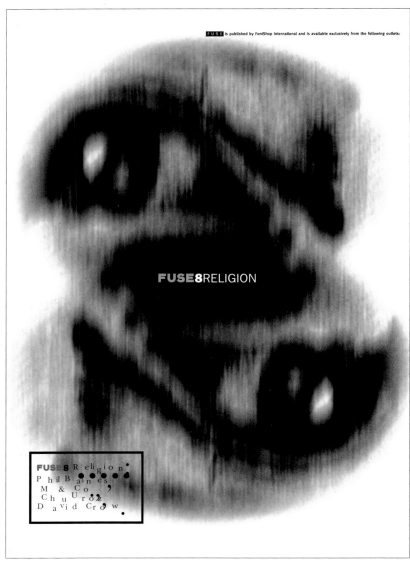

"Let us admit, once and for all, that the lines that we draw are not straight. Here we are. Let us say Yes to our presence together in Chaos."
John Cage, *Silence*, Calder and Boyars 1968.

Fuse has so far published nine issues. This first sequence demonstrates the massive changes happening to the visual word and the way it is applied, but it is also a setting-up procedure for what is to follow. Information will be increasingly animated by faster processing speeds. Our visual perception is undergoing a rapid overhaul thanks to everything from candescent bulletin boards to the current vogue for 'autostereogram' posters. By building a forum in which new ideas can be put forward, and by basing this dialogue around an abstract, intuitive and unconventional approach to print and digital communication – Freeform language – *Fuse* also reminds us of the need to nurture the wealth of human feeling and experience that cannot be programmed.

EDITOR: JON WOZENCROFT
DESIGNED WITH JOHN CRITCHLEY

**74. *F Obedience*, *Fuse 8*,
FontShop International 1993
75. Poster for *Fuse 8*,
FontShop International, 1993**
Fuse 8 underlined the religious attitudes we invest in language by contrasting the lapse of traditional faith with the rise of fundamentalism and NASA's initiative, the Search for Extra-Terrestrial Intelligence (SETI), which attempted to make contact with 'Alien' language from other planets. Such a project not only appears as a vivid and yet euphemistic distress signal as far as earthbound communications are concerned, but goes some way to legitimising William Burrough's claim that "Language is a virus from outer space."

Brody's three font designs for this issue were simple and direct, like typographic telegrams. The first, *Loss of Faith*, mixed the location of individual characters in the keyboard layout so that direct input became scrambled output; for *Order*, every key gave lower-case 'g' and every numeral '1'; for *Obedience*, the baseline and letter spacing

was kept constant while the size of each character was reduced to 40% around its centre to create a sense of forced humility and confusion within a strict discipline. For both *Order* and *Obedience*, the punctuation remained unchanged, implying the dominance and control of external forces.

Fuse is deliberately anamorphic. Our set of twenty six letters, punctuation and numerals is evidently not enough in a digital world. We have the option keys to a new door.

Opposite:
**76. Poster for *Fuse 9*,
FontShop International, 1994**
AutoFuse takes the premise that the car, initially an invention that liberated us, now threatens to choke and enslave us, serving as an example of the hidden consequences of excessive automation and our vacillating relationship to machines. Those who live and work in a brutalising urban environment express themselves accordingly – leading to a breakdown of common civility and manners.

FontShop Austria
(02 22) 523 29 46
Fax (02 22) 523 29 47 22

FontShop Benelux
(09) 220 65 98
Fax (09) 220 34 45

FontShop Canada
Mac 1-800-36-FONTS
PC 1-800-46-FONTS
Local (416) 348 9837
Fax (416) 593 4318

FontShop France
(1) 42 99 95 61
Fax (1) 42 99 95 01

FontShop Germany
(030) 69 58 95
Fax (030) 692 88 65

FontShop Italy
(2) 70 10 05 55
Fax (2) 70 10 05 85

FontShop Switzerland
(41) 44 326 26
Fax (41) 44 326 27

FontWorks UK
(071) 490 2002
Fax (071) 490 5391

FontShop USA
Mac 1-800-36-FONTS
PC 1-800-46-FONTS
Fax (416) 593 4318

FUSE is published by FontShop International and is available exclusively from the following outlets:

FUSE Fuse
Neville Brody Jon Wozencroft
Mario Beernaert Malcolm Garrett
Russell Mills Vaughan Oliver

"Technology, technique and metaphor fuse into a new language of being, and the ancient rift between science and music is apparently healed. The distinction between man and machine is replaced by a continuum in which the rational and the imaginary amalgamate. In a sort of state of zen, where meaning floats, we live the fascination of traversing and transgressing that old frontier and entering, as it were, a fourth dimension. But perhaps all this is merely the latest version of a boy's adventure story."
Iain Chambers, *Migrancy, Culture, Identity*, Routledge 1994.

**77. *F Virtual, Fuse 5,*
FontShop International 1992**
Virtual reality can be contrasted with the tribal practice of shape shifting, whereby shamen would create states of altered consciousness before adopting the guise of an animal or a tree in order to connect with the primal forces of nature, using this energy as a form of healing.

The plastic, virtual environment will transform our perception of reality; we will once again lull ourselves into thinking that we can exert the same power in the real world as we can in an artificial zone. The hallucination of virtual reality is an unedited, intensified and private perversion of the collective rituals and visions common to all societies and all time.

Brody's font explores the plasticity of an artificial language based on universal forms. An exploded diagram of Disneyworld.

**78. *F Crash, Fuse 7,*
FontShop International 1993**
No straight lines appear on *Crash*, reflecting the erosion of conventional forms through the passage of time and the blunt edges that result from the constant collision of information against data, truth against truth. In spite of the sophisticated field of ISDN and fibre-optic networks, an Ariadne's web, the primitive forms of *Crash* suggest organic and flowing shapes tangled up within a language out of control. For this image, Brody placed the outlines of all the characters in *Crash* on top of each other.

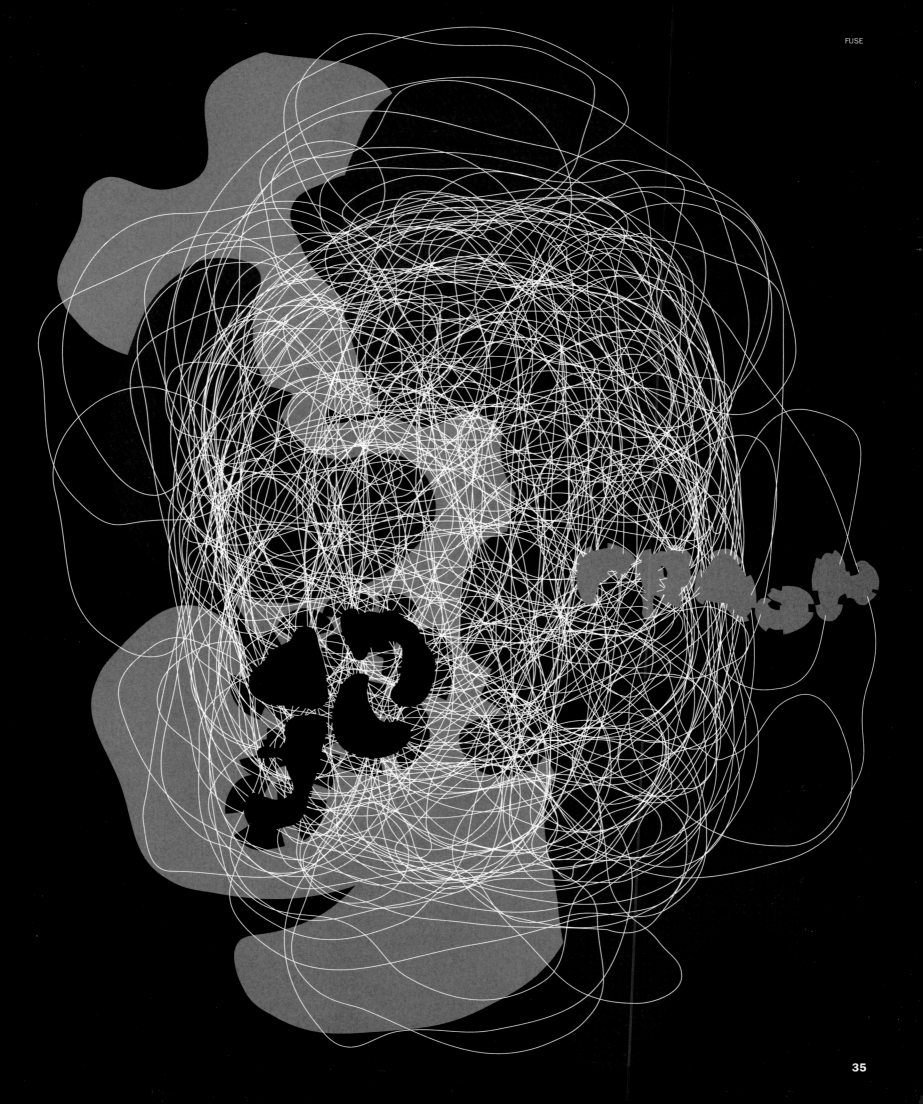

ABCDEFGHIJKLMNOPQRSTUVWXYZabcdef
ghijklmnopqrstuvwxyz1234567890!?*

79. *FF Gothic*, FontFont, FontShop International 1993
Originally reproduced in the Vienna exhibition catalogue, Brody's page design for *FF Gothic* highlights the strict geometric lines of this utilitarian typeface, created as a "*Bank Gothic* for the 1990s". Brody reversed *Bank Gothic*'s customary use at small sizes for commercial print applications – business cards and letterheads often use the font – adding a series of boldly underlined lower-case characters to further disrupt the even flow of the traditional gothic. The typeface's name was originally going to be *Gold*. The final designs were digitised and interpreted by Tobias Frere Jones at the Font Bureau, Boston.

80–81. Stamps for the *Floriade*, PTT, The Netherlands 1991
The completely digital designs for the Dutch Telecom were created by taking a circular route. The original symbols were drawn in FreeHand, turned into Pict files by using the screen capture function, and then imported into Photoshop, processed and colourised. The images were then brought back into FreeHand and the typographic information added.

PTT, THE DUTCH TELECOM, commissioned Brody to create a set of stamps to commemorate the four-yearly *Floriade*, the country's biggest flower show. This coincided with his acquisition of the Macintosh programme that enables image manipulation, Adobe Photoshop. The job came with the benefits of a long lead time, and over a four-month period Brody settled down to an intensive exploration of the programme's capabilities. Having travelled through the learning curve, Brody decided to use softened geometric forms to allude to the organic shapes of flowers and their patterns of movement.

Immediately, the idea of using flowers to illustrate the *Floriade* was rejected in favour of an expressive and apposite alternative that created the effect of the images themselves coming into bloom. This choice of representational graphics

**82–85. Stamps, First Day Cover
and franking logo for the *Floriade*,
PTT, The Netherlands 1991**
Brody supplied the PTT with four final
designs from the myriad of possibilities
he had created in Photoshop – only three
were used, the stamp shown below
bottom right being the odd one out.

was a step beyond the use of the computer to perform a process of literal translation.

The next consideration was the size and scale of the stamps themselves: how to create a delicate yet distinctive and eye-catching image. Contrasting the softened shapes with a hard-edged application of the type information was achieved by combining Photoshop with QuarkXPress. This had the side effect of making Brody aware that different Mac programmes could be combined – you did not have to rely on just one application to complete a commission. This sounds obvious now, but it is another example of how long it takes to break certain habits that come part and parcel with digital design.

PTT liked the designs because they saw the process of representing the flowers as a metaphor for business – computerisation made into an aesthetic. There were enormous problems in matching the printed colours to the conceptions Brody had produced on screen, but this was finally overcome by using ink-jet Iris prints for the film-making.

As a first step to realising the possibilities of digital painting, the stamps became billboards in scale.

THE COMPUTER IS NOT A TOOL. Just as the first TV sets looked like radios, whose early broadcasts were seen as a form of domestic theatre, in its infancy the personal computer has been used to emulate electronically the physical processes it has replaced. In the space between input and output, the PC will colour and contaminate an idea, making original intentions *swerve*. Often, in frustration that the computer will not work as expected, one wishes a hammer were close to hand.

This means that every user is forced into bilingualism, having to learn how to translate analogue brainwaves into digital. Because the computer is such an obviously powerful machine, in the early stages of its use it is unavoidable that its potential is tempered by making it perform tasks that can be easily classified in terms of function. The first temptation is to see it as a labour-saving device – no messy artwork, typesetting turned around in a fraction of the time – but as soon as one has learnt the basic parameters of a programme and starts to divine what should or could be the computer's "natural" language, it fast becomes apparent that this is the equivalent of trying to find the stop point on a Moebius strip.

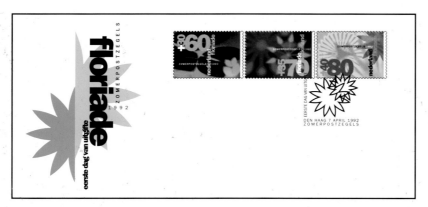

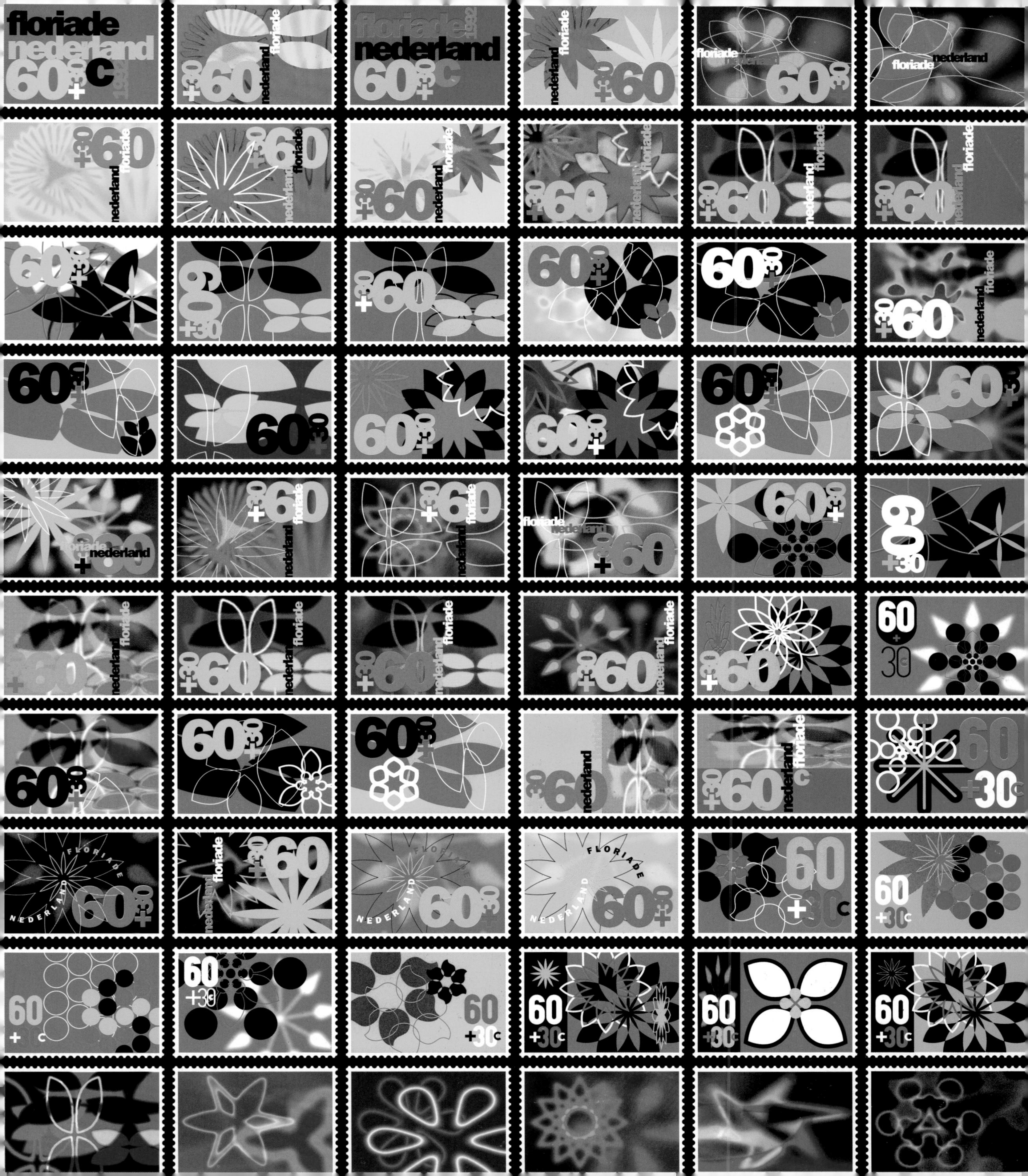
floriade
nederland
60
+30
c
1992

87. Divider page for the
***Fuse* section, *FontBook 1993*,**
FontShop International 1993

Right:
88. Divider page for
***FontBook 1993*,**
FontShop International 1993

Below:
89. Covers for *FontBooks*,
FontShop International
1991 and 1992
The *FontBook* is updated
annually: the most recent
edition was an ambitious
undertaking, with a current
print-run of 20,000. Edited by
Ed Cleary, Jürgen Siebert and
Erik Spiekermann, each font
was fully run out and annotated
detailing original designer and
digital translator – a logistical
nightmare in terms of organisation and artwork.
  Brody's design takes the
word "font", rotated, enlarged,
and fragmented alongside the
scrambled instruction "only print
out black and yellow films."
  For the previous two editions,
MetaDesign devised the binder
format and Brody designed the
wrap-round labels.

FONTSHOP

When Erik Spiekermann travelled to the USA in the 1980s, he
was often asked to bring back typefaces that were not distributed or difficult to find in Europe. At this time, the production,
sale and distribution of fonts was in the hands of four major
companies: many designers did not even realise that fonts
could be purchased for personal use. When the PostScript
language was developed by Adobe in
1984, the outputting of digital type
was no longer restricted to 'bitmap'
outlines and the new standard
was taken up by Apple
Computers. With his partner
Joan Spiekermann, Erik
established the first
FontShop in 1989 in
Germany to import,
market and distrib-
ute typefaces by mail-
order, the operation run from
their Berlin apartment.

Neville Brody, London, UK

**90. Logo for FontFont,
FontShop International 1990**

**91. Logo for FontShop
International 1990**

**92. Insert for FontFont jewel-case,
FontShop International 1990**
The first format for FontFont packaging
included a liner card that described the
installation procedure necessary before
digital typefaces could be used on the
Mac, and a full keyboard layout to highlight the location of option-key characters. All FontFonts are now sold in
recycled board containers similar to
those used for *Fuse*, and include the
alternate character information on a
read-me file on the actual disk.

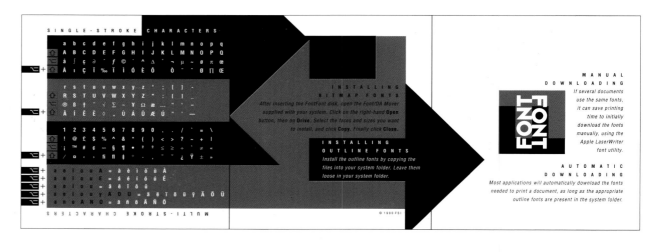

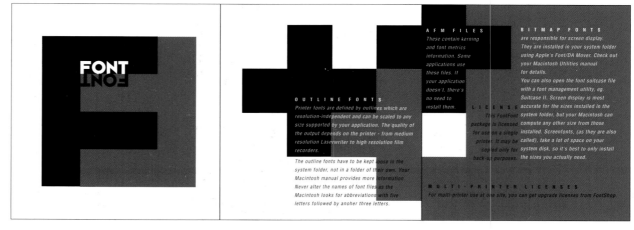

FontShop set a precedent that the fast-growing demand for digital typefaces was best developed by those who were working in its midst – designers rather than middle management. In the same way that traditional repro and typesetting can be bypassed in the print process, type manufacture and distribution has been returned to the domain of the designer.

In 1990 Brody formed FontWorks UK with Stuart Jensen soon after Ed Cleary set up FontShop Canada. A franchising system was then established, with FontShop International created to organise the expanding network. Erik Spiekermann had already created a yellow-and-black design template; yearly *FontBook* catalogues, a quarterly FontZine and *Fuse* are published by FSI, also acting to help the launch of new FontShops and link together those that already exist in Austria, Benelux, Canada, France, Germany, Italy, Switzerland, UK, USA. FontShop dealers are now being established in other countries to distribute FSI's own type label, FontFont, plus other independent publishers and *Fuse*.

FontShop exemplifies the composite minicorporation that will emerge increasingly as digital technology changes modes of production and distribution. The effect of independent type producers like Emigre and Font Bureau in the USA and FontFont in Europe has been to create font pop, combining this with the same structural influence that independent record labels had in the 1970s.

In the USA, *Wired* magazine includes a Top 10 typeface chart – *RayGun* lists font designers on its credits page as if they were authors or photographers. For graphic designers, the choice of typeface increasingly carries the identity of a design. Independently produced typefaces spring up in every context from corporate advertisements to techno 12" singles. This results in a continual watch for the latest font and the latest language. FontFont now releases ten new families of type designs every three months. The FSI typeboard attempts to attract young designers to submit their work. The lifespan of typefaces is in general drastically reduced, though like LPs they can sometimes lie dormant and then suddenly ascend. First designed by Erik Spiekermann for the German Post Office in 1985 but never used, the FontFont *Meta* has rapidly become the *Helvetica* of modern times.

FontFont also promotes experimentation – an early release being the "random font" *Beowolf*, designed by Just Van Rossum and Erik Van Blokland, which mutates to varying degrees each time it appears on screen. The pair are also responsible for the Instant Font series, a step towards the idea of *Dirty Faces*, digitising a classic typewriter style (*Trixie*), the look of a rubber stamp (*Confidential*) and container box-labelling (*Karton*).

The Font Bureau, based in Boston USA, and FontFont are now the largest and fastest-developing independent type libraries in the world. From the transient to the longer-lasting, FontFont provides an outlet for young designers and for typefaces that would be thought too rough and radical for the major font producers. And *Fuse* provides the outlet for type designs thought too radical for FontFont. Why join a band when you can have a hit typeface?

93. Disk label for *FF Blur*, FontShop International 1992

94. Brochure cover for FontFont 5, FontShop International 1992
The design shows all the typefaces included in the fifth FontFont release.

95. Brochure cover for FontFont, FontWorks UK 1994
A new 64-page A5 brochure displays all the FontFont designs to date. The final cover was printed yellow and black.

Panel 1 (top left)

FontShop International

FontShop

FontWorks UK
65-69 East Road,
London N1 6AH
Tel: 071 490 5390
Fax: 071 490 5391

FontShop Deutschland
Bergmannstraße 102
D-1000 Berlin 61
Tel: (030) 6900 6262
Fax: (030) 6900 6277

FontShop Canada
401 Wellington St. West
Toronto Ontario M5V 1E8
Tel: 416-348 9837
Fax: 416-593 4318

FontShop Nederland
Laan von Beek & Royen ld
3701 AH Zeist
Tel: (31) 3404 24950
Fax: (31) 3404 24948

FontShop Belgium
Maallcenter Blok C
Derbystraat 247
9051 St. Denijs-Westrem (Gent)
Tel: (32) 91 262 628
Fax: (32) 91 203 445

FontShop Sweden
Tegnérgatan 37
S-1161 Stockholm
Tel: (46) 821 52 00
Fax: (46) 821 28 80

dousJuoy

FontShop stocks a growing resource of more than 2000 fonts, from leading manufacturers like Adobe, Agfa Compugraphic, Bitstream and Monotype to independent designers and suppliers like Emigre, FontBureau, ATF Kingsley, Giampa Textware, and many more throughout North America and Europe. All fonts are for the Macintosh and 70% and growing for PC.

FontShop was founded on a number of simple ideas, carefully researched, and put into effect to solve all your typeface problems.

The good news about Type

FontShop was set up by typographic experts, Erik Spiekermann in Germany, Neville Brody in the UK, Roger Black in the US and Ed Cleary in Canada are people with strong typographic backgrounds, so they know a good typeface when they see one. They select our fonts according to strict quality criteria.

Our catalogue shows the complete collection of more than 2000 typefaces and typefaces with extra pages were provided by internationally renowned designers including Hermann Garrett April Summer, Hans Vorken and H&Co.

Call and find out how to get your copy of the catalogue.

Set in ITC Officina by Erik Spiekermann and Devil, and Helvetica Ultra Compressed

Panel 2 (top right)

Whether you are working on a Macintosh or a PC, whether you like classical Typefaces or eccentric cuts, whether you want them in PostScript or TrueType format. **FontShop** has a carefully selected collection of typefaces from type foundries such as **Monotype, Adobe, Bitstream, Berthold** and **Agfa-Compugraphic**, as well as exclusive fonts from independent houses like **The Font Bureau, Emigre, Giampa, ClubType** and many others.

Catalogue

FontShop's prize-winning catalogue shows the complete collection of almost **3000 typefaces**. Internationally renowned design bureaus like **Emigre, H&Co, 8vo, Total Design** and **Eclat** have contributed unique a - z divider pages.

Ee1 **Ee1** **Ee1** Typefaces

The many faces of

This advert is set in Officina Sans and Serif, and Helvetica Ultra Compressed

 FUSE

FUSE is a new venture in type design, an interactive magazine and forum for a fresh approach to typography. Published quarterly, **FUSE** contains a disc featuring four experimental fonts digitised for Macintosh, accompanied by four A2 posters that show each typeface in creative application. Issue 1 includes four British designers: *Phil Baines, Neville Brody, Malcolm Garrett, Ian Swift.*

F FontFont

FontShop now releases exclusive type designs under the **FontFont** label. These faces range from classical text to modern headliners and more radical designs. In an age of rapidly changing tastes, we quarterly publish typefaces which are already digitised by their designers, ensuring that the fonts are immediately available.

International

The International **FontShop** network was set up by typographic experts: Erik Spiekermann in Germany, Neville Brody in the UK, Roger Black in the US and Ed Cleary in Canada.

FontShop Belgium
Maaltecenter Blok C
9051 St. Denijs-Westrem (Gent)
Tel: (32) 91 20 65 98
Fax: (32) 91 20 34 45

FontShop Canada
401 Wellington St. West
Toronto, Ontario M5V 1J8
1-800-36-FONTS
Tel: (1) 416 348 9837
Fax: (1) 416 593 4318

FontShop Germany
Bergmannstrasse 102
D-1000 Berlin 61
Tel: (30) 69 00 62 62
Fax: (30) 69 00 62 77

FontShop Holland
Laan van Beek
& Royen 1b
3701 AH Zeist
Tel: (31) 3404 32366
Fax: (31) 3404 24952

FontShop Sweden
Tegnérgatan 37
111 61 Stockholm
Tel: (46) 8 21 52 00
Fax: (46) 8 21 28 80

FontWorks UK
65-69 East Road
London N1 6AH
Tel: (44) 71 490 5390
Fax: (44) 71 490 5391

Panel 3 (bottom left)

TYPE

Whether you are working on a Macintosh or a PC, whether you like classical Typefaces or eccentric cuts, whether you want them in PostScript or TrueType format, **FontShop** has a carefully selected collection of typefaces from type foundries such as **Adobe, Monotype, Bitstream, Berthold** and **Agfa-Compugraphic**, as well as exclusive fonts from independent houses like **The Font Bureau, Emigre, Giampa, ClubType** and many others.

CATALOGUE

FontShop's new catalogue will be available in October. The most definitive guide to postscript type ever published, it contains reference to the almost 4000 fonts that we stock. Special divider pages have been provided by international type designers like **Hermann Zapf, Adrian Frutiger, Summer Stone** and **Aldo Novarese.**

FUSE

FUSE is a new venture in type design, an interactive magazine and forum for a fresh approach to typography. Published quarterly, **FUSE** contains a disc featuring four experimental fonts digitised for Macintosh plus four A2 posters that show each typeface in creative application. **Issue 1** includes four British designers: *Phil Baines, Neville Brody, Malcolm Garrett, and Ian Swift.* **Issue 2** featuring *Erik von Blokland, Max Kisman, Just Rossum* and *Gerard Unger* will be released on October 25

 FONTFONT

FontShop's exclusive **FontFont** label releases typefaces which range from classical text to modern headliners and more radical designs. We quarterly publish typefaces already digitised by their designers, ensuring that the fonts are immediately available. Out now are **Meta,**

TYPEFACE SIX,

Dolores, Jacque and **Marten**

FontShop

The International **FontShop** network was set up by type experts: Erik Spiekermann, Neville Brody, Roger Black, Ed Cleary, Petr van Blokland and David Berlow.

INTERNATIONAL

FontShop Belgium
Maaltecenter Blok C
Derbystraat 247
9051 St. Denijs-Westrem (Gent)
Tel: (32) 91 20 65 98
Fax: (32) 91 20 34 45

FontShop Canada
401 Wellington St. West
Toronto, Ontario M5V 1E8
1-800-36-FONTS
Tel: (1) 416 348 9837
Fax: (1) 416 593 4318

FontShop Germany
Bergmannstrasse 102
D-1000 Berlin 61
Tel: (30) 69 00 62 62
Fax: (30) 69 00 77 77

FontShop Holland
Laan van Beek
& Royen 1b
3701 AH Zeist
Tel: (31) 3404 32366
Fax: (31) 3404 24952

FontShop Sweden
Tegnérgatan 37
111 61 Stockholm
Tel: (46) 8 21 52 00
Fax: (46) 8 21 28 80

FontWorks UK
65-69 East Road
London N1 6AH
Tel: (44) 71 490 2002
Fax: (44) 71 490 5391

Set in ITC Officina by Erik Spiekermann and Typeface Six by Neville Brody

Panel 4 (bottom right)

Typefaces from FontShop

international

fuse

catalogue

FUSE 6 : CODE is now available. The new forum for experimental typography includes four fonts with accompanying posters from **IAN ANDERSON PAUL SYCH RICK VERMEULEN MARTIN WENZEL** plus a bonus fifth font.

fonts

All your typeface requirements are now supplied from one source. **FontShop** is the largest and most comprehensive worldwide supplier of typefaces for Mac and PC. We supply over 5000 fonts, many of which are exclusive, from over 30 manufacturers, including major vendors such as Adobe, Monotype, Agfa, Bitstream and ITC, plus independents like Emigre, Font Bureau, Electric Typographer and our own FontFont

catalogue

Our catalogue is the most comprehensive guide to PostScript fonts available. Contact your local FontShop to find out how to get hold of the catalogue including the latest update containing over 1000 new fonts

FontShop Austria
Seidengasse 26
A-1070 Wien
(02 22) 526 78 75
Fax (02 22) 526 78 75 22

FontShop Belgium
Maaltecenter Blok D
Derbystraat 119
B-9051 St. Denijs-Westrem
(091) 20 65 98
Fax (091) 20 34 45

FontShop Canada
401 Wellington Street West
Toronto, Ontario M5V 1E8
1-800-36-FONTS
Local (416) 348 9837
Fax (416) 593 4318

FontShop Germany
Bergmannstraße 102
1000 Berlin 61
(030) 69 00 62 62
Fax (030) 69 00 62 77

FontShop Holland
Laan van Beek en Royen sb
3701 AH Zeist
(034 04) 323 66
Fax (034 04) 249 52

FontShop Italy
Via Masotto 21
20133 Milano
(2) 7000 0555
Fax (2) 7000 0585

FontWorks UK
65-69 East Road
London N1 6AH
(071) 490 2002
Fax (071) 490 5391

Fonts used on this page are Advert, Clarendon, Vortex, Meta, Fago, Journal, Bodoni, Hus, Interstate and Franklin Gothic

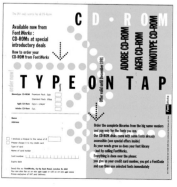

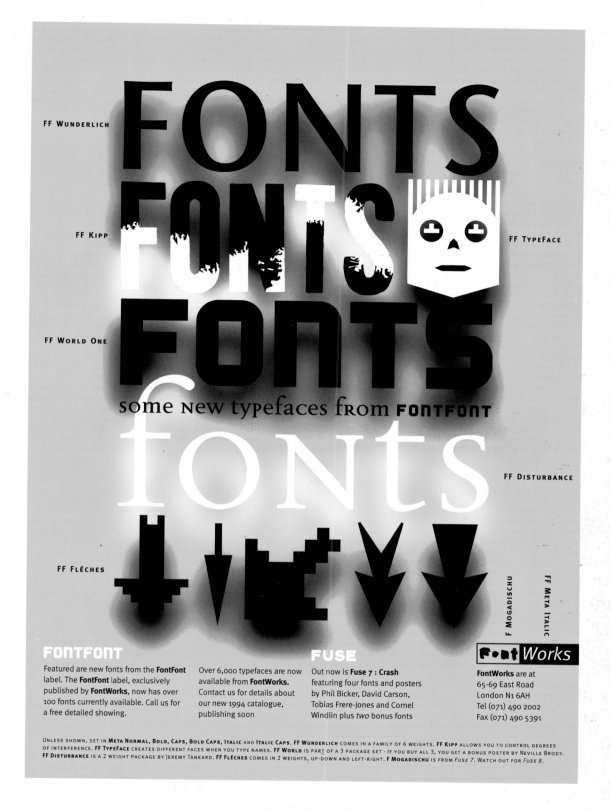

100. Advert for FontWorks UK, 1993

101. Postcard for *Typeface 6 & 7*, FontWorks UK 1992
Appearing as hand-drawn designs in the first book, *Typeface 6 & 7* were published by FontFont in 1992.

102. Postcard for Font Bureau's *Grotesque* family, FontWorks UK 1992

103. Mouse mat, FontShop Germany 1993

104–105. Flyer, front and back, for FontWorks UK, 1993
The flyers introduced the unlockable typeface libraries on CD-ROM. "Type on Tap" is not that simple just yet – users now have to unlock one or every typeface encoded on the CD by buying the appropriate serial number. This can be done by phone with a credit card, but the equation with municipal services has some way to go. Supported by the electronics industry, buying through CD-ROM is nevertheless seen as the digital transportation method of the near future, until ISDN and cable networks are fully operative.

Dirty Four

Dirty Six

Dirty Seven

Dirty Three

Bitmap

Dirty One

Dirty Five

Dirty One Bold

klmn
opqr
stu-
vwxy

**106. *FF Dirt 1–7,
Dirty Faces,* FontShop
International 1994**
The increasing interest in
Dirty Faces reflects the
present urge to process
letterforms. Rather than
use the Mac simply as a
typesetting facility,
designers are treating
text as image. This recon-
nects with the semantic
experimentation of Punk
graphics in the late 70s;
it is also a reaction to the
effortless clarity of digital
typesetting, now that
everybody can do it.

The seeds of the *Dirty
Face* were sown years
before the Mac became
widely available. Before
PC, these might have
been created by stu-
diously messing up type,
using scalpels, photo-
copiers and the PMT
machine, but it was a
laborious and often hap-
hazard process – this
being part of the attrac-
tion for those who always
sought to challenge the
regular image of printed
words.

Too abstract for
FontFont, too simplistic
for *Fuse,* the randomised
deformity of *Dirty Faces*
gives designers instant
access to distressed
typefaces and mangled
shapes. FSI produces
Dirty Faces at a lower
price, quarterly, including
a mix of contributors in
each pack with its accom-
panying poster. If clarity
is the traditional aspiration of any trained typographer, then *Dirty Faces*
demand... *BRING THE
NOISE!* Their design and
usage demonstrates the
desire for a more expres-
sive typographic lan-
guage, deviating from the
precision of the past.

107. *FF Autotrace family,* FontShop International 1994

Autotrace was an idea that originated with *Fuse 9* and the notion of automated language becoming automatic language, instant print, instant reaction, the closing down of the distance between thought and expression. To visualise this process of compression, Brody took a series of sans serif typefaces and using a computer font creation programme, he interpolated and combined their outlines, ending up with the ultimate – and the average – sans, *Autotrace One*, a *Univers* for

the digital age. Once this had been done, the autotracing facility in Altsys Fontographer was used to progressively distort the mean item, in the same way as information loses its original form when passing through the various stages of travel from source to destination. On reaching 10, the binary end-point was achieved by superimposing *Autotrace Two* and *Autotrace Nine* on top of one another.

AutotraceOne
AutotraceTwo
AutotraceThree
AutotraceFour
AutotraceOutline
AutotraceSix
AutotraceSeven
AutotraceEight
AutotraceNine
AutotraceDouble

Autotrace

108. China page for
***03 Tokyo*, Japan 1990**
The magazine *03 Tokyo*
devoted a special issue
to the first anniversary of
Tiananmen Square, inviting
designers to submit pages;
those living outside Japan
were asked to send their
contributions by fax.

109. *Images pour la lutte*
***contre le sida*, Artis,**
Paris 1993
*Images pour la lutte contre
le sida* was an international
poster project organised in
Paris to mark World Day
against AIDS.

110. *FF Blur*, FontShop International, Berlin 1992
111. Postcard for *FF Blur*, FontWorks UK, London 1992
Since typeset information is now read from the screen and viewed on the street as often as it is read from the printed page, the need for readability has been superceded by typefaces that attract instant recognition. The effect of data banks has been to remove the transmission of information from the role of typography. We no longer need books for

information storage. The present uses of typography are for entertainment, art and publicity. What should its new role be? To convey emotion? If so, what emotions? Will typography be liberated in the long term, resulting in a new language of abstraction, as modern art achieved

90 years ago? This assumes that data is analagous to photography, but whatever the outcome, the more typography is divorced from its text-informational role, the greater its potential as a tool to demonstrate the importance of presentation and context in all communications.

Like woodblock letterforms, *Blur* emphasises the process inherent in the technology with which it was created. The font projects a sense of humanity. It demystifies the authority of printed words and rejects the coldness and precision of digital language.

ABCDEFGHIJKLMNOPQRSTUVWXYZ
abcdefghijklmnopqrstuvwxyz()[.,:;!?"] 1234567890

ABCDEFGHIJKLMNOPQRSTUVWXYZ
abcdefghijklmnopqrstuvwxyz()[.,:;!?"] 1234567890

ABCDEFGHIJKLMNOPQRSTUVWXYZ
abcdefghijklmnopqrstuvwxyz()[.,:;!?"] 1234567890

Blur is a new typeface by **Neville Brody** in three weights **available** exclusively from FontShop

Light
Medium
Bold

51

112. Poster for *Werkschau Neville Brody*, Hochschule Für Angewandte Kunst, Vienna 1992

Right:
113, 114. Inside front cover and catalogue cover for *Werkschau Neville Brody*, DMC/ORF, Vienna 1992

The decision to use recurring shapes and symbols forms a narrative. These examples, used for the promotional material accompanying the *Graphic Language* exhibition in Vienna – the relocation of the Parco emblem, the skeletal figure first used for *Virtual Fuse* – represent a symbolic consistency in what seems a fragmented and volatile collection of work. In many ways, this is the case: Brody has used the various and often unanticipated commissions he has received over the last five years to probe the parameters of the computer, to investigate the ways it can be applied to different jobs and contexts. As such, the intentions that underpin the designs do not differ – they oscillate.

"Technology is the survival kit of the human race."
Lindsay Anderson/David Sherwin, *O Lucky Man*,
Memorial Enterprises/SAM Film Productions 1973.

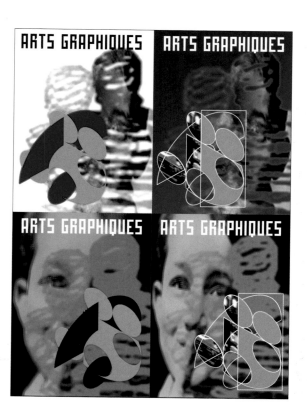

THE FIRST MEANING OF COMMUNICATION, its prime intention, is the direct transfer of ideas and information from one person to another, from subject to object, the voice to the ear. In this form of communication there is a clear bridge – a visible join. The process is inclusive. If someone asks you for a pen, they do not want to be handed a toothbrush. When a letter is addressed to Singapore, you do not expect it to be delivered to Moscow. However, such breakdowns have become more and more commonplace. We have invested so much faith into a better future based on "advanced" communications systems that our expectations are high and often thwarted. The system is called into question. Confidence subsides. Communication becomes a game of hit and miss.

At its origins, the function and motive of language is survival. A shout of **"FIRE!"** across a crowded theatre would remind us of this, creating an instant mix of panic and direct action: consequently, false alarms are punishable by law. It would be, nonetheless, a rare example of everybody receiving a singular message that was universally understood. For the greater part of human history, language has been used on this localised scale, paradoxically allowing it to be more effectively focused through the use of storytelling and ritual. Today, as McLuhan remarked, "the information environment in which we live is quite as imperceptible to us as water is to a fish".

The chaos of communication has to be kept tidy, thus as soon as human encounters ceased to be either original or impromptu (which is to say, relatively early in the day), codes are developed to hold fast the compartments. As the population and diversity of voices increases, so must the codes be made more rigid. Until communication, driven by mass media forms which expressly rely upon the concept of hidden (if not invisible) information, consists only of codes... then codes of codes of codes. Tabloidish, pastiche and self-referential terms

become a staple diet – "garbage in, garbage out", the saying goes. And we shout to make ourselves heard.

All forms of writing and typography are a means of information storage. This storage function is umbilically linked to the process of distribution. It is a link rarely severed, heavily policed. In the best of all possible worlds, nothing needs to be recorded because the experience of it is always available. As soon as a civilisation devotes its energies to upholding (and thus redefining) its "heritage", a storage problem arises – just like the housing crisis. As soon as the exposure and availability of any item or idea is restricted by the need to control the amount of people who wish to be exposed to it, the need to capture this information and to replicate it results. *How can a concept best be communicated?* becomes *How can a concept best be categorised?* Words and ideas, like cities, become overpopulated. In this way, communication is no longer guided by the desire to emancipate, but the need to edit. The notion that, in today's market, everything has to be commercial in order to achieve a high profile is often the end as far as meaning is concerned (and as for irony?!). Ours is an Age of Convenience, no matter what the cost, and the computer screen's underlying promise – "what you see is what you get" – promotes the illusion of substance, when any content can only be quantified in terms of amount.

The second meaning of *communication* is related to transport, from roads and waterways to the present intensified environment of air travel and cable networks. Human numbers have rapidly increased so that more and more are subject to these forms of freight, while less and less have direct contact, let alone control of their movements. The grid seems to be constantly shape-shifting, thus the process of any communication, as well as its style and content, becomes crucial – if fundamental changes to the process of transmitting language create fundamental changes in its expression, few are in the position to appreciate this because the terms of the new contracts are kept hidden.

Digital codification is a radical response to the problems caused by the volume of traffic. It is too early to predict how,

115–118. Cover designs for
***Arts Graphiques*, Paris 1992**
Four designs were submitted –
the one on the top right was chosen.

119. Colour variations for Vienna exhibition poster, 1992

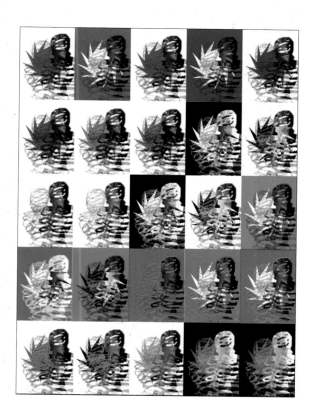

**120. Poster for
Glasgow Design Renaissance
conference 1993**
Icograda commissioned
a series of posters to be ex-
hibited during the conference.
The first question is, can a
Renaissance be claimed for
a protective industry close to
collapse, refusing to admit any
need for change? What is the
potential for long-term planning
and rebirth? More likely, the
design industry will batten
down the hatches and pursue
its policy of damage limitation
until choices vanish and
change is forced upon it.

Opposite, reading clockwise:

**121. Postcard for
Icograda, 1993**
Various designers were invited
to come up with a postcard to
commemorate Icograda's 30th
anniversary. Brody's contribu-
tion was designed around the
same time as the poster for
Fuse Codes (see p.28). He
wanted to suggest a sense
of protection, which is questioned by the image's ambigu-
ity – "The hand that is in need
of protection is nailed to the
hand that protects it."

**122. Telephone cards for
Prinz, Hamburg 1991**
Prinz is a listings magazine
customised for every major
city in Germany. Brody and
Austrian designer Lo Breier
were asked to produce telephone card designs that would
be distributed as a free gift
to *Prinz* readers. Brody's
Photoshop images were
thought too abstract and
not used.

**123. Party invitation for
"Think Big", Mattheo Thun,
Italy 1989**
The invite was designed as an
A2 poster that folded down to
A6, printed on airmail paper.
Mattheo Thun is a product
design agency, formed by the
ex-partner of the Memphis
group. For the other side of
the invite, drawings of Mattheo
Thun products were scanned
and enlarged from a fax
transmission.

**124. Advert for Apple
Computers Japan, 1990**
Produced specifiacally for the
Parco exhibition catalogue,
Brody wanted to promote the
Macintosh's creative potential,
suggested by the interlocked
and radiating forms.

exactly, the conversion from analogue to digital forms is going to affect human communication and interaction on an every-day level – already, it is possible to send computer files down a telephone line; we will soon all be able to publish our own faces on videophones hooked up to all corners of the globe; magazines with the wherewithal can retouch photographs to make smiles flash on full beam, yet the full potential of new technology is still beyond our means, the cutting edge is never accessible, and by its very nature it always will be. It is far more constructive to put the inaccessibility of "top perfor-mance" machines in perspective and work to regenerate the power of our own psyches and perceptions.

One outcome of this link between language and technol-ogy is the common feeling that you should "never believe" what you are exposed to in the media: a built-in feature of today's screen and print experience is the general awareness that "the whole picture" is not present. This may be evidence of a healthy scepticism, or further proof that oral and typo-graphic language have lost their power and are being over-taken (or even made redundant) by the more dramatic 'speech' of music and film?

Is language *always* evolving? If not, then what?

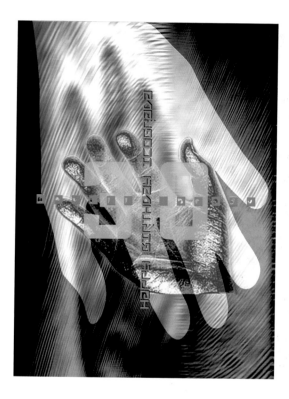

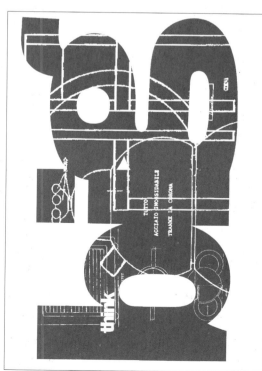

1 The AgfaType **CD-ROM** puts a complete type store on your desk. You can gain *instant access* to a comprehensive collection of **2,500** PostScript and TrueType faces in three ➜

2 Become part of the *Agfa Type Universe* – we can solve all your PostScript problems and put you in *type heaven...* ➜

3 The new *Agfa* **TYPE REFERENCE BOOK** *for PostScript users* is the definitive reference source for anyone working with faces from the Adobe or AgfaType ➜

CD-ROM VERSION 4.0

125–128. Promotional brochures for AgfaType, Agfa, Dublin 1993
AgfaType needed to high-light the different aspects of its PostScript service and commitment to desk-top digital typography.

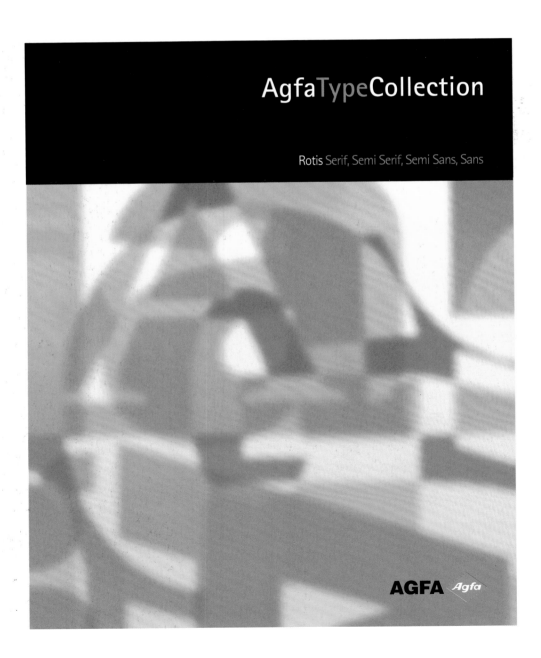

AgfaTypeCollection

Rotis Serif, Semi Serif, Semi Sans, Sans

AGFA *Agfa*

129. Roughs and preparatory sketches for the AgfaType collection, Agfa, Dublin 1993
In a rapidly changing industry, Agfa felt its AgfaType image to be outdated, wanting to present more the idea of creativity and interaction. The Brody Studio was commissioned to reconsider every aspect of AgfaType's visual presentation, developing a system which combined abstract typographic forms, giving flexibility to the company's visual identity, linked to a rigid structure that could incorporate variable information.

Shown opposite, the Photoshop-created image is contrasted with the clarity of the *Rotis* typeface, demonstrating the basis for an effective system.

DESIGNED WITH SIMON STAINES

The Hafler Trio: How to Reform Mankind
Hilmar Örn Hilmarsson: Children of Nature
Sandoz: Intensely Radioactive
Chris Watson: Atmospheres
John Duncan: Send
Albania: Songs as Old as the Earth
The Golden Hammer 1—6
Scanner series

Touch, 13 Osward Road, London SW17 7SS

coming attraction, the media performs its everyday hijack and exhausts the experience before anyone has the chance to explore it for themselves. Who could turn down this digital passport to paradise?

Virtual reality works by presenting each eye with a different image, making it seem three-dimensional; when you move your head, the image around you changes, with real time computer graphics recreating the scene in front of you 25 times a second, creating the illusion that you are moving around *inside* what is actually a stationary external world. According to the inventor of the term VR, Jaron Lanier, "We should think of the human being as a kind of spy submarine moving around in space, gathering information. This creates a picture of perception as an active activity [*sic*], not a passive one." Ultimately, VR might offer fantastic opportunities to transform the basis of visual language, but in the short term, the signs are not good. When researchers and manufacturers of VR machines talk about their quest to "personalise and humanise technology", they stress the interactive nature of VR and the "immersive" quality of the experience, though reading a book or driving a car never warranted this Pavlovian bell.

William Bricken, principal scientist at the Human Interface Technology Laboratory in Seattle, observed the behaviour of 20 people who had spent 10 hours on a VR machine; he noted: "VR effects dreaming strongly – it seems to provide tools for the control of the dream-life within the dream. The trouble is that we don't have the faintest clue what is going on." Such details do not bother Bob Jacobson of WorldDesign, another VR developer based in Seattle: "We only have a finite amount of time to prove the worth of what we're doing." His argument is based on economics .[1]

Some scientists are beginning to talk down supercharged expectations, warning that the technology is still at a primitive stage and that even the best VR displays can emulate just one-fiftieth of the detail of the human eye – equal to a car with a top speed of 3 mph. The laboratories worldwide working exclusively on VR all talk of the user's need for "cognitive plasticity", in other words the ability to form patterns from crude outlines.

This is what we should be doing with the very idea of virtual reality. "Given the rate of development of VR, we don't have a great deal of time to tackle questions of morality, personal identity and the prospect of fundamental change in human nature", says Howard Rheingold.[2] J.G. Ballard reckons "virtual reality represents the greatest step in human evolution", but in another breath he warns, "when VR comes on stream, we'll immerse ourselves in an ocean of rubbish".

VR is being proclaimed primarily for its potential to enhance entertainment: a fantasy factory that can fire the imagination and promote self-awareness in one fell swoop. But VR is reality made safe, as if Dionysian rituals, the alphabet, cinema, cities and money markets never existed, as if strokes and squiggles on a piece of paper never allowed us "to interact with other people almost as if it were part of the real world". And as if language itself wasn't virtual.

Virtual space provides a haven that appears to reconcile opposite extremes. It upgrades the continual human quest to find the means of escape from human limitations and thus assumes a mystical dimension. By providing the illusion of power to the socially and politically deprived, collective struggle can be removed from the streets and relocated behind the screen. As long as every digital Columbus can immerse themselves in their pixelated paradise, who gives a damn about hell on earth if everything else can look like a private heaven?

EVER SINCE MAN BEGAN TO BELIEVE he could control and transcend his environment, we have passed through various stages of virtual reality. We are, and always have been, living in the imaginary world of our own perceptions. For centuries, the role of artists, writers and musicians has been to challenge prevailing notions of reality – the modern day remix of Hieronymus Bosch's *Garden of Earthly Delights* is now promised to us mechanically.

It's a suspect idea, virtual reality, because deep down we know we've got it already, everywhere around us, but for some, spurred on by the last decade's success of selling us things we already own, such as water, gas, and electricity, it's a marketing opportunity not to be missed. To canonise the

1. Quotations are taken from Charles Arthur's article "Did Reality Move for You" in *New Scientist* No.1822, 23 May 1992. **2.** Howard Rheingold, *Virtual Reality*, Secker & Warburg 1992.

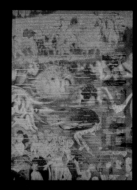

131. Poster for 1123, Berlin 1993

1123 is an art-sponsorship-project organised by Peter Gluckstein and Yves Senger who invite 1123 companies in each of five cities – the first having been Berlin – to contribute money towards the production and display of a double A0-sized poster printed in five colours. The poster from each city will eventually fit together and list the names of every sponsor. The project seeks to draw attention to the switch from state funding to the corporate sponsorship of the arts.

DESIGNED WITH JOHN CRITCHLEY

Opposite:
130. Poster for *Touch*, London 1994

For the last 12 years *Touch* has explored the language of sound and visual media and has experimented with different formats to try and arrive at the powerful feeling that Eisenstein called *The Film Sense*. Using the idea that music is the soundtrack, images the stills and text the script of an unedited film, *Touch* products appeal to the interactive involvement of the end-user. In this way, a narrative is established that deals with media techniques and their effect upon human perception: a step beyond commercialism.

**132. CD poster for *Gruppo Musicale*,
Ryuichi Sakamoto, Midi Records,
Japan 1990**
The design continues the quest to come
up with original variations on the CD format.
This "Best Of" compilation involved the inclusion of Japanese text, the first time that
Brody had worked with non-Western typography. Hence caution: he used the photocopier to distort the Kanji characters so that
they became totems as well as titles.

DESIGNED WITH TONY COOPER AND CORNEL WINDLIN

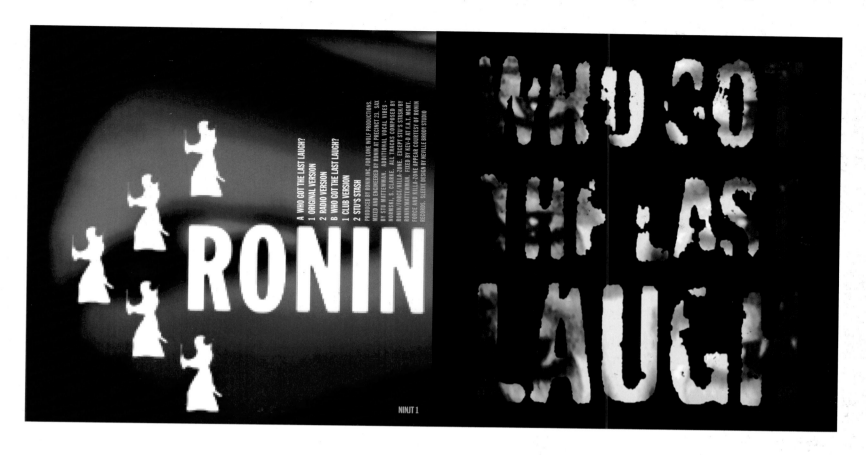

NINJT 1

WHO GOT THE LAST LAUGH?
1. ORIGINAL VERSION
2. RADIO VERSION
A 33RPM

RONIN INC.
FEATURING FORCE & KILLA ZONE
RONIN
?
NINJ D 1

133–135. Front, back cover and labels for
***Who Got the Last Laugh*, Ronin Inc.,**
10 Records 1991
Behind the front cover image is a spy from
a Chinese movie, repeated three times and
becoming progressively larger. The martial
artists on the back were originally used on
the cover of a previous release, *The
Assassins of Soul*, placed here in an arrow
formation. The yellow label features a question mark based on The Riddler's symbol
from the TV series *Batman*.

137. Cover for *Heaven Give Me Words*,
Propaganda, Virgin Records 1990
136–139. Poster, Front and back cover for
***1234*, Propaganda, Virgin Records 1990**
Covering all formats, the designs for
Düsseldorf-based group Propaganda focused
on the power of images. For *1234*, each side
of the outer and inner cover portrayed a
visual code – here, the art of Brancusi is set
against natural forms.

PHOTOGRAPHY BY JÜRGEN TELLER
DESIGNED WITH SIMON STAINES

PROPAGANDA
1234
THE ALBUM

PROPAGANDA
HEAVEN GIVE ME
WORDS

PROPAGANDA
1234

CABARET VOLTAIRE

140. Logo for Cabaret Voltaire, 1985
Never used, this Mexican symbol was designed to be part of the promotional material for concert dates.

141. Inside liner card for *Dont Argue* cassette single, Cabaret Voltaire, Parlophone Records 1987

Below:

142. Cover for *Joy's Address*, Float Up C•P, Virgin Records 1986
Their family tree going back to The Pop Group and Rip Rig and Panic, the jazz-dance ensemble Float Up C•P were too ahead of their time to last long on Virgin, yet brought a burst of exuberance especially to live performances that prefigured the rave scene. Brody designed this cover with the group's Gareth Sager. Vocalist Neneh Cherry – her eyes, taken from a childhood snapshot, peering out of the front cover – found success as a solo artist. Tragically, Sean Oliver has since died from sickle-cell anaemia.

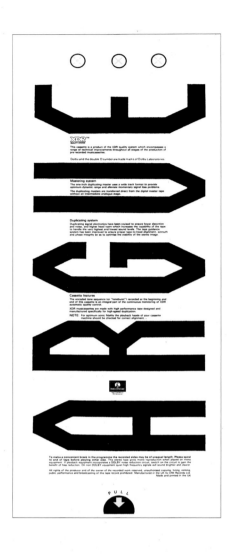

"**PEOPLE ARE NO LONGER CITIZENS**, they are passengers in transit," says French writer and weapons analyst, Paul Virilio. Visit an airport, free of the pressures of baggage checks and final calls, and you can observe the catalogue of parallel realities kept in line within the miniature city – a seamless quilt of shopping malls, banking services, telecom centres, restaurants and bars that keep the modern nomad occupied and animated in no man's land. These days, the pleasure of travel is not only to arrive but also to be wilfully detached from the process, somehow in a daze (though not immune to the tempting bargains that blare at you from the duty-free shops), and like the executive homeless, of no fixed abode – but as soon as the seat-belt sign lights up you can simultaneously be everywhere. A quick safety demonstration, and then the first thing the cabin crew do is calm you down by serving drinks, as advertised.

First of all, the formalities. British Airways might promise with a marketing blast, "Clearing the path from A to B," but they never tell you about the rest of the alphabet. Wherever you fly from, before you settle down to that drink and the in-flight magazine, you must wade through a torrent of typography. All you really need is a ticket, your passport and boarding card, but that would be too straightforward. Thus you travel through a maze of external information, carrying your bags, yet only at three stages do you actually intersect with the real reason why you are there.

Your broken trolley somehow navigates its way to the passport and security checks, and here the zone is free of service industry retouching: it's automatic techno. As your bags pass through the scanner, you concentrate on being the luggage, and the luggage being you – the perfect, virtual state of the telecommuter.

Like scanners, we become magnetic and lean against an illuminated advert. Smoke. Read a book. Get the GameBoy out. Watch the on-screen timetable. *Do anything*. This is no place to be placid. In any case, from here on it is easy – a moving conveyor belt helps you to the Gate Number (how could you stand still?), elsewhere a shuttle car perhaps, and then the whirr of the engines as you clamber aboard. You cannot allow yourself and must not be allowed any quiet, nor any solitude. If the blip drops off the radar screen, then where will we be?

All these shifts in perception link to stages of movement across the grid. The grid is electronic High Art. The information is a cocktail of hard/soft, concrete/plastic, real/imagined. On JAL, a computer screen changes every 10 minutes, showing your position, altitude, outside temperature and distance to the nearest city, marked out on a digital map. The pilot does not speak – the passengers like it that way. They've had enough, and need to recover.

Airports perform technology's circus tricks for us, and at the same time they are development sites where new techniques can be seen to operate freely. The mapping out of land and space has been achieved, so the energies of information technology are now devoted to the mapping out of time – "geography is replaced by chronography". SPACE = TIME = MONEY. Humans, however, create interruptions, hence delay, the enemy of progress.

It is clear that the connection between (information) technology and the creation of stress is residual. The connection between IT and the *manufacture* and *calibration* of stress is embryonic. As a result, we still have some chance of interacting, of understanding and therefore some hope of intercepting IT's negative and regulatory effects. Our future reality is based on the same age-old premise – an consensus made through communication.

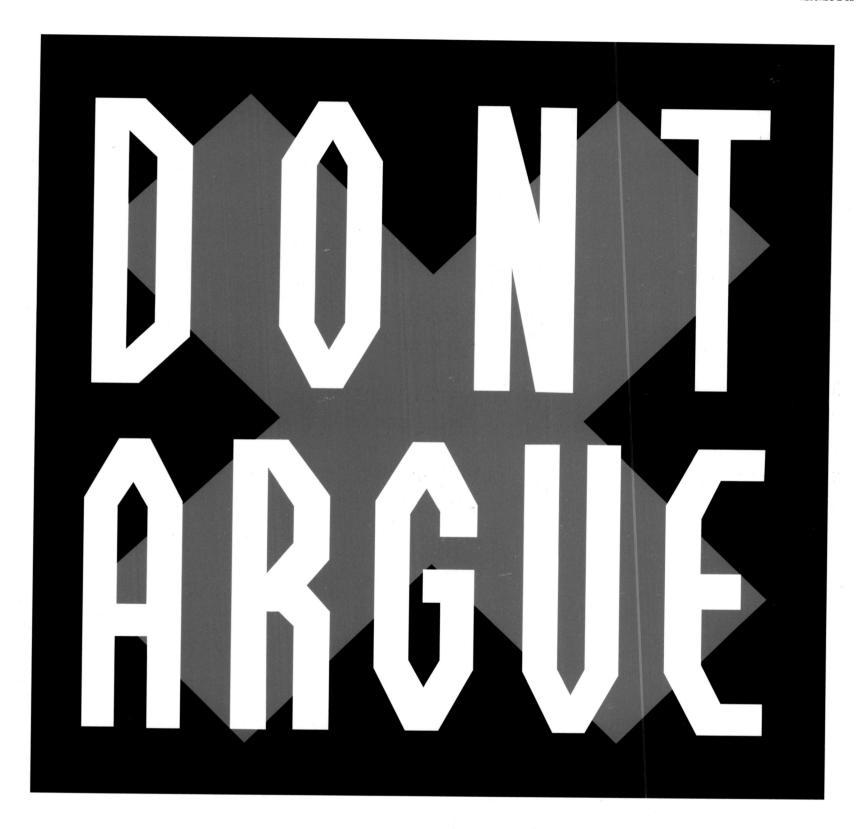

143–145. Cover logo for 12'' single, cover for 7'' single and cassette cover for *Dont Argue*, Cabaret Voltaire, Parlophone Records 1987
Newly signed to a major label, for the first time Mallinder and Kirk's portraits appeared on one of their covers. The type was drawn by hand. Reflecting the title, the logo is taken from product warning signs used on items like Tippex and aerosols.

DESIGNED WITH JON WOZENCROFT
AND PANNI CHARRINGTON

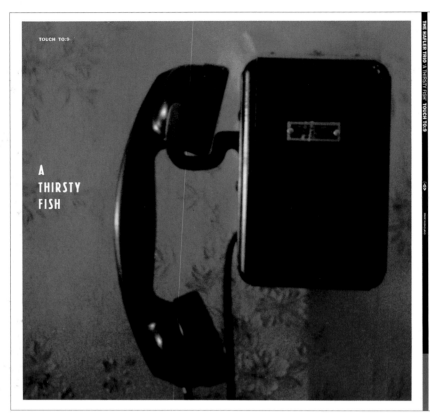

146. The Hafler Trio, *A Thirsty Fish*, Touch 1987

"You hunger for knowledge like a thirsty fish" was an admonition by a Zen master to his pupil and an apt title for this double LP by The Hafler Trio which created, collected and juxtaposed the sounds of religious observance and persuasion. Fish, apparently, have a memory span of 16 seconds. Fast-changing cut-ups of media babble segue into a muezzin call, shouting crowds, pure frequency and tone.

At this point, The Hafler Trio were extending Gysin and Burroughs' *Third Mind* and cut-up theory into a new sound. *The Third Mind* connects two apparently unrelated elements (people as well as any specific subject matter) to create a third "unspoken" meaning that favours intuition over reason; as Burroughs explains, "to make explicit a psycho-sensory process that is going on all the time anyway", breaking down the either/or proposition of Aristotelian logic, "one of the great shackles of Western civilization".

The photograph, taken by Ben Ponton, shows a telephone cradled on the flock-wall of The Beat Hotel in Paris where the cut-up technique was reputedly invented by Brion Gysin in 1959. The typeface *Erbar* was photocopied from a 1930s catalogue and retouched. The colour shift to green was achieved by switching the cyan and magenta films from the four-colour separations. A wrap-round sticker sealed the cover and included the evocative track titles, eg – *a loud egg, the blind table, an elderly testament...*

DESIGNED WITH JON WOZENCROFT

The Point as a symbol for unity and source.
The first move, creating a line.
The second move, the arc creating a boundary.
The closing of the circle to form a domain.

Sleevenote to *A Thirsty Fish*.
© McKenzie/Touch

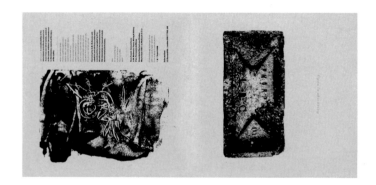

147–151. Mother Tongue, *Open in Obscurity*, Touch 1988
Mother Tongue was a collaboration between McKenzie of
The Hafler Trio, percussionist Z'EV and linguist Doro Franck
all of whom were expatriates living in Amsterdam. For the
cover we decided that every element had to come from
different objects and images in the immediate vicinity of the
Tottenham Court Road studio, each being put through a different process. The still-life painting by 17th-century Spanish
artist Juan de Zurbarán was found in a local bookshop and
polacolor-processed by Jürgen Teller. On the reverse was a
close-up of the alarm bell outside the delivery door at the
back of the local Virgin megastore, printed as a contact

sheet and then massively enlarged on a Canon colour xerox.
Hand-drawn type was contrasted with a hot metal antique
italic. On the inside cover, the PMT of a brick, lateral to a lino
print that Brody had done years before of an angel, moving
across what could be a blackened cloth.

The print process heightened the cover's strange ambience. The photographs were scanned as four-colour separations, then two of the films were jettisoned and the
remaining two assigned special Pantone colours. The
reversed-out type was printed as a third colour white on a
rough textured, straw-coloured board.

DESIGNED WITH JON WOZENCROFT

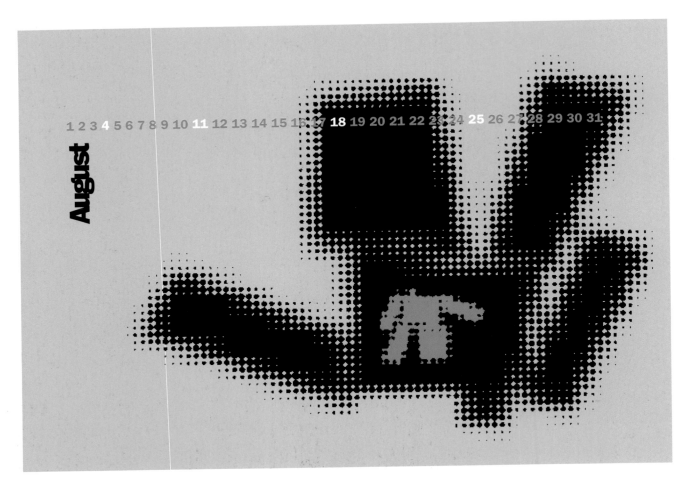

August

1 2 3 4 5 6 7 8 9 10 11 12 13 14 15 16 17 18 19 20 21 22 23 24 25 26 27 28 29 30 31

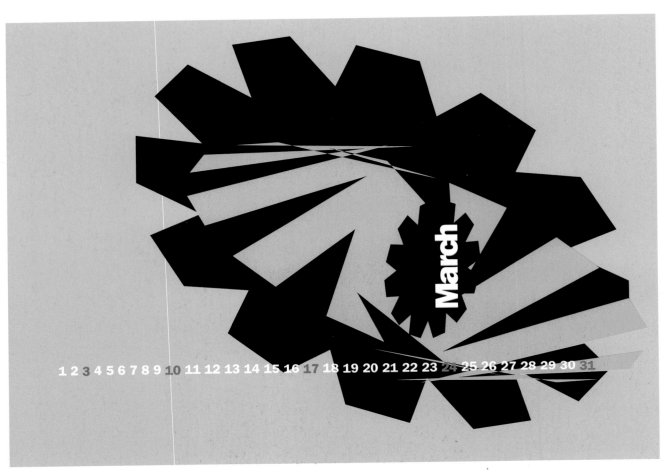

March

1 2 3 4 5 6 7 8 9 10 11 12 13 14 15 16 17 18 19 20 21 22 23 24 25 26 27 28 29 30 31

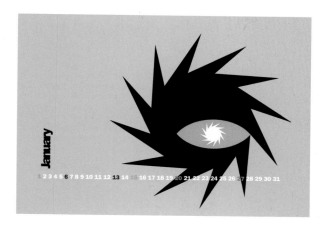

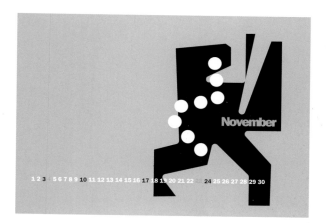

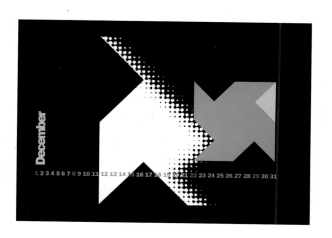

152–161. 1991 Calendar for Parco Department Store, Tokyo 1990

Parco, hosting the *Graphic Language* exhibition in October 1990, asked Brody to prepare several promotional items to tie in with the event which he focused around the calendar design. The work represented a watershed at the time in his understanding of the Mac's potential – the prime question being whether or not the machine's linear capabilities could be used emotively to create an expressive language.

Connected to the magazine layouts for *Per Lui* (see p.90), the monthly designs for the calendar create an interplay between different shapes and typographic treatments.

Beginning by drawing individual symbols in FreeHand, grabbing some and saving them as PICT files, Brody imported the designs into MacPaint and ImageStudio, distorting the shapes by using various filters that were then available, before bringing the processed results back into FreeHand for final artworking.

Each month was branded with a small logomark, also drawn in FreeHand. The finished designs were organised as three colour separations using two fluorescent Pantones and a spot colour white, output to film in London and sent to Japan for printing, using recycled Kraft wrapping paper.

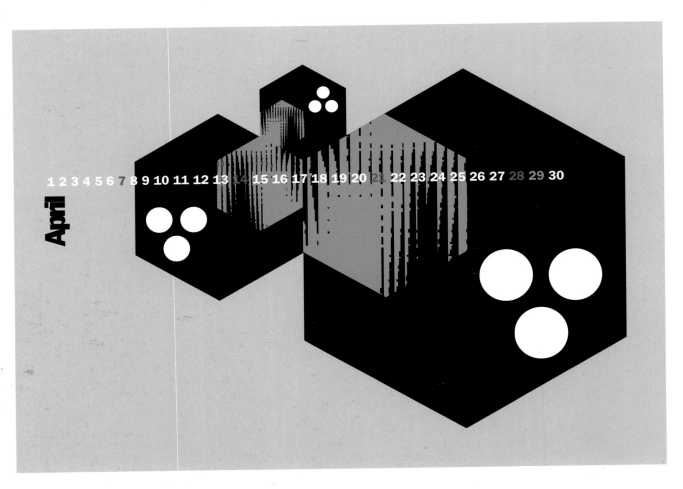

1 2 3 4 5 6 7 8 9 10 11 12 13 14 15 16 17 18 19 20 21 22 23 24 25 26 27 28 29 30

April

162, 163. 1991 Calendar for Parco Department Store, 1990
For the various calendar page designs, Brody wanted to explore the potential of a surrealism based on purely graphic form by joining unrelated elements abstracted from unlikely and unrecognisable sources. The desire was to create a dissonance whose heart echoed the impact of our everyday urban environment, but also returned the forms to their organic roots.

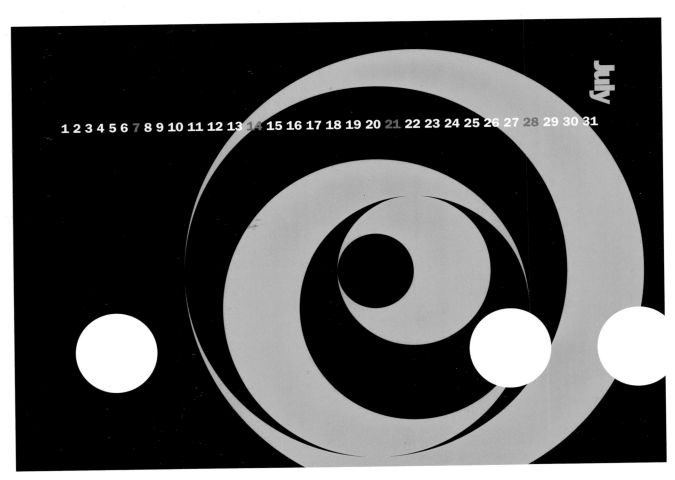

1 2 3 4 5 6 7 8 9 10 11 12 13 14 15 16 17 18 19 20 21 22 23 24 25 26 27 28 29 30 31

July

164. Promotional A4 for *The Graphic Language of Neville Brody*, Parco Space 3, 1990

165. Catalogue cover for *The Graphic Language of Neville Brody*, Parco Space 3, 1990

The emblem created for the cover sheet of the loose-leaf bound calendar became the exhibition logo. The playfulness of the design was later applied in a more serious context when reworked for the page in *Interview* magazine (see p.18).

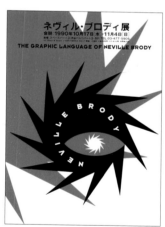

"No other people in history, perhaps, has been required to absorb such a plethora of new ideas as the Japanese were in the second half of the nineteenth century, following the Meiji restoration. The outside world had become a bazaar where one could pick and choose religion, moral standards, art and political systems to be used as tools for modernisation... Nishida Kitaro remembered how in 1914 his German-trained teacher Dr Raphael Koeber put it: 'We have people who are greatly admired for bringing the flowers, but we cannot find the plants that should be producing them.'"
Karel Van Wolferen, *The Enigma of Japanese Power*, Macmillan 1989.

SITUATED IN THE SHIBUYA DISTRICT, Parco is one of the largest department stores in Tokyo. Brody's Japanese agent Grant Gilbert and his associate Junko Wong had for many months been attempting to set up the *Graphic Language* exhibition in Tokyo following the initial work Brody had done for the fashion outlet Men's Bigi and the production company Overheat.

In the late 1980s, there were few foreign designers working in Japan. *The Face* was well-known there, yet very few people had any idea who was responsible for its art direction. Unwilling to take risks and even less likely to work with a small, independent studio, Japanese companies had to be carefully courted and convinced of the benefits of collaborating with an English designer.

The British Council was organising a series of exhibitions and cultural events under the banner "UK90"; Gilbert was already negotiating with Parco to bring over Brody's exhibition which the department store decided to present as the centrepoint of its "Alternative UK90" festival.

Men's Bigi, Brody's first big Japanese commission, had ended in disappointment. Shizuo Ishii of Overheat had introduced Gilbert and Brody to the company, the menswear division of Japan's largest clothing retailer, the Bigi Group. In response to the Japanese habit of using type on many items of clothing, usually to Western eyes in nonsensical "Jinglish" (such as "I am loving you go sporting"), Brody wanted to use the medium as an outlet for ecological messages.

The Green issue and global awareness did not figure in Japan at all. Brody's designs for Men's Bigi (see p.150) were nonetheless received enthusiastically, and working with Yuri Funatsugawa, Yuji Imanishi and Shinichi Kobayashi, the core team at Men's Bigi, Brody wanted to take things further to a "total design" by using naturally dyed cotton for the fabrics, recycled paper for all the packaging and a new emphasis on their promotion. The idea for an Anglo-Japanese production company, Global Force, grew out of this (see p.154), but in spite of the support of Men's Bigi's chief designer and principal protagonist, the management of the Bigi Group rejected the proposal.

As a result, Funatsugawa, Imanishi and Kobayashi all resigned to concentrate on developing the Global Force proposal in Tokyo. They have since formed the clothing company, Planet Plan. Brody's working relationship with Men's Bigi came to an end, though the company had nevertheless agreed to be the main sponsor of the coming exhibition at the Parco store.

As elsewhere, Brody's strategy in Japan was to create designs for clients based on his perception of what they needed, rather than working like a slot machine to provide what they wanted. At that time, Japan enjoyed the world's most dynamic economy, yet it maintained its traditional policy of protectionism at the expense of its potential ability to transform consumer consciousness. This lacuna was being increasingly acknowledged and acted upon by young people in Tokyo, but convincing companies that they should respond to this fundamental development involved a protracted process of invisible conversion.

Working relationships with large Japanese companies demand a firm understanding of the country's elaborate social rituals, most of them grounded in the art of camouflage and contradiction. Fundamentally, the job of Japanese executives is to import ideas and then translate and refine them for domestic consumption. The greatest problem foreigners working with big corporations in Japan have to face is the need to accept their ineluctable status as outsiders at the same time as learning to read as clearly as possible the complexities of these codes. As far as possible Brody was – and is – determined to do this.

For example, the word for "playback" in Japanese is "saisei", literally meaning "to live again". The process that allows the Japanese to freely consume foreign culture also acts to dilute dramatically the original content of whatever it is they are consuming. Brody's impression of this bizarre world of juxtapositions was reflected in the treatment of the shapes appearing on the Parco calendar. Gilbert's task when negotiating with Parco was to intercept and circumvent the possibility that Brody himself would be used as a commodity to serve the immediate interests of "Alternative UK90".

Although Parco's budget did not cover the costs involved in mounting an exhibition of the size that Brody had presented in London, Berlin and Hamburg, Syscom Ltd, an advertising agency, and Apple Computer Japan Inc. linked up with Men's Bigi to sponsor the project. Adobe Systems provided the money to produce a full-colour catalogue. Parco, who agreed to hand over their largest available floor space and transform it into an exhibition area on the top floor of their main store, proposed that Brody design exclusive items of merchandise which they could produce to coincide with the show.

The exhibition was set to run from October to December 1990. During August, Brody designed an A2 calendar and a wristwatch, both based around a logo that joined elements of the eye, the sun and the cutting wheel. The catalogue was completed a month later and included page designs for Men's Bigi, Syscom, Apple and Greenpeace Japan (see p.136). The exhibition travelled to Osaka and Nagoya.

On arrival in Tokyo, we were overwhelmed by the hospitality of our Japanese hosts at Parco, Hirotsugu Shibata and Keiko Nakano, and helped considerably with the frantic last-minute preparations by Junko and Malcolm Wong: who amongst other things, organised the facilities for recording and mastering the exhibition's soundtrack. Mixing sleepless nights and raw sushi with the airless environment of Shibuya further enhanced the impact of this exposure to Japanese culture. With the support of Tadakatsu Kobuchi to encourage us, we were left even more determined to pursue the idea of Global Force, to create a platform for future cross-cultural collaborations: a view of globalism based on the gathering of opposites, not the assimilation of the one into the same.

166. Parco Graphic Watch, 1990
Inspired by Brody's visits to Tokyo, the watch face reflects the collision of the city's speed of life and obsession with time against the effects of sensory overload and jetlag.

167–169. Invitation cards for the opening of *The Graphic Language of Neville Brody*, Parco Space 3, 1990

Opposite:
170. Poster for World Heavyweight Championship, Tokyo 1988
Using letterforms specially drawn for this poster, Brody opts for a simple structure. The weight of the design suggests its collapse; it is held fast by the strength of the two bars and the choice of a strong second colour.

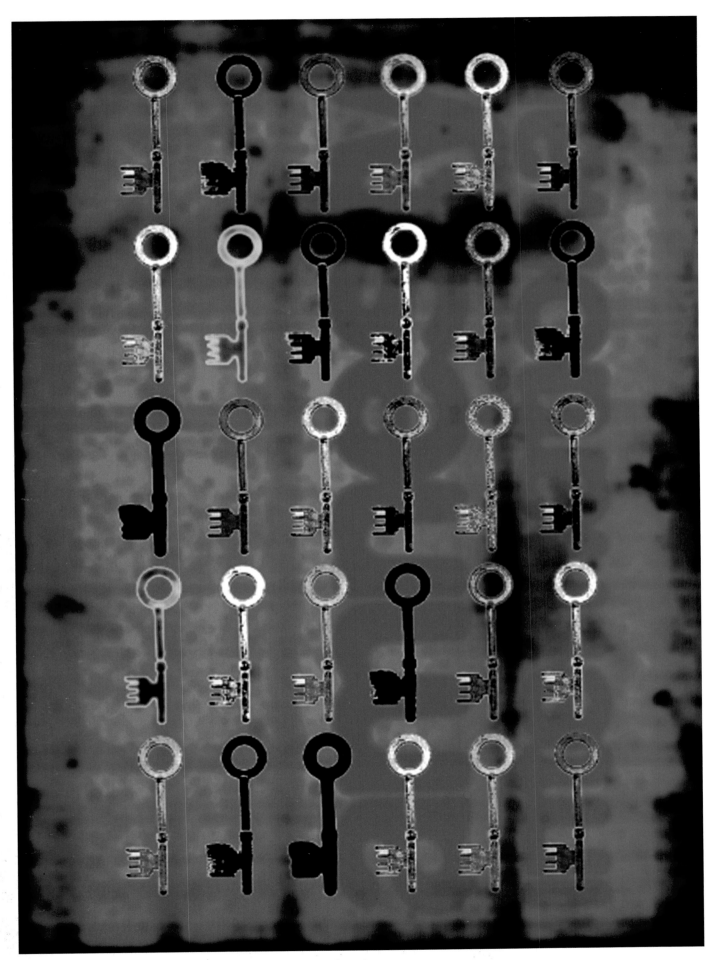

171. Design for the 30th Anniversary of Amnesty International, Holland 1992 Commissioned by Wabnitz Editions.

"Our thinking machine possesses the ability to be convinced of anything you like, provided it is repeatedly and consistently influenced in the right direction."
George Ivanovitch Gurdjieff, *Views from the Real World*, Arkana 1984.

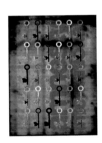

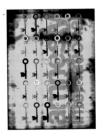

Deutsches
Schauspielhaus
in **Hamburg**

**172. Montage of central ideas
for the Schauspielhaus,
Hamburg 1993**

(040) 2 48 71–0

173, 174. Letterhead and Fax for the Schauspielhaus, Hamburg 1993

The Schauspielhaus is one of the largest theatre and opera houses in Germany. Director Frank Baumbauer and Creative Director Wilfried Schulz hold their tenure for five years and work with the same basic troupe – all originating from Switzerland's Theater Basel – determined to present modern theatre in a radical way. Stefanie Karp contacted the Brody Studio wanting a visual identity that did justice to their experimental aims.

Brody's first step was to insist they set up an in-house Macintosh facility and employ a designer to manage the day-to-day design work internally. Andreas Homann became the studio's main contact.

The initial roughs were reworked, having been considered not radical enough. The final design was developed in close collaboration with Baumbauer, Schulz and Homann, fixed on the concept of discovering at what point chaos becomes structure. This was exemplified by the dislocated and disjointed use of *OCR*, the computer recognition typeface, normally employed for the accurate digital transfer of information.

Colours, typefaces, symbols and shapes were taken to the point of collapse. Pictograms were extensively used because of their theatrical connotations, to achieve a sense of visual mime. Initially, the theatre-going Hamburg public disliked the new Schauspielhaus design.

DESIGNED WITH SIMON STAINES AND ANDREAS HOMANN

Left:
176, 177. Front and back of theatre membership card and ticket design for the Schauspielhaus, 1993

Right:
178–182. Promotional posters and press folder for the Schauspielhaus, 1993
Just as the unusual bi-monthly programme folds out into a concertina, the theatre did not want normal promotional posters to announce their first productions. Different phrases were taken from plays being presented in the season, selected for their dramatic, provocative content. The full repertoire is run out at the base of the poster.

Opposite page:
175. Bi-monthly programme for the Schauspielhaus, 1993

Above:
183. Two covers for the bi-monthly programme, the Schauspielhaus, 1993

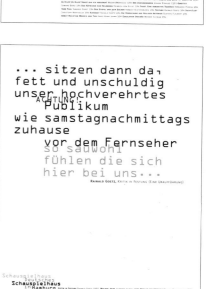

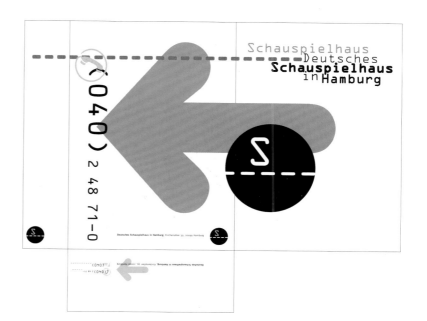

Left and below:
184, 185. Letterhead and image for Christopher New, London 1989
The commission was a Post design with Fwa Richards and Tim Soar, assisted in the studio by Tony Cooper. Fashion retailer Christopher New had leased space in a new mock-Georgian office development in Richmond, designed by Quinlan Terry. Post was given the opportunity to evolve the shop interior from scratch. For the letterhead, Brody twisted a metal coat hanger into the shape of a fish, and for the last time in recent memory used the PMT camera. The design was printed grey on one side to create a translucent effect with the negative image appearing through the gold reverse. The version below was achieved by photocopying the fish direct on the glass with the lid of the studio copier closed.

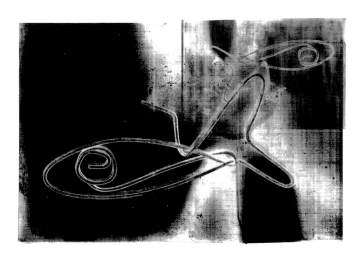

186. Business card for Christopher New, London 1989
The closed copier strikes again.

187, 188. Shop interiors, Christopher New, London 1989
Brody, Richards and Soar spent six months sourcing original materials and working with the owners to furnish the space so that it merged a brutal mix of natural surfaces with hard metallic edges. The shelving system was developed by Post with a rail of machine cogs. The wooden floor was highly polished. The heavy column-mounts were sand-blasted to reveal the rough life-lines of the wood.

Opposite:
189. Carrier bag for Christopher New, London 1989

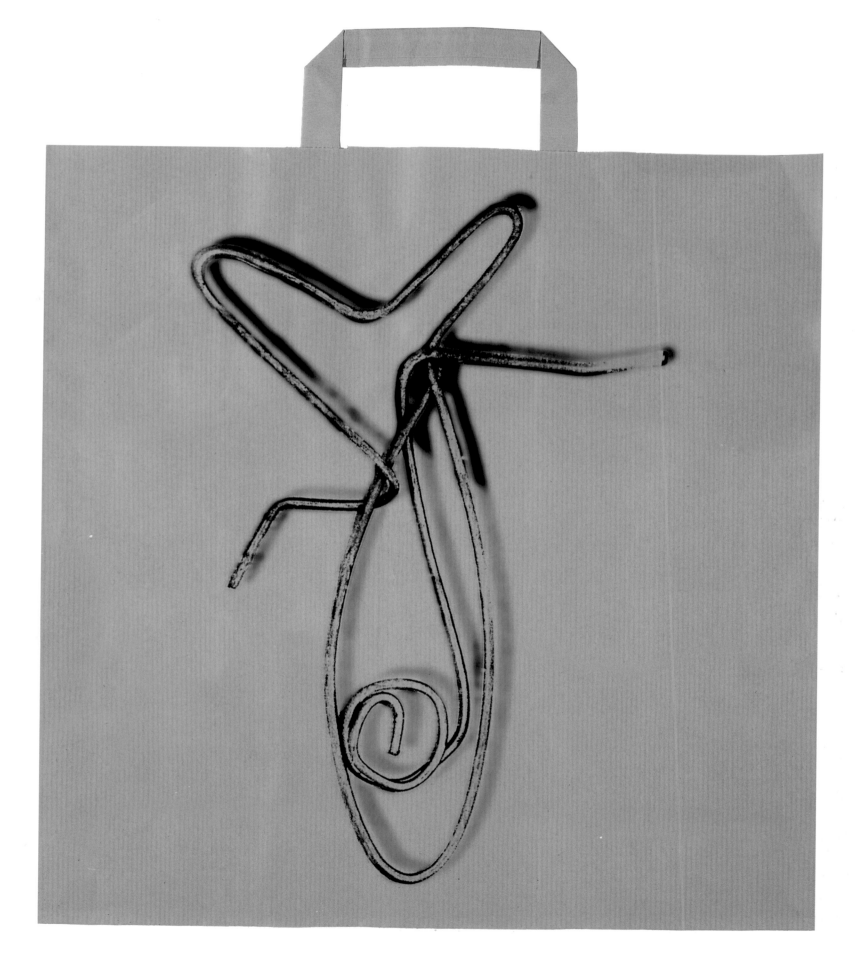

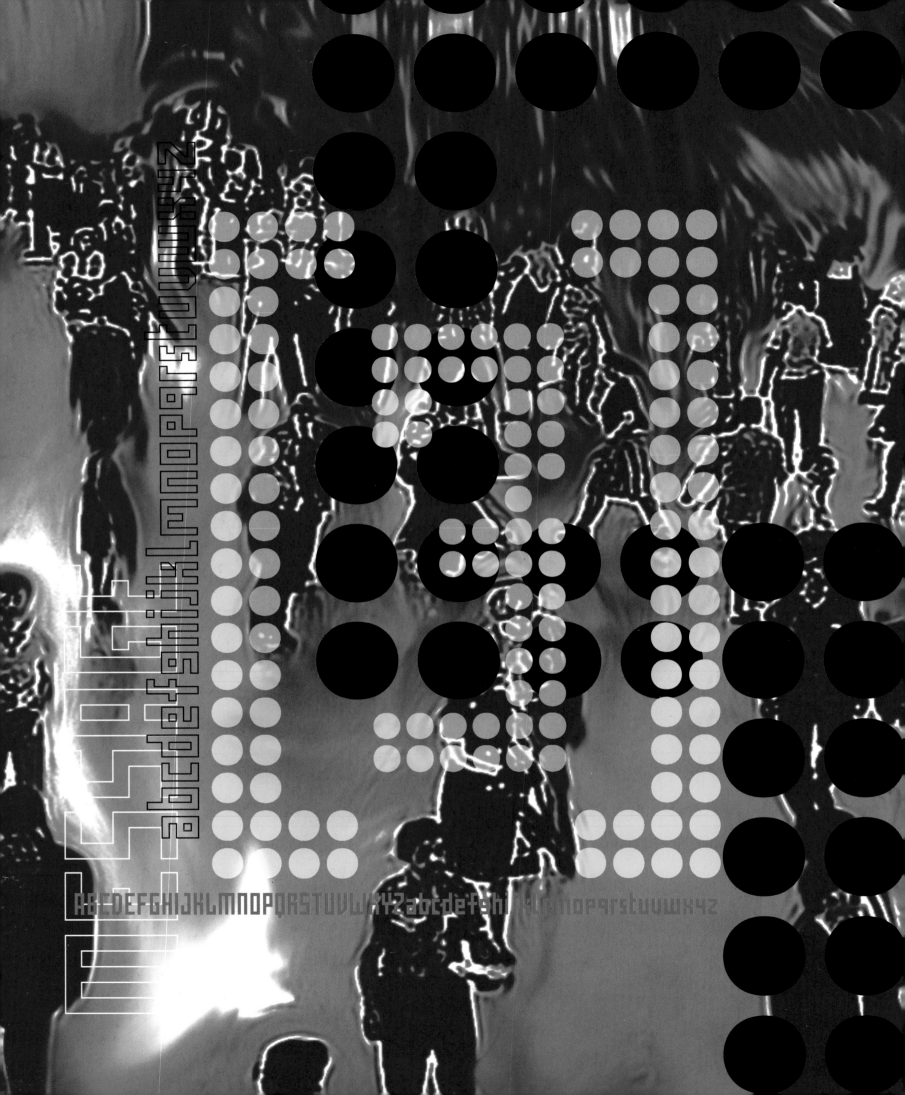

**190. FF Pop/Pop LED,
FontFont, FontShop
International 1992**

Pop was originally developed
for a German music-TV programme called "Pop". Anticip-
ating the need for fast moving
but clearly identifiable credits,
the electronically utilitarian *Pop*
was designed with sharply-cut
corners and arrowed edges on
some of the characters.

Later, *Pop LED* was digitised
because the Kunst und Ausstellungshalle needed an electronic display font. Both versions
were finalised for FontFont
release by David Berlow at the
Font Bureau.

"If, against all the evidence, men
dream of original and brilliantly
thought-out machines, it is
because they despair for their
own originality, or prefer to part
with it in favour of the sheer pleasure of machines that grant them
this by proxy... Firstly, what these
machines do is offer the spectacle of thought, and men, as they
manipulate them, devote themselves more to this spectacle
of thought than to thought itself."
Jean Baudrillard, *Xerox and
Infinity*, Touchepas 1988, also
included in *The Transparency
of Evil*, Verso 1993.

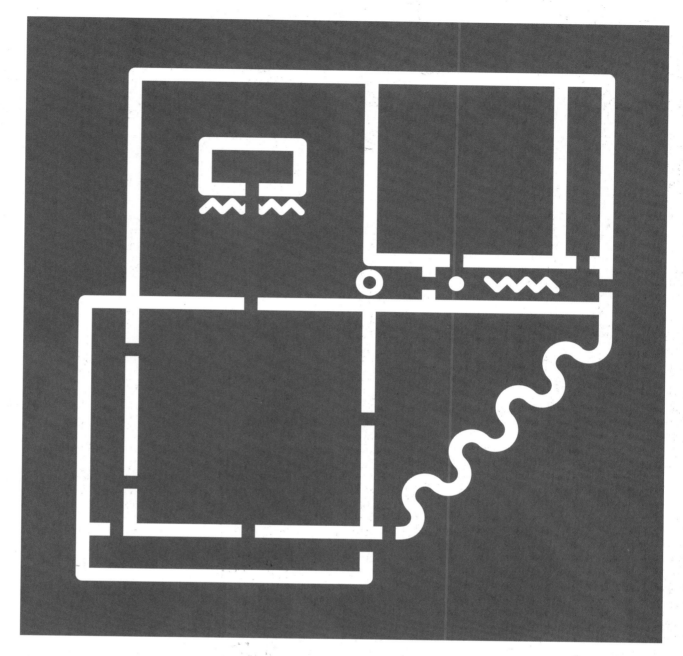

FOLLOWING AN INTERNATIONAL COMPETITION in 1985, Viennese
architect Gustav Peichl won a commission from the German
Federal government to build a new arts centre and exhibition hall
in Bonn – a modern National Gallery to improve the capital's
status as a cultural as well as a business centre. Sited in the
Rhine Valley, Peichl created a monumental space whose forebod-
ing exterior contrasted with a series of intersecting rooms that
broke with the rectangular construction.

**191. Ground floor map, Kunst und
Ausstellungshalle, Bonn 1992**
The layout of the relevant floor space
is displayed at the entrance to every
room, and subtitled with the name of
the exhibition presented therein.

**192. Gallery brochure, front and back,
Kunst und Ausstellungshalle 1992**
The basic information provided to each
visitor on arriving at the centre.

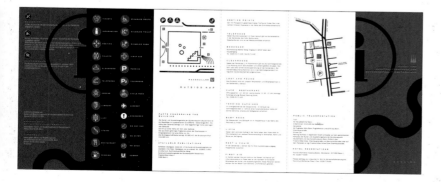

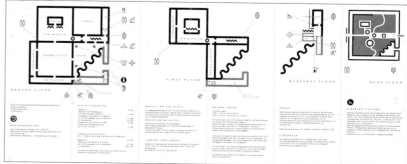

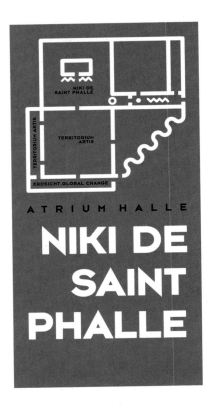

In 1991, Brody was invited to design the signage system for the new complex, alongside the station identity and television graphics project for ORF, his largest ever commission. Working closely with Giles Dunn at the Brody Studio and Jo Hagan, an architectural consultant responsible for all the construction drawings, the system needed to be not only modern, unique and unlike any other contemporary example, but for a building which would represent Art and Culture in the new Germany, it had to be enduring, valid in twenty years' time.

The first priority was to set up a system that effectively guided the public through the building itself. The signage had to work hand in hand with the challenging architecture of the complex, leaving the public with the impression that they had just visited a creative, exciting and modern environment. Alongside this, it was important that the people who would work in the building on a day-to-day basis felt at home and were inspired by their environment. Several months of intensive research was undertaken to explore the huge number of creative possibilities.

At the centre of the system Brody designed a new typeface and a new set of symbols – both had to work on an international level. Many existing typefaces and symbol systems were studied, but none managed to harmonise to form a single identity. Taking hieroglyphics and Aztec patterns as a starting point, Brody produced this graphic language for use on the Apple Macintosh, making it easier for the Kunsthalle to control their graphics in-house.

The system needed to communicate both permanent and changing information. The signage avoided any conflict with the building by being based on squares, allowing the information to complement the space. It was proposed that directional information should be kept away from any wall surfaces and still be recognisable as directions. The materials and colours used to produce the signage were in keeping with those used in the construction of the building. A means of showing the plan of the building and the visitor's location within it was also needed.

Top left:
**193. Map point,
Kunst und Ausstellungshalle 1992**
The marker, "You Are Here".

Above:
**194, 195. Monoliths,
Kunst und Ausstellungshalle 1992**
These large display columns use a number system to guide the visitor around the space, and double as easily identifiable meeting points.

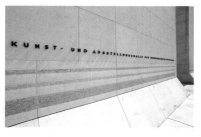

204. Door plate,
Kunst und Ausstellungshalle 1992
Used for the administrative section of the building, the information is screen-printed onto transparent perspex; the door plate can be easily detached and replaced.

205. Utility block,
Kunst und Ausstellungshalle 1992
Designed to the same dimensions as the monoliths, the utility blocks are fixed to the wall.

Clockwise:

196, 197. Cloakroom
and Telephone symbols

198. North-facing
outdoor Monolith

199. Building inscription

200. South-side view

201. Exhibition banners
The five main exhibitions on show are indicated in the foyer of the building.

202. Outdoor banner
Fixed to the north-facing wall.

203. View of Ground Floor
Hallway, Kunst und
Ausstellungshalle 1992

ABCDEFGHIJKLMNOPQRSTUVWXYZ1234567890

To accomplish these aims, Brody intended to make the architecture "speak to the public", with the signage as its voice. He did this by using the concept of "extensions" whereby the building extends itself into the public environment by way of extra walls, like the monoliths in Kubrick's *2001 – A Space Odyssey*, as if in some way the floor grew into the public space, but still connected to the building.

It was important to differentiate the public space from the administrative space of the building. This was achieved by creating two systems, applying the same basic language in a different way. The information displayed by the monoliths was

given flexibility by embedding LED panels and LCD monitors within them, so that the solid squares could be removed and replaced by screens.

To create a plan, the building itself was considered as a self-contained area. A system was created that gave each zone a different identity by using letters and sequential numbers. This was applied to the individual monoliths, so that finding one's location is very simple. This system, or plan, was printed on a guide which is presented to each member of the public when they enter the building. The guide is international, using the symbols and room names as its basis.

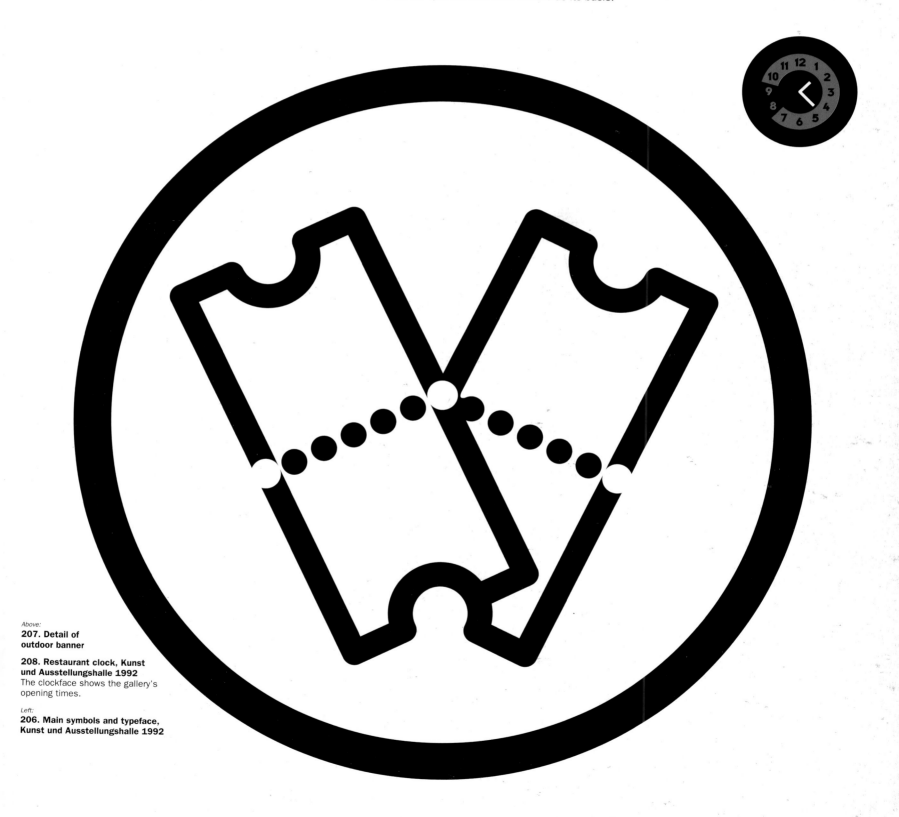

Above:

207. Detail of outdoor banner

208. Restaurant clock, Kunst und Ausstellungshalle 1992
The clockface shows the gallery's opening times.

Left:

206. Main symbols and typeface, Kunst und Ausstellungshalle 1992

**209. Carrier bag
for Bloomingdales,
New York 1988**
The highly decorative design
for Bloomingdale's new year
season represents the last
phase of Brody's hand-drawn
designs. Using Rotring pen,
graph pad and PMT camera,
the finished artwork was
printed in two colours on
recycled paper.

**210. Catalogue cover
for Repetto, Paris 1988**
Working with fashion editor
Elisabeth Djian whom Brody had
met whilst designing the Paris issue
of *The Face*, and co-ordinated by
Yannick Morisot, this A3 sized
dancewear catalogue featured a
number of Paris and London-based
fashion photographers whose individual styles were held together by
distinctive typographic treatments.
Printed with a special gold Pantone,
the cover features an early example
of Brody's computer-generated type,
achieved here by using the programme SuperPaint.

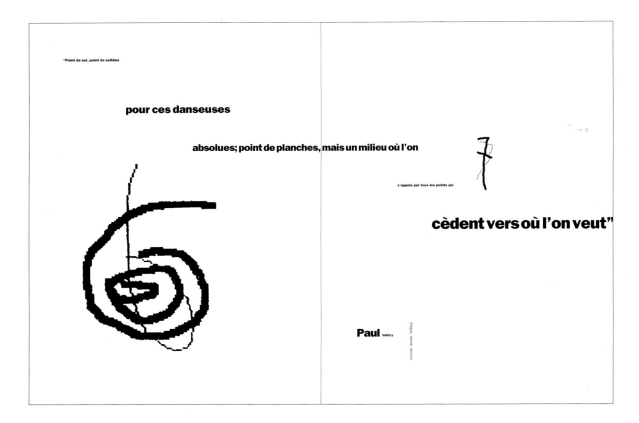

"Point de sol, point de solides

pour ces danseuses

absolues; point de planches, mais un milieu où l'on

s'appule par tous les points qui

cèdent vers où l'on veut"

Paul Valéry

(Degas, danse, dessin)

"Rythmes,

figures, coulisses. Et

les mouvements

goutes de

cris

goutes

de cristal

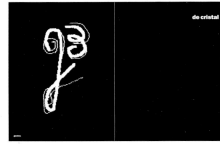

bo nbes sonores

danse

bombes **son** ores

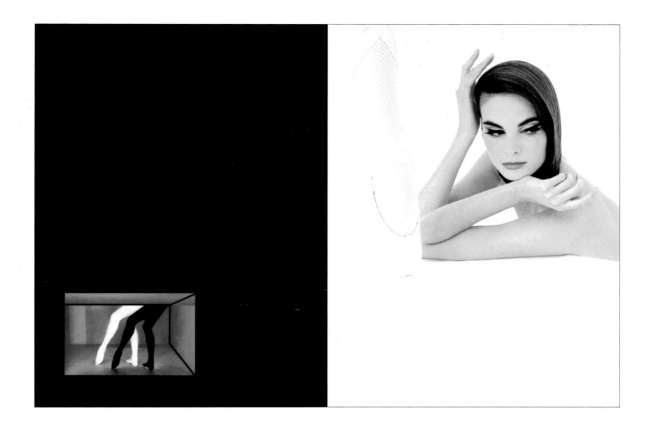

**211–219. Spreads for
the Repetto brochure, 1988**
The unsettling use of white space and the
wild structure of the design was based on
onomatopoeia and concrete poetry, using
Franklin Gothic Heavy in the spirit of Brody's
concurrent designs for *Arena* magazine
(see p.110), contrasted with manic computer
bitmapped graphics printed out on an
ImageWriter and then PMTed for artwork.

The 606 Universal Shelving System ia a highly flexible storage system. it may begin with a small number of components and be expanded and rearranged over the years. High quality, durability and classic design ensure that it will never be rendered obsolete by the changing requirements of the user.
designed by Dieter Rams, the system has been in continuous production in Germany for three decades. Many parts are now made under licence in Great Britain and are readily available from stock.
Shelves and cabinets are suspended from aluminium uprights allowing frequent alterations to be made. The uprights can be wall mounted, semi-wall mounted, freestanding or clamped between the floor and ceiling.

606
UNIVERSAL
SHELVING
SYSTEM

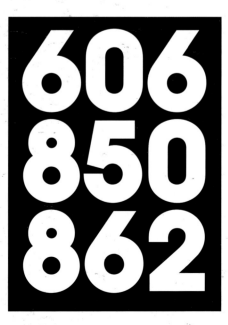

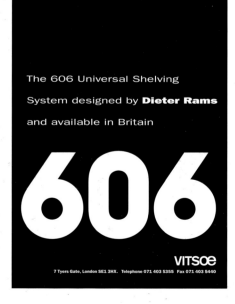

The 606 Universal Shelving

System designed by **Dieter Rams**

and available in Britain

606

vitsœ

7 Tyers Gate, London SE1 3HX.   Telephone 071 403 5355   Fax 071 403 5440

220–222. Catalogue cover, postcard and advert for Vitsoe, London 1989
The design aesthetic of Dieter Rams is based on the maxim "form follows function". Each item in the Vitsoe catalogue of Rams' furniture for home and office use was identified numerically – consequently Brody based the design around the bold use of these numbers.

223. Cover for *New Year*, Michael Tippett, Schott, London 1989
Brody extended the experimental use of imagery he had formerly applied to Cabaret Voltaire's record covers (see first book) for the front of this sheet-music publication, pursuing a similar obsession with the loss of human identity in a world of information bombardment. The accuracy of the notations within were contrasted by a front cover design that suggested white noise.

224. Postcard for *Aqua Planet*, Tokyo 1989
Commissioned by Junko Wong, this design was one of a collection of postcards concerning environmental awareness, published periodically by the *Aqua Planet* gallery.

DESIGNED WITH YUKI MIYAKE

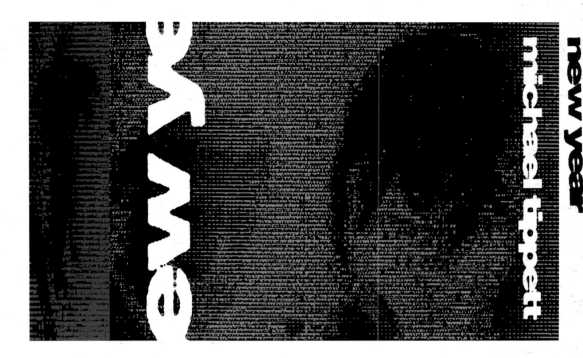

N° 80, Marzo 1990

L. 3.500

per Lui

Mensile del Gruppo Vogue

Sakamoto: oltre i confini della musica

Grandi Forme
energia e sesso
moda macchine e caos

Disegnare un mondo nuovo per gli anni '90

PER LUI

Italian Condé Nast commissioned Brody to redesign the men's fashion magazine *Per Lui* in 1989 after the title had lost its mid-eighties' vitality and descended into repetition and mediocrity. It came at the same time as a redesign for the magazine's sister-title *Lei* (see p.98), so for the next year Brody made monthly visits to Milan, home of the fashion and advertising industry in Italy, working closely with editor Donata Sartorio and in-house art director Olivier Maupas.

The magazine not only needed to be redesigned but restructured from the ground up. Brody wanted to move away from *Per Lui*'s traditional profile as a style magazine and shift its editorial policy towards more serious material, bringing a new sense of organisation to the use of imagery – previously, the difference between a feature article and a fashion spread had been unclear. Certain issues were made thematic – "Brasil" and "Italia" for example – to give a new focus to the art direction.

Brody used type and image to create a distinctive and simple design based on an emotive combination of shapes. The clarity and dynamism of these shapes were enhanced by the use of closely-cropped photographs. The circulation figures of *Per Lui* rose steadily and the magazine enjoyed a new lease of life before it was mysteriously closed down by Condé Nast at the end of 1990.

Left:

225. Front cover for *Per Lui* No.80, March 1990, Condé Nast, Italy 1990

226, 227. Italia issue, *Per Lui* No.78, January 1990
The type is influenced by the woodblock aesthetic of early 20th-century political manifestos and posters.

228, 229. "Transessuali" and "Università" features, *Per Lui* No.75, October 1989
Brody's early designs revolved around the use of *Franklin Gothic Heavy*, expanded to 140% width.

United Shapes of America

OVVERO, FORME UNITE D'AMERICA. UNITE CIOÈ ACCOSTATE, PENSATE, RIPRESE, RUBATE DALLE ARCHITETTURE CITTADINE, DALLA NATURA, DA SCULTURE E MONUMENTI. E RICREATE CON IL CORPO, PER FORMARE PIRAMIDI, ANGOLI, CERCHI, IMPRONTE E PROFILI. DI UN MONDO IN CONTINUA TRASFORMAZIONE, DOVE I CONTORNI SI PERDONO, SI CONFONDONO, SI INTRECCIANO. E MUTANO SENZA SOSTA, DIVENTANDO ESSI STESSI SCULTURE IN MOVIMENTO

falso movi- mento

L'abito fa la forma: e cambia lo stile di chi lo porta. Ne condiziona le posizioni, i gesti, gli atteggiamenti. Modella il corpo, lo libera, lo ingrandisce, lo arrotonda

pieno vuoto

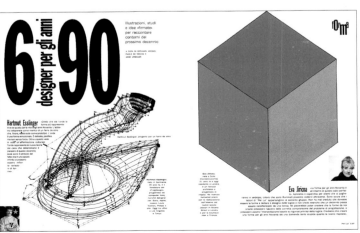

6 designer per gli anni 90

Illustrazioni, studi e idee «firmate» per raccontare contorni del prossimo decennio

Hartmut Esslinger

Eva Jiricna

deformazioni professionali

Stéphane Sednaoul, ovvero quando la fotografia oltrepassa i propri limiti. E diventa arte

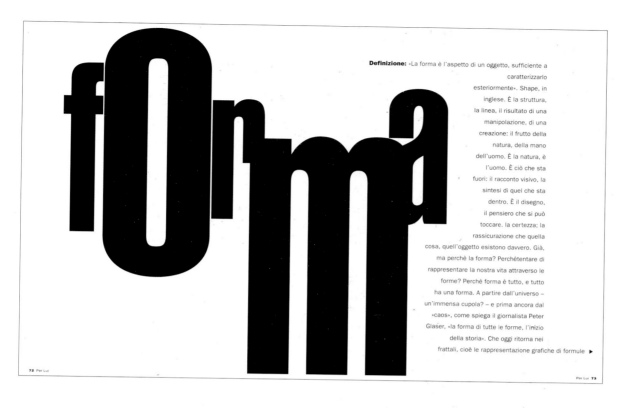

Definizione: «La forma è l'aspetto di un oggetto, sufficiente a caratterizzarlo esteriormente». Shape, in inglese. È la struttura, la linea, il risultato di una manipolazione, di una creazione: il frutto della natura, della mano dell'uomo. È la natura, è l'uomo. È ciò che sta fuori: il racconto visivo, la sintesi di quel che sta dentro. È il disegno, il pensiero che si può toccare. la certezza; la rassicurazione che quella cosa, quell'oggetto esistono davvero. Già, ma perchè la forma? Perchétentare di rappresentare la nostra vita attraverso le forme? Perché forma è tutto, e tutto ha una forma. A partire dall'universo – un'immensa cupola? – e prima ancora dal «caos», come spiega il giornalista Peter Glaser, «la forma di tutte le forme, l'inizio della storia». Che oggi ritorna nei frattali, cioè le rappresentazione grafiche di formule ▶

◀ sempre, purtroppo, è come lo vorremmo. Eppure ritoccarlo, e senza ricorrere alla fantascienza, si può: un taglietto qui, un'aggiuntina là e il gioco è fatto, ecco che il nostro aspetto si tras-forma, diventando più sexy, più anonimo, più gentile, più... normale. Siamo forme, quindi, in un mondo di forme. E la nostra vita, come racconta il filosofo Salvatore Veca, è da «predatori di forme. Non c'è qualcosa come un ''contenuto'' da una parte e dall'altra una ''forma'' da mettergli addosso. Qualsiasi

Al centro. La forma della natura: una foglia di corbezzolo. Qui sopra. La forma del look: quelle particolarità (il taglio di capelli, un vestito, un paio d'occhiali) che distinguono i personaggi famosi tra di loro e li caratterizzano nella nostra mente (da sinistra: David Bowie, Elvis Presley, John Lennon, Elton John, Mick Jagger).

oggetto, concetto, immagine è un ''mix'' es senzialmente strutturato, configurato, modellato». La prova? Basta pensare a un mondo senza forma: il nostro smarrimento sarebbe totale. Un mondo dove la Ferrari non ha una linea personalissima, la caffettiera non ha un design che ne ▶

230–239. Forma issue,
***Per Lui* No.80, March 1990**
The theme of shape was central to the philosophy behind the visual restructuring of *Per Lui*. This issue explored every aspect behind the meaning and perception of shape: its hidden use in commercial branding, its psychological impact, scientific significance, adaptability – from genetics to product design – and aesthetic power.

Shape was used as a metaphor for our increasingly sculpted environment over which we have less and less control.

240–248. Brasil issue,
Per Lui No.77, December 1989
Photographed by Jürgen Teller and edited by
Paul Rambali, this special issue was essentially a cinematic journey through Brazilian
life, culture and politics.

Ragazzi perduti

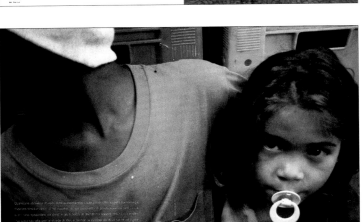

Brasil
Moda

Basta poco,
pochissimo per vestirsi
dove è estate dodici
mesi all'anno

JÜRGEN TELLER

Qui sotto. Camicia in cotone stampata.
American System by Oimes Carretti
(88mila lire). In basso, sulla spiaggia di
Buzios. Camicia in cotone e pantaloni
stretch, Katharine Hamnett Uomo;
gilet in velluto, Spector's (150mila lire)
in vendita da Energie, Roma

Gilberto Gil

I Fellini

Portfolio

Eurythmics, ritratto

Un'immagine della campagna stampa per il periodico Light

Ritratti, videoclip, campagne pubblicitarie. Il tutto giocato sempre all'insegna della fotografia elegante e ironica. Per Lui presenta Jean-Baptiste

mONdino

A vent'anni dalla morte, gli ultimi giorni di Hendrix

ELLIOT LANDY/GRAZIA NERI

heyJimi

Con la sua magica ___ Fender bianca stava scrivendo uno dei più emozionanti, insuperati capitoli della storia del rock di tutti i tempi. Fino a quando un venerdì di settembre di vent'anni fa morì improvvisamente a Londra, in un appartamento al numero 22 di Lansdowne Crescent, per un'intossicazione da barbiturici. Ma Jimi Hendrix, di cui ricostruiamo le ultime settimane di vita, era già entrato nel mito

● ENZO GENTILE

«If I Don't Meet You In This World, I'll [Meet You In The Next World, So Don't Be Late» («Se non ti incontro in questo mondo ti incontrerò nel prossimo, cerca di non tardare»)

(J. Hendrix, da Voodoo Chile)

E ra stato un settembre molto piovoso, quello del 1970
Una di quelle mani anonime che vergano scritte sui muri, sui tabelloni pubblicitari o lasciano biglietti d'amore per i pro- ▶

46 Per Lui

252. Jean Baptiste Mondino,
Per Lui **No.82, May 1990**

253. Jimi Hendrix,
Per Lui **No.84, July/August 1990**

At this point, Brody introduced *Franklin Gothic Condensed* as the main headline font, applying it with a painterly structure first explored in *Arena*.

Antichi riti, spiriti, morti viventi: primo piano su atmosfere, maschere e tradizioni del culto magico che viene dalle Antille. Tra moda e attualità

Attenti al Voodoo

sono una rock model

Sarah Stockbridge si esibisce e canta. Divisa tra cinema, musica e trasgressione, interpreta le provocazioni della sua maestra di vita: Vivienne Westwood. Mettiamola a nudo

etno in eruzione

Sound senza barriere

Viene dal Pakistan, dall'Egitto, dalla Turchia, dall'India. Si rifà a ridolì e tradizioni percossi il sarà la colonna sonora del Duemila. È la World music, un'anima musicale senza confini che sta annientando il predominio del rock. E che ne ha in un'etichetta discografica e in Peter Gabriel i suoi punti di riferimento ideali, tra le presentiamo

Sulle navi negriere, insieme alle genti catturate viaggiavano, invisibili e potenti, i loro dei. Nelle terre straniere, gli schiavi misero in comune i riti. Nacque così il Voodoo

Le metamorfosi di Jeff Goldblum

Il diavolo in corpo

La natura gli ha regalato un aspetto diabolico, il cinema l'ha reso uomo-mosca prima e Satana poi. Eppure lui si tira indietro e dice di essere una persona normale: ma dove recita di più, sul set o nella vita? Difficile dirlo. Intanto c'è qualcuno che lo aspetta in un ristorante di Los Angeles.

mass media

moda e modi

perLui

Voglia di volare, voglia di sognare. Cosa si nasconde dietro lo scimmeggiato. Aquile. Pag. 136. Creduloni e contaballe. Quadri, scritti, documenti, scoperte scientifiche. Busta che siano falsi e finzioncine gonfiati dai mass media. Pag. 144. Spettacolo, business, tecnologia. Lo sport dul Duemila sarà tutto da visionoleonare. Col telecomando. Pag. 148. S.O.S. Mamma: atbisso sulle discoteche, viva il mattcardo. Ma è tutto un bluff. Pag. 166.

Ai confini della realtà: viaggio nel mistero del voodoo. Tra moda e attualità. Pag. 96. Uno stilista scandalizza Parigi: Martin Margiela inaugura l'era del post-Gaultier. Pag. 110. Ispirazione campeggia: pezzi comodi per una storia d'amore a tre. Pag. 114. L'atcel in primo piano: il Gim e la sua miscele. Pag. 128. Torta in faccia: Sergio Saviane racconta com'è maleducata l'Italia a tavola. Pag. 131.

IL BUSINESS DELL'EROTISMO

Tutti i prezzi del sesso

Noi per sesso ora per denaro: sorna mercificato, reclagro, venduto e comprato. È anche piaculo, un giani piacetto ieu par sempre un giorno. Seduzioni premiate? Persuasini gratuiti? Fopins oure dal logoris della vita moderna? Per Lui seconde in campro, trabigando in un mondo numeroso, fiori dalla righe e taburità dalla logge: oggetti del desidorio, forni e salloveleso, prestazioni, manoali e longhi, Un'inchiesta da cifre che parlano da sole e che raccomo poi incrapoloza nuose vende

97

LE SCELTE DI LEI

sera
Gli indispensabili

FOTO BETTINA RHEIMS STYLING CHIARA SCIOLLA

Ovvero i capi-base che non possono mancare in un guardaroba che si rispetti. Da mescolare a piacimento

Ecco le scelte della nostra redazione per una serata, un Capodanno da vivere con «grinta»

Scialle di lana lavorato all'uncinetto, Dolce & Gabbana (L. 510.000 circa). Orecchini dorati, con grosse pietre multicolore, Eric Beamon

94

Sette idee preziose per...

sera oro

FOTO BRUNO CASCIARO STYLING CECILIA CRISTOFORETTI

LOOK RÉTRO

Scarpe color bronzo con «ricciolo», Kenzia (L. 75.000 circa) e modello in tinta oro con tacco a rocchetto, Campomaggi (L. 140.000 circa)

62

63

262, 263. Opening spreads for feature articles, *Lei* **No. 146, December 1989, Condé Nast, Italy 1989**
The word *sera*, 'evening', was used as a constant theme throughout a special fashion issue. Combined with the vertical and horizontal use of *News Gothic*, cut-outs were employed extensively on *Lei* as a way of adding dynamism to an A4 page size.

Opposite, top:
264. Front cover for
Lei **No.146, December 1989**
265. Front cover for
Lei **No.154, September 1990**

Opposite, left:
266, 267. Opening spreads for feature articles, *Lei* **No. 146, December 1989**

Opposite, right:
268, 269. Opening spreads for feature articles, *Lei* **No. 147, January 1990**

Opposite, far right:
270, 271. Opening page and turn page from "Commenti", *Lei* **No. 147, January 1990**
The architectural simplicity of the design was applied to the front section of the magazine, covering various cultural subjects.

LEI

Again based in Milan and published by Condé Nast, *Lei* was a young women's fashion magazine which, like *Per Lui*, had fallen into a dull routine and needed revitalising. Reflecting the magazine's readership, Brody developed a design structure for *Lei* that contrasted a bold, information-led approach with a softer and more subtle use of typography.

However, because of Condé Nast's editorial and marketing policy, *Lei* went through two redesigns in 12 months, including a change of editor and in-house art director. For this second reincarnation, Brody created a more refined, classical look by choosing *Didot* as the headline typeface, a bold departure when seen alongside the even greater prominence given to the images in *Lei*.

ART DIRECTORS EMILIA CAPOLONGO ELLI AND OLIVIER MAUPAS

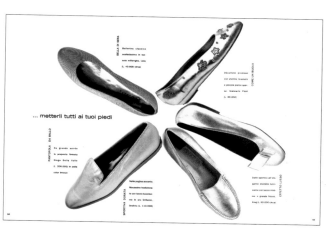

272–277. Feature articles,
Lei **No. 154, September 1990**
As part of the second redesign, Brody shifted the structure towards a more classical feel, contrasting the exaggerated thicks and thins of *Didot* with bold bars and expanded *Franklin Gothic* caps. Both white and black space were enhanced by the use of single large words in lower case with full page images.

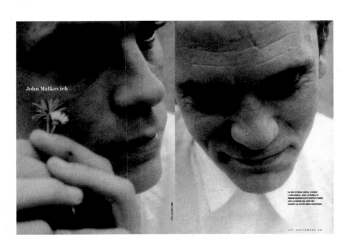

278. Front cover for *Actuel* **No.1, January 1991, Paris 1990**
With a new logo, the cover line for the first issue celebrating a decade of *Actuel* reads, "Ten years, that's enough!"

279. Front cover for *Actuel* **No.2, February 1991**
The early issues of the redesigned magazine suggest a return to hard journalism, indicated by the torn paper.

280. Front cover for *Actuel* **No.4, April 1991**
Actuel was never afraid of sensationalism.

ACTUEL

Based In Paris, *Actuel* was established in 1969 as a response to the riotous events of May 1968. Rather than take to the streets, founder-editor Jean-François Bizot wanted to "make a revolution with ideas and colours", and for five years *Actuel* became part of the Underground Press Syndicate that included *Oz* and *International Times*. For France, this was a unique venture. From the beginning a collective enterprise, *Actuel* tried to match the energy of Anglo-American pop culture with the French tradition of investigative New Journalism exemplified by 19th-century writer, Balzac, and contemporaries like Josef Kessell, author of *Belle de Jour*.

Bizot had wanted to break open a free space but found *Actuel* falling into the same ghetto as many other anarchic magazines of the day. *Actuel* was "disbanded" for many years before re-emerging in the late seventies to become a contemporary of *The Face* and *i-D* in England. It was relaunched without any capital and employed young reporters whose proactive techniques sent the circulation soaring to 250,000 within six months. Journalists would adopt a range of personae, as Bizot says, "To get the

truth. TV was shit. We wanted stories and pictures that showed what's moving in the world."

When the Socialists came to power in France in 1980, *Actuel* lost its earlier left-wing distinction. TV began to imitate the investigative techniques the magazine had pioneered in France. Attempts to make stronger links with *The Face* got no further than the Channel. Notwithstanding, Bizot started a pirate station, Radio Nova, and has since linked *Actuel* to France's Minitel computer network.

Actuel was in the singular position of being politically driven and content-led, but the only magazine of its style in France. As TV further caught up with the magazine's syntax, with the number of commercial TV channels increasing to 6 in 1985, *Actuel* set itself a new editorial brief, to investigate the role of magazines themselves in the TV era. The same bias existed in favour of English language culture – the magazine is if nothing else "anti-MTV" – and instead of following the "American Hong Kong in London", Bizot picked up on the developing World Music culture in Paris, *Sono Mondiale*. Still focused on an 18–30

"The structure of the city is a lot like television. The 'design' of TV is all about erasing differences... The new city likewise eradicates genuine particularity in favour of a continuous urban field, a conceptual grid of boundless reach. The new city threatens an unimagined sameness even as it multiplies the illusory choices of the TV system." Michael Sorkin, *Variations on a Theme Park*, The Noonday Press 1992.

281. Paul Bowles, *Actuel* **No.137, November 1990**
Actuel always looked for incisive and original ways of storytelling. Images were not selected for their beauty, but for their role in enriching the narrative.

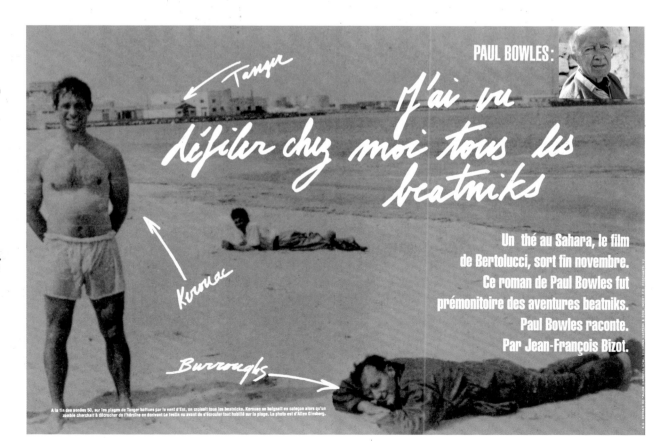

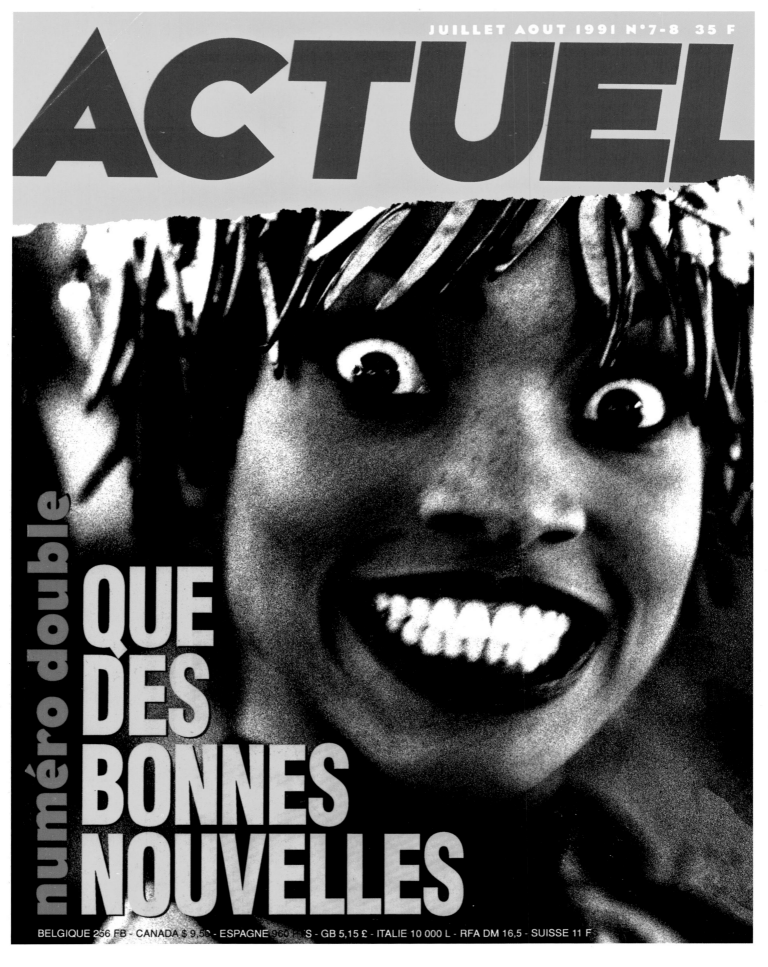

JUILLET AOUT 1991 N°7-8 35 F

ACTUEL

numéro double

QUE DES BONNES NOUVELLES

BELGIQUE 256 FB - CANADA $ 9,50 - ESPAGNE 960 S - GB 5,15 £ - ITALIE 10 000 L - RFA DM 16,5 - SUISSE 11 F

282. Front cover for *Actuel* No.7-8, July/August 1991

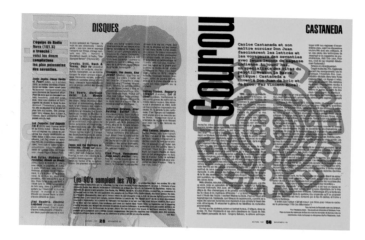

Left:
283. Front cover for
Actuel **No.136, October 1990**

Above:
284, 285. Sampling and Carlos Castaneda, *Actuel* **No.136, October 1990**

Below:
286–289. Four Features from *Actuel* **No.136, October 1990**

For the issue *1990 meets 1970*, each spread was a chaotic contrast between left and right-hand page. The magazine was about to enter its second rebirth: accordingly, the spreads appear as items thrown together as a scrapbook, left to create their own logic.

290. Front cover for
Actuel No.136, October 1990

291–296. Articles and features from
Actuel No.136, October 1990
This issue featured the 100 people that *Actuel* considered central to the definition of our culture at the end of the 20th Century. Scrawled left-hand writing was combined with a bold use of *Helvetica Ultra Condensed*.

DESIGNED WITH SIMON STAINES

Opposite, clockwise:
297–301. *"Je Suis"* features
Actuel No.1, January 1991
Actuel No.4, April 1991
Actuel No.3, March 1991
Actuel No.1, January 1991
Actuel No.3, March 1991

As a departure from the normal magazine interview format, *Actuel* opted for a more direct approach whereby the interviewee spoke in his or her own words, allowing personal stories to unfold – a mix between *cinema verité* and the home movie. This allowed for greater diversity of subject matter. Editor Jean-François Bizot felt that, spiritually, many of *Actuel*'s readership were part of a lost generation who lacked belief in their world and were searching for something more tangible to invest their faith in.

readership, *Actuel* changed its formula once more and set about the task of creating a magazine that challenged the lure of TV. In 1989, *Actuel* eventually linked up with *The Face* and *Tempo* in Germany to organise a "Fax China" protest campaign, following the repression of the Tiananmen Square demonstration in Beijing.

Brody's work for the magazine came about thanks to a timely convergence. Bizot had admired *The Face* and in 1989 contacted Brody for a new redesign. Having left *Arena*, Brody was interested to see to what extent design could be minimal behind the content of a magazine. This turned out to be totally opposite to Bizot and *Actuel*'s feeling that the construction of a magazine should be a crazy play with preconceptions. Brody, strapped for time, wanted method not madness. Bizot insisted he wanted "grunge before grunge".

"Neville was right, the bastard. It was ahead of its time, but 'today, design has to be minimal', I hated that phrase! We did three great issues, but time was a big problem for Neville. The relationship stopped but could be picked up again at any time."

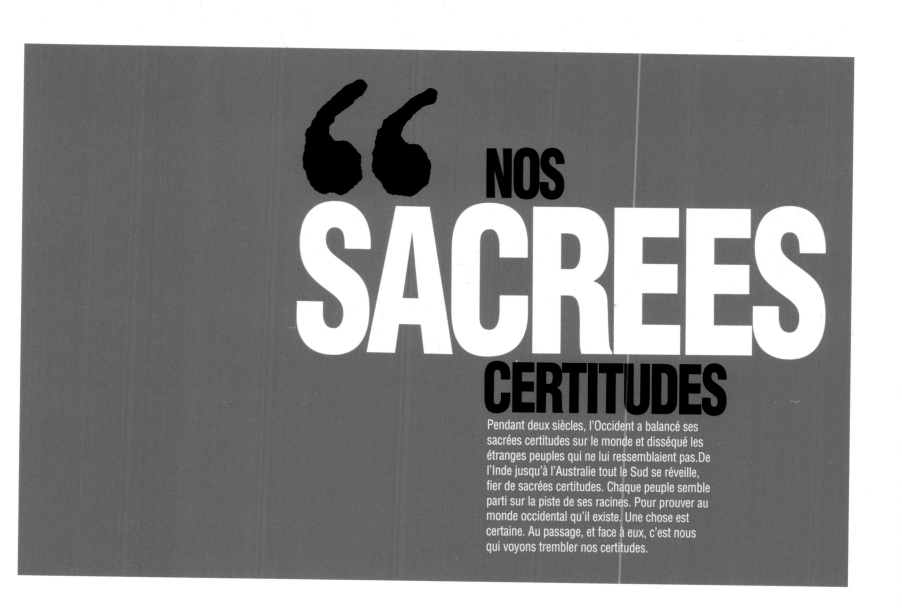

Premier étranger dans le Grand Nord russe depuis le goulag

TOUNDRA PARADIS PERDU

302–304. Feature
on the Russian Tundra,
Actuel No.3,
March 1991
Photojournalism was
central to *Actuel*'s
editorial policy. With
the help of the maga-
zine's picture editor
Claudine Maugendre,
the power of the image
was placed in pole
position.

Right:
305–307. Feature
on the Camcorder,
Actuel No.10,
October 1991

LES POMPIERS SE FILMENT DANS LES FLAMMES

RIEN n'échappe au CAMESCOPE

Les puits de pétrole abandonnés esquintent la
toundra
pour
des siècles
et le fils
du chaman
a vendu
son tambour
pour acheter l'eau de Cologne qu'il sirote

LA POLICE SURPRISE EN PLEIN TABASSAGE

Les derniers nomades des îles arctiques vivent toujours sous des teepees

LES PARENTS ABSENTS, LA NURSE COGNE

AH! SI DAVID VINCENT AVAIT SU...

308, 309. Feature
on Virology,
Actuel No.7-8,
July/August 1991
Inspired by a page
for Ionesco's *Délire
à deux* designed by
Massin in 1966.

épidémie
choléra,
origine du SIDA,
moustiques
et
tiques,
fièvre de Lassa
virus
d'Ebola,
ils sont partout traqués par
les
chasseurs
de *virus*

ACTUEL

Les
nouveaux
détectives...

Allô,
la fièvre
hémorragique
"rongeur"
renaît au Nigéria.
Qui
va enquêter?
Pasteur ou
Atlanta?

Left:
310, 311. Feature on New Orleans, *Actuel* No.3, March 1991

Right:
314–316. Feature on Surrealism, *Actuel* No.5, May 1991
Surrealism was the perfect companion to the typographic experimentation in *Actuel*.

Left:
312, 313. Feature on Lithuania, *Actuel* No.2, February 1991

Right:
317. Feature on Athletics, *Actuel* No.7-8, July/August 1991

BITE FANATISME RUSES POESIE ISRAEL LEURRES HADITH DJIHAD ETC...

LES DOUZE MOTS CLE DES ARABES

Qui les comprend vraiment en Occident? Nous avons rencontré un vieux sage, René Khawam, Français d'origine syrienne, traducteur du *Livre des Ruses*, un vieux manuel qui serait le vrai Coran de Saddam.

Entre le monde arabe et l'Occident il y a eu de nombreuses époques d'affrontement mais aussi des phases de complicité et de coopération. Les exemples ne manquent pas : la première mosquée de France fut érigée en 1187 par un Croisé bon chrétien qui voulait ainsi rendre hommage à la générosité de Saladin dont il fut le captif à Jérusalem. En 1535, François 1er fit appel aux musulmans

pour l'aider à libérer Nice des mains de Charles Quint. Et le rêve fou des Saint-Simoniens et de Napoléon III n'était autre que la création d'un grand royaume arabe en Afrique du Nord, associé à l'Occident. Aujourd'hui Dieu sait combien les médias nous parlent des Arabes et de l'Islam, sans pour autant nous expliquer grand chose. Les Arabes ont une autre vision du temps,

du langage, de la religion de l'histoire et même des gestes. Vision qu'il faudra bien comprendre un jour. On ne peut expliquer les événements d'aujourd'hui sans revenir au passé : la détermination de Saddam, ses appels à la guerre sainte, la rue arabe qui vibre pour lui de Rabat à Amman. *Actuel* a rencontré René Khawam. Erudit, traducteur du Coran et des *Mille et Une*

CRU, VRAI, HARD. VOILA LEURS VALEURS. L'AVENIR, C'EST LE MIX. ILS SE BATTRONT POUR LE METISSAGE

A la télé, les banlieues de France sont connues pour leurs casseurs. Leur musique explose ce cliché. Une génération de groupes refuse de se faire "golfiser". On ne déchirera pas ce mix qui vomit la guerre. *Par Bernard Zekri. Photos J.P. Plunier.*

MESSAGEMAN Nous parlions sur eux ! Cinq groupes français. La Mano Negra 91 se cache là. Choisissez ! Le funk bondissant de FFF, les raps sensuels de MC Solaar, le hip hop live de Babylon Fighter, le reggae-transe de Human Spirit ou l'existentialisme black d'I Am. Ils ont poussé en dehors des travées du showbiz. Ils ont déjà un public, une carriè-

re. Ils tournent sur Paris, en France, à l'étranger. Ils déjouent les images. Regardez toutes les photos. Essayez de dénicher parmi ces groupes même flous et artistiques celui qui apprend le russe ? Lequel est féru de théologie ? Cette année, ils signent leur premier contrat d'enregistrement. On va les voir, les entendre ! Ils sortent de la zone bourrés d'énergie street. Cru, vrai, hard,

voilà leurs valeurs. Qu'est-ce qui les fait courir ? L'avenir, c'est le mix. Ils se battront pour le métissage. L'éloge de l'individu, la réussite trottinent à bout de souffle. C'était hier. Aujourd'hui, ils refusent la frime, les discours et se méfient des médias. On ne se fera pas avoir. C'est aussi leur attitude par rapport au showbiz. Vestiges de l'attitude des indépen-

MARCO PRINCE, DU GROUPE FFF. PLUS FRANKAOUI, TU MEURS. « LAISSE TOMBER CES RACES OU LE GOLFE. LA MUSIQUE A DE L'AVANCE. LES JAZZMEN ACCOMPAGNENT LES RAPPERS QUI COPIENT LE REGGAE. C'EST LE FEELING JAM DE L'EPOQUE, LE PLAISIR DES BŒUFS, CE QU'ON APPELLE LE FUNKY TRASH. TU ME SUIS ?»

Above and opposite:
318–320. Three spreads from a feature on Islam, *Actuel* **No.2, February 1991**
The editorial use of a large word within columns of text punctuated the feature.

Left and opposite:
321, 322. Two spreads from a feature on Multicultural Music, *Actuel* **No.2, February 1991**
Lines of different point sizes were set touching each other.

Right:

323–325. Pages from the "Tout Nu" section, *Actuel* 1991
"Tout Nu" was an ironic look behind the scenes of various media events which
also involved penetrating reportage. Influenced by America's now defunct *Spy*
magazine, it was given a look emanating from French magazines from the
1950s to underline its main area of concern.

326. Contents page to the "Stop" section, *Actuel* No.5, May 1991
"Stop" was a round-up of cultural reviews and social trends.

109

Opposite:
330. Cover for *Arena* No.12, Autumn/Winter 1988

Below:
327. The Chill Factor, *Arena* No.7, Winter 1987/88
328. Tuscany, *Arena* No. 11, Summer/Autumn 1988
329. Yohji Yamamoto, *Arena* No.8, Spring 1988
At this stage, Brody restricted the headline
typography to *Helvetica* caps.

ARENA

The original intention of *Arena*, the men's magazine launched in 1986 by the publishers of *The Face*, was to create a new title for readers who had "grown out" of *The Face*'s target readership. By doing so, they opened up a hitherto unexplored area in magazine publishing, quickly exploited in the UK by other titles such as *GQ* and *For Him*.

Initially edited by Nick Logan and Steve Taylor, and subsequently by Dylan Jones, *Arena* rapidly established itself. For three years, Brody was the magazine's art director, his overriding concern being to utilise "a straightforward, informational approach" that challenged the over-exposure of design at that time and its tendency to smother editorial content with another "new look". He drew a logo by hand, suggesting an international, mock classical feel by echoing an IBM golf-ball typewriter face, and for the early issues (illustrated in the first book), he combined *Garamond*, *Helvetica* and *Kabel* with an emphasis on white space, giving the magazine a bland but subtle elegance.

Brody wanted the design to be boring, but soon became "bored with the boredom". He had chosen to focus the design on the use of *Helvetica* – a typeface he had hitherto studiously avoided – in an attempt to make an unemotional type create an emotional response. "I wanted to pursue the power of simplicity." Initially he had tried to use *Helvetica* as a means of avoiding a strong design identity, but not only was this approach instantly imitated, dissatisfied with the limitations he had imposed upon the early issues, Brody decided to pursue a more expressive, fluid and painterly use of the type during the later phase of his work for *Arena*.

The imagery in Arena was emotive, placing a great emphasis on the power of photography. Photographers were commissioned who could push the boundaries of their medium, pioneering several new techniques and aesthetics that have now become commonplace in fashion magazines.

Both approaches reflected Brody's response to design solutions that relied wholly upon the choice of typeface to fix their identity. Instead, for *Arena* the challenge was to develop a visual language that was defined by form and structure. This intention was enabled by the changeover to computer generated artwork. Adobe FreeHand made it easy to overlap words and letters, a treatment that had been almost impossible to specify to the traditional typesetters that *Arena* used. The page layouts were no longer based around a rational, cold display of information, and from here Brody set off on a new exploration of typographic treatments, conspicuously processed images that highlighted the effect that the Macintosh would have on the design process.

From the page design for *Vagabond* (p.13) to the poster for *AutoFuse* (p.33), Brody's later work for *Arena* is the source and embarkation point for much of his current typographic expressionism.

DESIGNED WITH SIMON STAINES AND IAN SWIFT

AUTU... ...50 US$3.95

ARENA

WHAT'S IT ALL ABOUT, ALFIE?

my name is michael caine exclusive interview by tony parsons

body count despatches from the war zone; by john sweeney

trouser snake! sir les patterson's wardrobe

bedtime story fiction by raymond carver

the bachelor pad/alexandra pigg/jean-michel basquiat
dean stockwell/maria cornejo/museums/the beer belly
thinking man's crumpet/travel writing/haoui montaug

36 pages of fashion: white shirts/man in
a suitcase/accessories/the colour of money

A12

SIXTIES CAINE: PHOTOGRAPHED BY DAVID BAILEY

0 74470 72697 5   11

MEN AT WORK

a head for heights: architect **richard rogers** has a towering international reputation but his dreams of an aesthetically revitalised london remain on the drawing board. his anti-nostalgic designs aren't made for today's climate, his ego unlikely to bend. how far can this maverick recast the establishment's view of itself?

ARENA **43** WINTER

331. Richard Rogers, *Arena* No.13, Winter 1988/89

332. Cover for *Arena* No.13, Winter 1988/89

The architectural use of type, image and space in *Arena* found its perfect application in this spread.

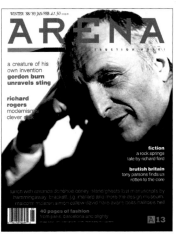

333. Hombre,
Arena No.13,
Winter 1988/89

334. Body Heat,
Arena No.11,
Summer/Autumn 1988

335. Fatal Attraction,
Arena No.8,
Spring 1988

At this stage Brody began to use all lower-case, building shapes with the type and bleeding headlines off the page, creating a dynamic by exploiting the heavy weight of *Helvetica Black*.

336. Reflections in a Golden Eye,
Arena No.12,
Autumn/Winter 1988

337. Café Noir,
Arena No.14,
Spring 1989

338. Faith,
Arena No.13,
Winter 1988/89

The main fashion photographers working for *Arena* at this time included Nick Knight, Jürgen Teller, Norman Watson, Michel Haddi, Kevin Davies, Marcus Tomlinson, Julian Broad, Martin Brading, Mark Lebon, and Stephan Sednaoui. Simon Foxton, Ray Petri and David Bradshaw were the main stylists.

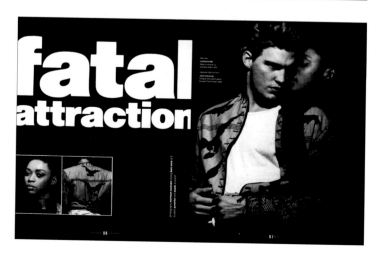

Grip

Treading dangerously

photography **marcus tomlinson**
art direction and fashion **david bradshaw** assisted by **simon steel**
machinery kindly supplied by **valentine lindsey** at V12

ARENA **109** SUMMER

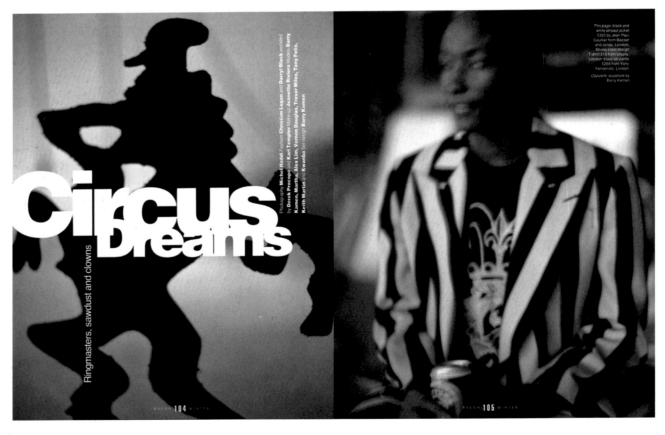

Circus
Dreams

Ringmasters, sawdust and clowns

Photography **Michel Haddi** Fashion **Christian Logan** and **Darryl Black** assisted by **Derek Procope** and **Karl Templer** Make-up **Jeanette Riviera** Models **Barry Kamen, Martha, Alex Lim, Vernon Douglas, Trevor Miles, Tony Felix, Keith Martin** and **Kwamba** Set design **Barry Kamen**

ARENA **104** WINTER

ARENA **105** WINTER

341. Cover for *Arena* No.8, Spring 1988

342. Cover for *Arena* No.20, Spring 1990

Left:
339. Grip,
Arena No.16, Summer 1989

340. Circus Dreams,
Arena No.19, Winter 1989/90

Letters begin to overlap and vary in
size – words interconnect, forming
isolated shapes.

Right:
343. Streets Ahead,
Arena No.18, Autumn/Winter 1989

344. Sport,
Arena No.18, Autumn/Winter 1989

345. Boss City,
Arena No.16, Summer 1989

346. Norman Mailer,
Arena No.16, Summer 1989

20

Deutsche für die **90er**

TEMPO präsentiert die
Top Twenty der
Neuen Zuversicht. Und
eine Reihe weiterer
Namen, die uns durch
das nächste Jahrzehnt
begleiten werden. → Frank Arnold, Ozonloch-Stopfer-

Andreas Lukoschik, 35 Jahre. Der Columbo unter Deutschlands Klatschreportern. Eine Mischung aus Ilja Richter und Alfred Biolek. Seine guten Manieren, sein meisterhafter Smalltalk und seine perfekte Primanertarnung sichern ihm Sympathien in den besseren Kreisen. Unfein wird Lukoschik dagegen an jedem Mittwochabend im dritten Programm des bayrischen Fernsehens. Unter dem Pseudonym Leo führt er dummerhafte Schickis vor, zerlegt stadtbekannte Nullen und plaudert aus dem Nähkästchen der Münchner Prominenz. Die Sendung, Pflichtprogramm in Bayern, hat Lukoschik die herzhafte Feindschaft seines allerden, zahllosen Kollegen Michael Graeter eingetragen. Ab Herbst 1989 werden wir Leo bundesweit erleben.

Frank Schirrmacher, 29 Jahre. Deutschlands Großkritiker Marcel Reich-Ranicki ernannte das Wunderkind des Feuilletons zu seinem Nachfolger als Literaturchef der „FAZ". Frank Schirrmacher selbst fand diese Revolution „nicht überraschend". Er ist einfach besser als die anderen. Nur einer wie er kann es sich leisten, Frankfurt als kulturelle Provinz zu bezeichnen. Nur er kann die Alt-68er als Geheimdienste des Geistes beschimpfen. Er wird die intellektuelle Onanie beenden, die heute noch die Kulturseiten befleckt, und das „FAZ"-Feuilleton zum Zentralorgan des kritischen Geistes machen.

Neu er Wilder Sänger · **Katharina Fritsch**, Bildhauerin und Kunsthoffnung · **Thomas Gögele**, Bernhard-Langer-Erbe · **Ben**

Marianne Sägebrecht, 42 Jahre. In den 80er Jahren brachte sie es zur Schauspielerin und Schutzpatronin aller Dicken. In den 90er Jahren wird sie „Oscar"-Preisträgerin und Schönheitsideal. Ihre satte, authentische Ausstrahlung ist unschlagbar. Marianne Sägebrecht ist allerdings mit sich selbst vergleichbar. Nur so konnte das dicke „Zuckerbaby" ausgerechnet Amerika erobern, die Supermacht der Null-Diät. Nur so konnte sie als Jasmin Münchgstettner das Titelbild der französischen Zeitschrift „Actuel" entern. Die 90er Jahre gehören einer Frau, die das pralle Leben verkörpert: sinnlich und erotisch.

Ulf Schirmer, 29 Jahre. Noch fünf Jahre, dann wird ausgerechnet Wiesbaden die beste Adresse für Avantgarde-Opern sein. Dank Ulf Schirmer, dem jüngsten Generalmusikdirektor Deutschlands. Für die laufende Wintersaison setzte er zunächst auf Selbstgänger: „Lohengrin" und „Die Hochzeit des Figaro". Im Februar schlägt Schirmer dann zum ersten Mal zu: Er bringt die Oper „Stallerhof" von Gerd Kühr auf die Bühne, eine Perle der Münchener Biennale von 1988. Wenn Wiesbaden richtig top ist, wird Schirmer garantiert von den Berliner Philharmonikern abgeworben.

Stefan Aust, Spiegelin, Spieglein in Privatternsehhand · Walter Dahn

ny Härlin, grüner Gen-Technik-Torpedo im EU

347–354. **Contents page, Feature articles and Front cover for TEM90, _Tempo_, Hamburg 1989**
The incongruous montage of the Aeroflot jet flying across the contents page and the crowded shapes on the architecture page (opposite, top right) predate Brody's approach to the design for _Actuel_ (see p.101–109). The running credit line used on "20 Deutsche für die 90er" anticipates the notion of the Internet. The large numbers appear as speed restrictions.

AT THE END OF 1989 Brody was asked by Tempo's editor Markus Peichl to collaborate on a "divided" issue of the magazine, split as far as the centrefold between a review of the 1980s and a preview of the coming decade, the pages of one section connecting with the other upside down. Lo Breier, from the Hamburg and Vienna-based design agency Buro X, art directed the 1980s' half; Brody, working with Cornel Windlin, tried to fathom the look of the future.

The design of the 1990s they decided would be dictated by a return to geometric lines and clarity, the image of order in the face of mounting urban chaos. "If the shape of the 80s was a square, man-made, then the shape of the 1990s would be a circle, suggesting a more spiritual, inward direction." The layout of the section was worked out so that it unfolded like a journey of sharp contrasts, photographic spreads being followed by essays from well-known German writers and philosophers, profiles, prophecies. The typeface *DIN* – "the return to an orderly system" – was used ironically, a reference to Germany's road signs.

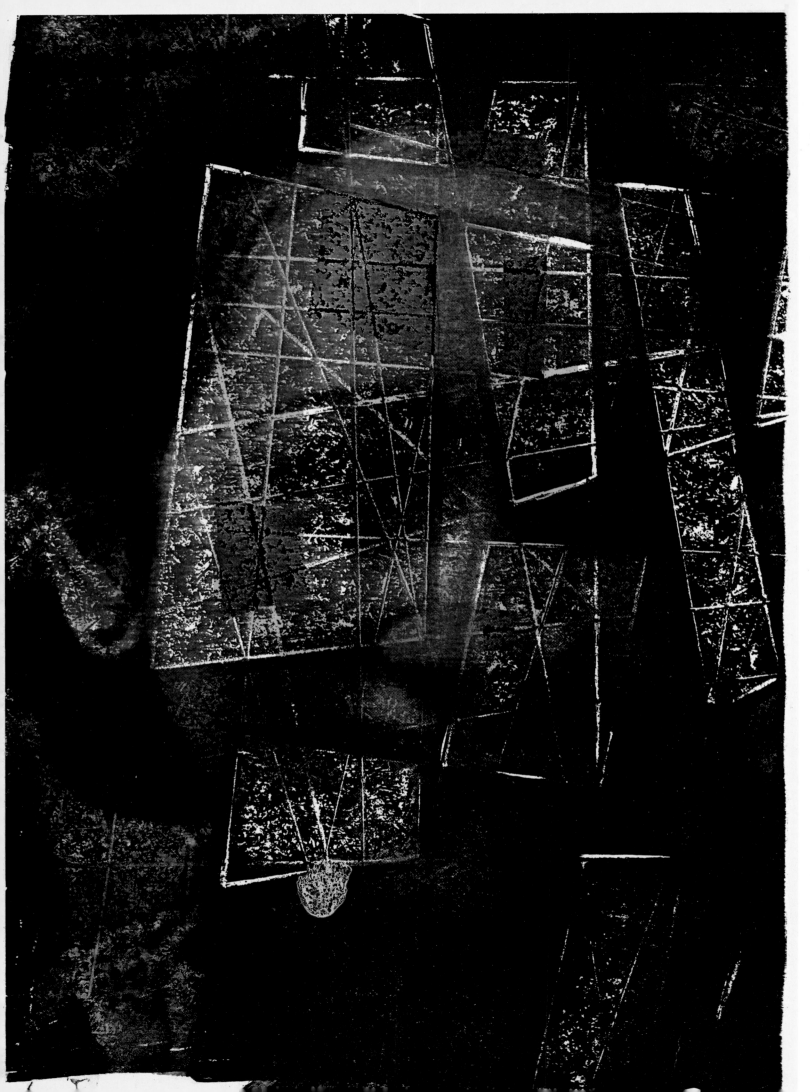

355. Sadie, poster for *Touch*, London 1988

Cyberspace is a by-product of the US military's attempt to keep communications possible after a nuclear war. The language of virtual space is typified by terms that suggest not only well-structured organisation, but an underlying immobility. The Net, the Grid, and the Matrix are like the harness strapped around the shoulders of a child out shopping with its mother to prevent any sudden dash onto the main Highway and into the on-coming traffic.

The Information Superhighway itself has yet to appoint its traffic police; nevertheless, already reports are coming in of users stuck in a digital queue waiting their turn to "log on" to the Net. The FBI has also been taking an interest, agents adopting electronic guises to monitor the communications taking place.

If the situation regarding regulation is as yet unclear, then at least one publisher in the US has recently compiled the *Net Guide*, the virtual version of the breakdown and rescue services on our car-clogged roads.

In a bid to come up with a more fluent image for information trafficking, according to *Wired* magazine, the latest term for the unwieldy "Information Superhighway" is the speedier-sounding "Infobahn".

356–362. *Skin Deep – The Portraits of Alastair Thain*, **Viking, London 1991**
Alastair Thain had worked with Brody at *Arena*, and on being given the chance to publish a monograph of his photographic work, he asked the Brody Studio to design the book. Featuring artists, musicians and performers, the photographs were naked and unglossy portraits that broke beneath the surface of the subjects' usual media representation; they were used uncropped, often full-bleed. Jane Withers supplied an essay on the contemporary art world – at the back of the book were short biographies of all the photographic subjects included. The work reveals a darker side to celebrity, verging on the grotesque.

DESIGNED WITH GILES DUNN

THE PORTRAITS OF ALASTAIR THAIN

'PROTECT ME FROM WHAT I WANT'

HAUS DER KULTUREN DER WELT

AFTER THE V & A EXHIBITION in London, Brody was interviewed by the German magazine *Der Spiegel* in the summer of 1988 and invited to design the six-page article himself. The magazine had never covered design issues before, let alone allowed an outsider to artwork its pages – the interview had been set up by one of their journalists to stimulate debate on the subject. Brody's piece was pre-empted by an editorial in the same issue which insisted that this was the first and last time an outside design would be allowed. Nonetheless, *Der Spiegel* was redesigned shortly afterwards.

One of the comments in the interview advocating "a modern outlook with a strict system to support it" caught the eye of Gunther Coenen, then head of London's Goethe Institute. Coenen had just been appointed the inaugural director of a new cultural institute in Berlin, Haus der Kulturen der Welt, based at the Kongressehalle, a building donated to the Berlin people by the United States at the end of the Second World War.

The working relationship was unusual. Brody and Coenen set up a close collaboration, expanding the brief into many non-related areas in order to find a language that HdKdW

Opposite:

363. Poster for Kleine Kulturen in grossen Staaten, HdKdW Berlin 1988
The first A1 poster that Brody designed for HdKdW. Publicising one of the centre's frequent cultural debates, the emphasis is on information. Personality is kept to a minimum - thumbnail photographs.

364, 365. Mittwochskino, front and back, HdKdW 1988
To publicise HdKdW's monthly film programme, Brody devised an A2 poster for display purposes that folded down to an A5 self-cover brochure.

This page:

366–370. Logo for HdKdW, 1988
Hand-drawn and assisted by Cornel Windlin, the logo was devised to be used in different colour combinations for each item of HdKdW stationery, and again changing for the reprint of each piece.

inka-peru

3000 Jahre Indianische
Hochkulturen durch drei
Jahrtausende 8. Mai bis
30. August

HAUS DER
KULTUREN
DER WELT

Di - So 10 - 20 Uhr. Sa, So und feiertags 12.00-21.00.   Eintritt: 8, - Dm ermäßigt 6, - Dm Haus der Kulturen der Welt (Kongreßhalle),
John-Foster-Dulles-Allee 10, 1000 Berlin 21 Telefon: 397 87 - 0 Verkehrsverbindungen: Bus 100 und 248,

Opposite:
371. Poster for Inka Peru, HdKdW 1992

This page:
372–375. Book covers for HdKdW, 1991
376. Poster for Kaukasien festival, HdKdW 1991
As well as holding exhibitions, HdKdW promotes concerts and performances, screens films, organises lectures and debates, and publishes books and compact discs to tie in with its focus upon a particular area of cultural activity. The book covers reproduced above were all associated with the festival of culture from the Caucasus, a series of events that reflected the re-consolidation of national identities following the collapse of the Soviet Union.

377. Symbol for Inka Peru, HdKdW 1992

SM 1509-2

SIERRA MAESTRA
Son Highlights
from Cuba
★

Alejandro Suárez vocal, claves
Alberto Valdés vocal, maracas
Luis Barzaga vocal, cowbell
Carlos Gonzalez bongo, congas, batá-drums, cowbell
Carlos Puisseaux güiro
Jesus Alemany trumpet
Eduardo Himely bass
Juan de Marcos González vocal, tres
José Antonio Rodríguez vocal, guitar

**378. CD booklet cover
for *Sierra Maestra***

**379. CD booklet cover
for *Soinari*, HdKdW 1993**

For the centre's series of compact discs which are released
approximately every two months,
Brody and the studio have developed a system of photographic
processing that avoids the predictable practice of using in-
concert or travelogue photos.
Visual material is supplied which
acts as the basis for the design:
often a small section of a photograph is selected, scanned, and
then processed and colourised
in Photoshop. The Georgian
script on the cover of *Soinari*
was drawn with a calligraphy
pen from a supplied example.

DESIGNED WITH SIMON EMERY

SOINARI
Folk Music from Georgia today

SM 1511-2

380. CD label for *Sierra Maestra*, HdKdW 1993
For every CD in the HdKdW series, one letter
is taken from the title, cropped and highlighted
on the label design.

would be at home with on a daily basis. Brody and Coenen
finally decided that everything should be contained within a
basic shape, choosing a square to symbolise a physical
centre and point of focus for world cultures, in preference to a
circle which would represent a more generalised globe. An
adaptable colour system was set up to identify the HdKdW's
different activities and print requirements, an organic design
suggesting the breadth of culture that it would present.

Brody drew up a new typeface with Cornel Windlin that
visually unified the range of HdKdW's work. Once the basic
design had been finalised, the Brody studio worked directly
with HdKdW's Harald Jähner to produce its promotional mate-

rial for the next five years. The design for each project is
structured on a rotational system within the studio. The prime
intention has been to raise the image of non-Western culture
from its tourist, travel-brochure ghetto without resorting to
false exoticism and cliché.

The Haus der Kulturen der Welt is itself a place of great
political significance. Less than five minutes' walk from the
Reichstag and the Brandenberg Gate, its very survival is currently under threat due to the German government's cut-back
on the funding of international cultural activities and its plans
to relocate itself in Berlin.

INDIEN

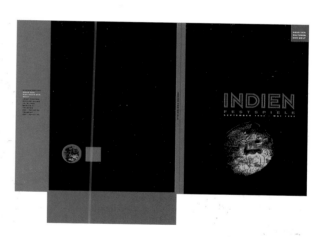

381–386. Brochure, Logo, Press folder, Early rough,
Colour system and Press Release, Indien festival, HdKdW 1991
HdKdW organised a German-wide festival celebrating Indian culture, and for its publicity material Brody was determined to develop a design that avoided the obvious
use of Indian typography and iconography. A colour system was developed both to
reflect the life and culture of India and to suggest a modern, dynamic nation. For the
main brochure, Brody used an ancient Indian coin to underline the deep roots of its
civilisation. An earlier rough shows a typographic treatment that was discarded in
favour of the understated application of *Akzidenz Grotesk* expanded.

"EXCITING AND BODACIOUSLY ENTERTAINING! SEXY, FUNNY AND WICKEDLY STYLISH. SHEER JUBILATION." WASHINGTON POST

FOREST WHITAKER GREGORY HINES ROBIN GIVENS ZAKES MOKAE and DANNY GLOVER as 'EASY MONEY'

A RAGE IN HARLEM

a PALACE presentation in association with MIRAMAX FILM CORPORATION of a PALACE WOOLLEY/BOYLE PRODUCTION FOREST WHITAKER GREGORY HINES 'A RAGE IN HARLEM' ROBIN GIVENS ZAKES MOKAE and DANNY GLOVER as 'EASY MONEY'
music by ELMER BERNSTEIN production designer STEVEN LEGLER edited by CURTISS CLAYTON director of photography TOYOMICHI KURITA executive producers NIK POWELL HARVEY WEINSTEIN BOB WEINSTEIN WILLIAM HORBERG TERRY GLINWOOD
co-producers FOREST WHITAKER and JOHN NICOLELLA screenplay by JOHN TOLES-BEY and BOBBY CRAWFORD based upon the novel by CHESTER HIMES produced by KERRY BOYLE and STEPHEN WOOLLEY directed by BILL DUKE

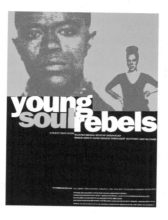

Opposite:
**387. Poster for *A Rage in Harlem*,
Palace Pictures, London 1991**
Part produced by the now defunct Palace
Pictures, *A Rage in Harlem* was directed by
Bill Duke with an all black cast and crew.
Shown here is the film's promotional poster
as used in England.

Left:
**388. Poster for *Jamon Jamon*,
Lolafilms S.A., Spain 1992**
Directed by Bigas Luna, *Jamon Jamon* was
promoted with the catchline, "Where women
eat men and men eat ham." Taking the most
graphically suggestive still from the film, the
end result was that Brody's poster was displayed worldwide but passed over by the
film's British distributors who commissioned
a different design.

DESIGNED WITH JOHN CRITCHLEY

Below:
**392. *FF Harlem*, FontFont,
FontShop International 1993**
Under the influence of *Helvetica Ultra
Compressed*, Brody's type design for the film
poster was extended into a full character set.
The font was enhanced and digitised by
Tobias Frere Jones at the Font Bureau,
having been emulated by MTV for their main
information font.

Above:
**389. Promotional poster for *Young Soul
Rebels*, British Film Institute, London 1991**

**390. Proposed poster for *Young Soul
Rebels*, British Film Institute, 1991**

**391. Front and back cover for *Young Soul
Rebels*, Various Artists, Big Life Records,
London 1991**
The title song for Isaac Julien's film was
performed by Mica Paris and released on
a single, whose cover design was similar
to that of this soundtrack LP. The story was
centred around life in Notting Hill Gate in the
late 70s.

ABCDEFGHIJKLMNOPQRSTUVWXYZabcdefghijklmnopqr
stuvwxyz1235678900ABCDEFGHIJKLMNOPQRSTU
VWXYZabcdefghijklmnopqrstuvwxyz1235678900

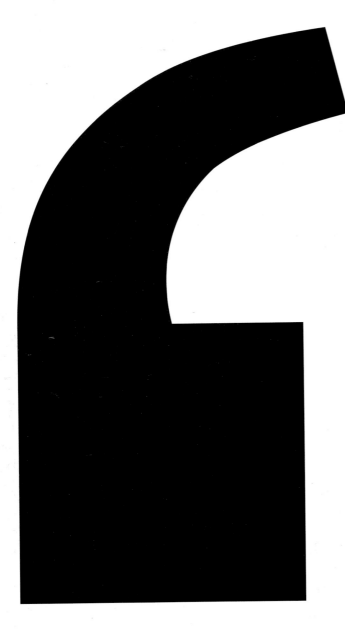

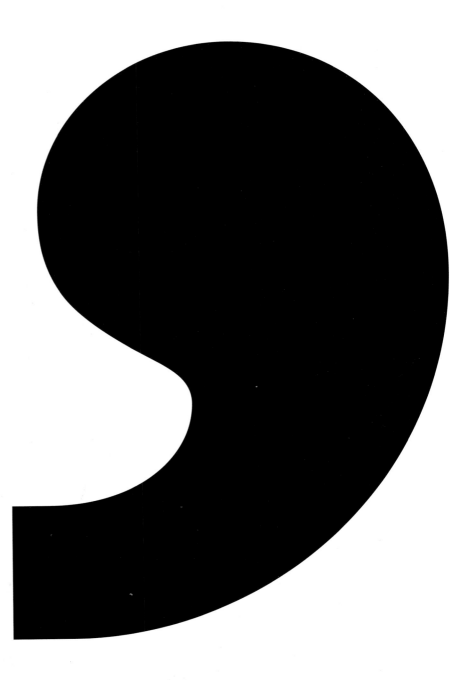

392. Logo for the Font Bureau, Boston 1993
Run by David Berlow with partner Roger Black,
the Font Bureau supplies customised fonts
specifically commissioned by publishers and
corporations, working either directly from past type
designs which are then digitally translated, or from
broader briefs. The Font Bureau also markets original fonts that their own designers have created.
The company has set up a model for the future
office network: their designers work on the basis
of a six month in-house "indenture" before being
sent out into the field and setting up as satellites,
transmitting finished type designs to the central
Font Bureau via fax and modem.

November 23, 1992

Font Bureau Retail VIII

Mac PostScript Type 1

Bodoni, Bremen,

Caslon, Century,

Cheltenham, Munich

FSI

Master

18 TREMONT STREET BOSTON, MA 02108-2301
TELEPHONE 617-742-9070 FAX 617-742-8464

Fax Letter

David Berlow → Erik Spiekermann
0101 617 742 9070
23.11.92. This page only

Erik – The Font Bureau, Inc., the Boston based independent type founder announced today the release to font distributors of its seventh retail font issue. This issue contains six condensed serif display styles from the **Cheltenham**, **Bodoni** and **Caslon** families. In addition The Font Bureau is proud to release three styles each of the **Bremen** and **Munich** families, a collaboration between The Font Bureau studios and type designer and calligrapher **Richard Lipton**.

The latter, new designs created by Lipton, are based on German poster design of the early 20th century and are ideally suited to striking decorative type for invitations, announcements and signage. As with all Font Bureau display faces, this issue is developed with extreme craftsmanship and care to set smoothly, without manual kerning in headlines and logotypes. This is of course true of the condensed serif faces as well. *"Designers have been waiting too long for a good set of condensed serif faces to use with the many serif text faces available today,"* explains famed design director and Font Bureau partner **Roger Black**. *"Most good text faces are not good for display, but many designers settle for their use in display sizes or choose a sans display faces to contrast with the text."* With the Font Bureau's new serif display faces designers now have much better choice.

The Font Bureau was founded in 1989 by Roger Black and **David Berlow** to provide custom fonts to the emerging market of graphic arts users based on the Macintosh. This market, starved for fonts by

David Berlow

18 TREMONT STREET
BOSTON, MA 02108-2301
TEL : 617-742-9070
FAX : 617-742-8464

The Main List of Things

82

393–397. Press folder, Disk label, Fax letter, Business card and SyQuest cover for the Font Bureau, 1992
The design focuses on quote marks and exploits their expressive function. Each inverted comma is taken from a different Font Bureau retail font, and is reproduced in black and white, with the added bonus that the design can be easily output from a LaserWriter and is readily faxable. The contrast between size and weight makes the design effective for fax purposes.

398–400. Identity, Letterhead and Invitation card for The Photographers' Gallery, 1990
Akzidenz Grotesk with white space.

DESIGNED WITH JOHN CRITCHLEY
AND PAT GLOVER

Right:
401, 402. Letterhead for Barfield Marks, London 1989
Introduced to Brody by David Rosen of Pilcher Hershman, Barfield Marks is an architectural partnership whose designs are usually based on a vertebral structure. At the time, they were working on a Bridge Building proposal for the canal docks at King's Cross in London. On the reverse of the letterhead is a light grey, three-backboned angel fish.

DESIGNED WITH GILES DUNN

THE PHOTOGRAPHERS' GALLERY

Thursday 25 January from 6 to 8 pm   **Private View**
                                              Invitation

The Trustees and Director of the Photographers' Gallery
request the pleasure of your company at the private view of

Martin Parr:
The Cost of Living 26 January - 3 March
Nick Sinclair 26 January - 3 March
Mihoko Yamagata: 2 January - 17 March

at the Photographers' Gallery,
5&8 Great Newport Street, London WC2

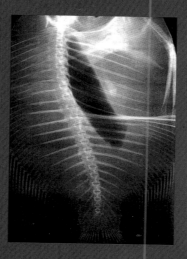

403. Poster for *Mountain Language*, Harold Pinter, National Theatre, London 1989
Harold Pinter's play explored the effect of a repressive political climate upon language and its usage. For the poster, the hand-drawn type was repeatedly photocopied until the letterforms started to merge.

Below:
404. Lecture slides for Texas AIGA conference, 1989
Using a double projector, Brody wanted to emphasise the absurd vacuity of the proliferation of design styles, and at the same time to highlight the persuasive power that the choice of typeface can command.

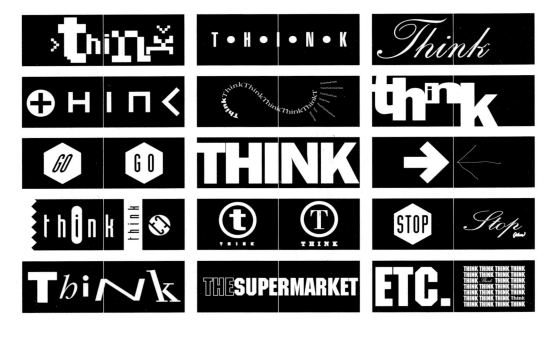

"It is essential in the early stages that all printed propaganda should have a *normal* appearance in the eyes of those to whom it is addressed. The slightest abnormality gives an impression of inefficiency and even absurdity: the document ceases to be serious."
Robert Byron, "Preparation of Leaflets, 23-30 Sept. 1938" (to be dropped from the air on enemy territory), quoted in Ellic Howe, *The Black Game*, Queen Anne Press 1988.

THE ADVERTISING BUDGET of the British Government during the 1980s expanded as the social deprivation caused by its policies increased. The London-based design industry freely colluded with its new paymaster's short-term party political and economic interests, prostituting its integrity to decorate asset-stripping policies like the various privatisation campaigns – mostly out of greed but also in an attempt to consolidate its new status as the "key to national salvation".

The aim of the article we were asked to produce for the *Guardian Review* was to question the speed and glee with which the design industry had invented this "protective, quasi-mystical status for itself" by insisting its stylistic devices as a vital part of every communication. "Refining and *redefining* techniques of manipulation... design is being used to conceal a social system on the brink of collapse." We extended this and argued that the design industry itself had become "a luxury item" and consequently its services would soon be deemed unnecessary. So it has proved.

Hit by the recession and the effects of new technology, by 1990 large design groups had either gone bankrupt or had been drastically reduced in size. The late 1980s showed design to be a failure as a business commodity and the industry's earlier boom to be no more than hype.

The present reality is that we are left to live with the corporate kitsch of this period. We need clear-headed, long-term design strategies to help structure the current revolution in communications, but the legacy of these emperors' new clothes has made the general public more than suspicious of design – the public no longer cares.

405. 'Protect the Lie', *Guardian Review*, London, 2 December 1988
The first *Graphic Language* was top of the *Guardian*'s list of best-selling art books in 1988; we were invited by the *Review* section's commissioning editor Waldemar Januszczek to write and design a front page as the first in a series created by independent artists. The Futurist manifesto published in *Le Figaro* in 1909 was a starting point. The text took two weeks to write, and for the page layout Brody adapted the paper's recent redesign by David Hillman of Pentagram from an eight to a six-column grid, with a staggered depth at the foot of the page. Various weights of *Franklin Gothic* were used for the main text.

The newspaper was not yet produced digitally. These were the last days of strength of the traditional print industry and, in spite of News International's new regime at Wapping, the *Guardian*'s presses were still union-run. Flat artwork was delivered, typeset by Brody (NGA member) at an NGA-appointed agency. Everything had been vetted by the *Guardian*'s arts editor, but compositors in the print room had not been told that they would be receiving alien artwork. Although the problem was resolved at the last minute, just before the page was to go on press they had protested and said they were not going to run it.

25

All information is seen as a threat until it is made familiar

27 Books — **The medicine men of the Third Reich**

30 Records — **Bon Jovi: Wouldn't you rather have pop?**

31 Records — **Four young fiddlers tackle Tchaikovsky**

32 Arts — **The alternative Emma Thompson**

Friday
December 2
1988

Review **Guardi**

What assumptions lie behind modern design? **Jon Wozencroft**, editor for the audio-visual publishers, *Touch*, is also the author of *The Graphic Language of Neville Brody*, The Guardian's best-selling Art book of 1988. **Neville Brody** is best known for his design on *The Face*, and is currently one of Britain's busiest art directors. Together, they challenge the corporate cover-up.

Late 1980s Britain, and the influence of design and of the Design Industry on everyday life is greater than ever. The declared intent is to present ideas, products and information as directly as possible. But the actual direction is towards the refining and *redefining* of techniques off manipulation. Design is no longer just a creative process – it is being used to conceal a social system on the brink of collapse.

Protect the lie

DANGER

British Steel, Barclays Bank, Nine-o-Clock News. We have to establish the scale of what we are dealing with. 'Television is working on us. Film is. We're not sure how yet. We wait, and count the symptoms. There's a realism problem, we all know that. TV is real! some people think. And where does that leave reality?' What Martin Amis says in *Money* applies equally to the current state of design.

DESIGN, *DE*sign, dsgn. The word itself has grown tiresome. In Britain, furthermore, we have inherited a literary culture that from the onset of the mass media age ha viewed design with deep suspicion.

We are not about to detail the distance between this dismissal and design's current state of hysterical self-indulgence. Ten years on from the liberating energy of Punk, we have witnessed design's accelerated shift from Form to Formula. This is increasingly acknowledged by 'style commentators', though rarely with any insight into what the present design mania implies – a massive and carefully controlled contrivance. What *is* happening now, and what does this suggest for the future? To set the wider frame within which the industry has developed, we must first look back to 1945.

The social catharsis that resulted from the Second World War gave the opportunity for economic, political and social reconstruction that was to be carefully *designed*. This was the promise: the world (which, as usual, meant Britain) was going to be a better place. Not only had Fascism been 'defeated forever', there was a real chance to learn from all the hardships and upheavals of the 1930s and before. The Ministry of Information made great efforts to ensure that 'we win the peace'. And to get this message across, the government immediately enlisted the services of the design trade.

In the New Society, to be young was not only to be good: the emergence of 'Youth Culture' in the 1950s offered princely possibilities of transformation.

To transmit this promise, all forms of design were necessary – for behind the bold typefaces lay a new form of Imperialism: the emergence of television and of an advertising industry, a system more pervasive than Hollywood had ever been. As Neil Postman wrote in *Amusing Ourselves to Death*, once there was 'no business like show-business', today the *only* business is show-business.

Design has been a prime agent in the compression of life into television time. A *creative* form, it quickly shifted its attention from social reconstruction, towards the new post-war consumerism, imported from the U.S. The earlier promise was overtaken by Superman comics and fast cars.

According to Robin Kinross, one of the few so far to have attempted an overview of this shift (*Blueprint*, No. 46, April 1988), design was soon forced to abdicate any distance its practitioners sought from the new world of advertising and entertainment. 'In Switzerland, design and advertising cohabited in self-restrained Calvinist order; but in ramshackle, free-for-all Britain, that was not on'. Rather than struggle to maintain their independence, most designers chose to conform (with exceptions, such as the opponents of advertising's takeover of the Designers' and Art Directors' Association in 1964).

CONFORMISM is no longer a tendency. It is a financial and political imperative in the face of increasing censorship and oppression. Design is now the focal point of cultural expression. It controls the image in the marketplace – an economic order that is by its very nature unstable and unpredictable. To consolidate this confidence trick, the design world glorifies the consumerist values the market place depends on for survival. Design becomes 'inflated into a way of life, a key to national salvation' (Kinross). It promotes itself as a vital mechanism of the system to its corporate patrons; furthermore, the design world believes itself to be essential to *any and every form* of communication. Nothing is left naked.

But at what cost? The marketplace has created artificial wealth in the short term, but in doing so it has brought us to the verge of cultural bankruptcy. As we seek to 'look sharp', have we cut off our heads?

'I think the fact that you see our work all over England almost ends up looking like a corporate identity for the country. We never set off with this in mind, but that's the way it seems to have evolved'. – Margaret Calvert, assistant to Jock Kinneir, designers of England's trunk road, airport and hospital signposting systems.

ARRIVALS, Departures, Accident & Emergency, WAIT, SLOW... NO ENTRY. The chaos of modern society requires such commands, categories and regulations: graphic design. Today, this colludes with commerce to insist that the only doors you pass through are the entrances to shops. Airports are chockablock with consumption: Sky Shop, Duty Free, Bureau de Change. Hospitals, as they veer increasingly towards private medicine, advertise themselves as hotels where room service comes complete with plastic surgery. In Money Culture, a shop is any service, system or outlet that depends on advertising. Britain is a supermarket. Our leader is a shop assistant. Culture is up for sale. Tourism, after all, saves us from facing up to the real lessons of history. Our past comes gift-wrapped, and it's on special offer!

Britain's signposting system is a model of efficiency, but many of its creators have been unaware of two areas vital to any communication – process and context. Firstly, it is necessary to clarify the motivations and their process, so that design can be a popular rather than an elitist form. Secondly, the willingness of designers to perceive *and* interact is gone – both with the context of their work, and the effect that it has on everyday life.

It is a question of responsibility, and research. From Top Shop to Virgin, what do the designers of our High Street shops think they are doing when they clutter the environment with appropriated graphics that are obsolete before the signs are even fastened to the wall? They are, of course, 'following the brief', making a fortune, and flooding our eyes with rubbish. The client wanted it.

Where does the brief come from? That's a good question. Does it come from the supermarkets themselves? From television? From the success of 80s 'lifestyle' magazines? Does it come from Rupert Murdoch? Or dies it come from the public? Shopping has become a vital means of expression during a time of authoritarianism. We are a long way from 1945. There is no longer any plan – simply a conspiracy of shared interests. On the one hand, greed, on the other, the need for economic survival. Money, the ultimate protection racket. The modern system that facilitates this is *signification* – the process by which all cultural ideas are reduced to mere codes and a method that enables design to appear to share the common language of its target market with no more meaning than commercial familiarity.

Culture is not a bottomless pit that can be infinitely ransacked

As Jon Savage put it, 'how did it happen that the current pinnacle of pop culture should be found in adverts?' This is the frame. You are the integral part of the set-up.

The real success of the Design Industry has been its ability to change its skin so often that you rarely, even in *The Guardian*, get more than a glimpse of the whole picture. This might begin to sound alarmist, but after working at the heart of design culture, we feel it is time to call a halt. The speed and the scale: billboards ever increasing in number, neon lights flashing faster and faster – we are deep into psychic assault of epic proportions.

STYLE IS A VIRUS. It is a means of self-flattery, and has become a way of countering the threat of individually. Like design, 'style' is now a badly infected word.

Such language problems allow no middle ground, no balance. 'Style Revolution' really means imitation overload – a complete loss of nerve on the part of writers, musicians, editors, designers, when it comes to releasing experience. It's so much easier to act the part than to live the life.

The notion of creativity itself has been colonised by advertising. Never have so many 'creatives' unleashed such destructive forces in their bid for your minds. This language no longer leans towards the opening of possibilities, but to the integration of all forms of expression and identity into plain commercialism. The new 'Silk Cut' ad rips the 'L' from LIFE. Integration becomes disintegration.

Cultural expression rests upon the visible plane of an invisible strata. All forms of Media operate on the surface of this strata. During the last decade, its layers have been intensively sucked to the surface and eaten away through the total reliance upon signif-ication, imitation and nostalgia. Everyone, from pop musicians to politicians, wants you to belong – ie, pay up – and the new promise is that fulfilment comes as part of the total package, *the product*. Like the ad boards in *Blade Runner*, advertising and design fix the scattered details that travel across the busy surface of the strata, and their 'finished' product is presented as confirmation of unity. The latest designs for Midland Bank, for example, mix antique globes, marble end-papers and grainy/moired photography with 'classical' small cap. and italicised type: banking is no longer thought of as a service, but comes as part of 'The Meridian Range of *products*' (my italics). 'The Meridian Range' (a package of banking services) is no different, or less transient, than a spring fashion collection.

The only reason why advertising and design have got away with this for so long is due to the prior depth of the strata: British Culture, European Culture, World Culture, Third World Culture. If design had true confidence in itself, would it feel the need to change constantly? Or is it the public that demands constant change? This reflects a desperate need to avoid being pinned down and revealed. Keep running.

Design is an animal hungry for 'fresh' supplies The process is reductive and the design world faces an abyss of its own making. In the end, design will eat itself. Culture is not a bottomless pit that can be infinitely ransacked – it needs a purposeful present, *lived* experience with which to nourish its context and vocabulary. This is now night on impossible. Consider the latest fashion in London. 'Acid House', a hybrid of 60s libertarianism and 80s compression ... glued together by the insistent bond of *the beat*. It harbours allusions towards past freedoms (which in the present climate is at least to be welcomed, if not swallowed whole) – freedom of movement, freedom of expression, freedom to take strange chemicals without worrying about the consequences. But even more so than previous subcultures that cross-over, 'Acid House' proclaims itself as a *designed* invention, matching past form to past form to dance and smile away the present. It's fun, a celebration, but of what?

The main lesson of 'Acid House' has been its speed of assimilation – approximately nine months – from London's scene to prime time Radio One DJs wailing 'acieed': across the airwaves and onto the front page of *The Sun*. Bans and moral outrage are par for the course, more so now – for the present puritanical climate. Fun must be strongly resisted. It should come as no surprise, therefore, that the most radiant smiles of young people, as pictured in the media, can be seen on the faces of those who jive in front of a cashpoint machine.

'Acid' is simply a quest for freedom, a craze that expresses young people's desire for sensory stimulation. It is actually celebrated within an environment that creates sensory *deprivation* – inside the club, hot, airless, loud and crowded. But who cares? 'We're out of it'.

Design is a process that creates sensory deprivation. It promises desire will be fulfilled, thus many have little trouble in parting with their money for more of the same.

THIS VENEER of happiness is closely linked with the success of style magazines, now style television, and their triumph of form over content. The public is more aware of design, but what kind of design, borne of what motives? Whilst many more people notice the process of design, there are just as many who resent the form for its glamourisation of trivia, and its easy translation from editorial page to advert. Meanwhile, the editorial recedes – the offer of more advertising revenue is too tempting, the subject of advertising becomes the editorial and vice versa. In many publications the editorial has disappeared as a means of stating one's position in relation to content.

So with design, you could argue that we are back to square one: the continued dominance of scepticism and suspicion, if not outright disavowal. And still some way from understanding.

What is "square one"? We long for a return to basics. Complexity and challenge do not fit the brief, and 'difficult' material is kept outside the frame of reference. The illusion of depth is provided by the screen of interchangeable surface details, like a loop. Understand its strategy. In past cultures, the by-product of philosophy was revolution; in the late 20th Century, the by-product of philosophy is style. Marx meets Sparks.

DANGER. It is clear that design is a political process, where all information is seen as a threat until it is made familiar, assimilated, and codified. Information is transmitted as a set of references, never as itself. Codes not only provide a system of classification – they encourage exclusion. Design is simply *the* process through which media systems present themselves, as elite clubs, whose membership policy is tightly controlled. Design is also an attempt at *sophistication*, tempting us to feel good about ourselves in the face of ever-mounting evidence to the contrary.

Design, then, is really no different to editing, the silent craft of the late 20th Century. Editing is a crucial part of everyday life – what you react to, what you ignore and what slips in unseen. The problem is not too little information of real quality, there is simply *too much* information with no substance, shining bright like a stroboscope.

Design is camouflage, and sophistication is, in reality, cheap simplicity. What is 'substance'? What is information? The Media Lab, based at the Massachusetts Institute of Technology has come up with a definition: 'Information is any difference that makes a difference'. Design accelerates homogenisation. As a manipulative force, design has not only been greatly refined since the days of WW2 propaganda, it has redefined, totally, the landscape of everyday life. According to Jean Baudrillard in *Rituals of Transparency*, faced with ever-increasing levels of exploitation, 'we don't look for definition or richness of imagination in (synthetic) images; we look for the giddiness of their superficiality, for the artifice of the detail, the intimacy of their technique. What we truly desire is their technical artificiality, and nothing more'.

There is no longer any plan – simply a conspiracy of shared interests

The consequence of sophistication – the need to refine, reduce and dress existing models, rather than to invent new forms – is stagnation. In a bid to invest this technique with some measure of progression, the Presentation industry, when it chooses to caption itself as Design, is fully supported by its associates in magazines, in the music business and on television. The Media is a *designed* phenomenon. It consolidates its power through ritual, the main event, the magnanimous gesture (charity), the beam to the camera, 'not to bring about a specific personal or group awareness, but to bring a seeping loss of power to the mass'. (Jon Savage, *Touch Ritual*).

Design is not the religion itself. The creed of the moment is celebrity and self-gain. But it is the major form through which this religion manifests itself. To the Design Industry, this has been a lifeline – design is a tool of communication. Today, the main message is the hollowness of our present culture and the bankruptcy of meaning, but there seems still to be plenty of money in the corporate pot bidding for the Magic ingredient of design. What else is there for it to do but continue the pretence?

As Gysin and Burroughs once suggested, 'exaggerate your weaknesses'. We allow this to persist: Money Culture insists you alleviate your insecurities and fears, both for the present and for the future. Design is a grotesque attempt to re-form and re-present our lives as perfect.

Man made God in his own image, and design is doing the same – through cloning. It takes parts of the body and tries to reassemble them as one being. The result is subhuman. As the year 2000 approaches, we should be moving forward and inventing new forms that clarify communication. Out of fear, we do the opposite. We should be taking more risks, but design in its present state is all about the elimination of risk – the hard sell with pretty pictures, its typography clean and precise, pompous neo-classical expression ('be Prudential'), representing a false image of purity against the threat of imminent contamination, Pillars built upon a bedrock of decay. Blindness is the order of the day, for 'not only do we seem completely unprepared to learn from our mistakes, but also from our successes' (A.M. McKenzie/The Hafler Trio).

TECHnology plays a part in all this. It is seen as the great liberator, but when machines are left to do all the work, the result is processed mediocrity. Lousy, ill-considered typography plastered onto images – from *Sunday Sport* to record covers, it's everywhere. There are also the dangers of tradition, designers who follow old rules that no longer apply to the present. There is either no discipline – the downside of Punk graphics – or the discipline passed on from tutors, usually with little experience of working in the commercial world. Rules have to be learnt before they can be broken, but you're never even shown that you can try the latter. The Design Industry wants good professionals. So does the Army.

For example, desk-top publishing, DTP, gives designers the opportunity to take total control of typesetting operations, but in the rush for deadlines, few have the patience. Unlike its hot metal precursor, this new technology does not require manual craftsmanship in the same way – the designer must now become adept at accessing a machine's capabilities through its system of codes. The real task that confronts designers should be to extend programmed limitations and to experiment with the technology.

At present, this is rarely happening. The easy availability of typesetting facilities and 'instant print' services has created a design supermarket. Most top Design groups, like Fitch & Co., will meet a client with three presentation boards, hoping to hit the right target. The first will feature 'the Youth Look' – the right magazine clippings, the trendiest typefaces...The second will have a 'nostalgic' feel, and the third, neo-classical. Ad nauseam. Immortality, comfort and tradition, all perfect frames of reference with which to create a seamless ambience: the disco pub, the DTI, Terminal 4. Solutions in search of a problem. If you approach design as problem solving, all you can ever hope to communicate is the problem itself.

E X A M P L E
Brasserie Media

e x a m p l e
Much ado about nothing

X
By self-appointment

E*xample*
The Modern identity

As far as the Design Industry is concerned, desk-top technology poses a serious problem. It will soon become obvious that design not only has no 'magic ingredient' other than an individual's skill and imagination, but furthermore, Design is a luxury item in its present and most widespread form. Or to go one step further – Design is unnecessary.

STOP. To prevent this from becoming too readily apparent, the Industry has invented a protective, quasi-mystical status for itself. Call it Designerism. This is self-anointed omnipotence. Why, then, have people welcomed (and endorsed) companies like Next whose design strategy reinforces the syndrome of plunder and abbreviation (the 'N' logo, cf. 'Q', 'M', 'W', etc.)? Fake universality – Is this the "return to basics" that people want? This ritualised compression is one step away from religious fanaticism, which is set to become one of the growth industries of the 1990s – promoted no doubt (for currently we cannot expect it to be otherwise), by Design.

Design may be unnecessary, but it is not irrelevant. The key is this: Design communicates the fact that Design communicates itself. This matters enormously.

Why does information about ourselves (or otherwise) have to be made more palatable? Information is biased by the means with which it is made appetising. What role does design perform in society? Is this a new need? Data does, after all, require a certain degree of translation and of entertainment. Colour is a primary means of differentiation, humour a vital element of life itself. Gatwick needs its sick bags.

FUNCTION follows form, form follows motive. There is more to motive than money, protection and *travail*. Design has forced itself into this system of contrivance. It turns a vicious circle, and keeps its cartel in the hands of careless people, protecting the wrong reasons. It communicates greed, promotes envy, and causes misery.

In *Hiding in the Light* Dick Hebdige writes that 'the circle is a metaphor that can contain everything and nothing. It can signify a black hole and the whole wide world...And everything turns within the circle. Everything there is'.

The Design Industry pretends to represent everything there is. It is not a question of good or bad design, but of the attitudes that lie behind it. What measures can be taken to move forward from design's sick condition and the stasis it promotes? Look to its antithesis as a starting point so that design might once again become a dynamic form, both socially responsible and aware.

The antithesis is chance, intuition and spirituality. How, then, can any movement seeking to counter Designerism avoid the existing frames of signified rebellion ('CCCP' T-shirts and 'radical chic')? Categorisation is a bullet to the brain. Learn how to step beyond the firing line, or better still, unload the guns. How could a humanistic approach deal with a communication process where speed, volume and scale rise above all other considerations? Coverage counts, not quality.

We must address such questions, without fear and without fail. We must create a context for a more active dialogue between designers and those that live with their effects (re-education, from both sides); moreover, we must recognise that an education in design and media awareness should start in schools. Ignorance is one of the oldest forms of protection.

To co-exist (and not *only* survive) alongside modern media systems, you need to develop your abilities to decode and deconstruct what is presented to you. Design has to encourage a critical perspective: It should challenge perception, and not deprive us of it. You need insight, but the mass media ritual attempts to deny you any space for insight.

Do not accept

THE SET UP

Martin Amis, *Money*, Penguin Books, 1984. Neil Postman, *Amusing Ourselves to Death*, Heinemann, 1985. 'A to Z', *Signals*, Channel 4, October 1988. Stewart Brand, *The Media Lab*, Viking/Penguin Books, 1987. Jean Baudrillard, *The Ecstasy of Communication*, Semiotext(e), 1988. Jon Savage, *Touch Ritual*, Touch, 1986. Brion Gysin/Terry Wilson, *Here To Go*, Re-Search, 1982. The Hafler Trio, *The Gathering of Opposites*, Touch, 1989. Dick Hebdige, *Hiding in the Light*, Routledge, 1988. ***The Graphic Language of Neville Brody* is published by Thames and Hudson.**

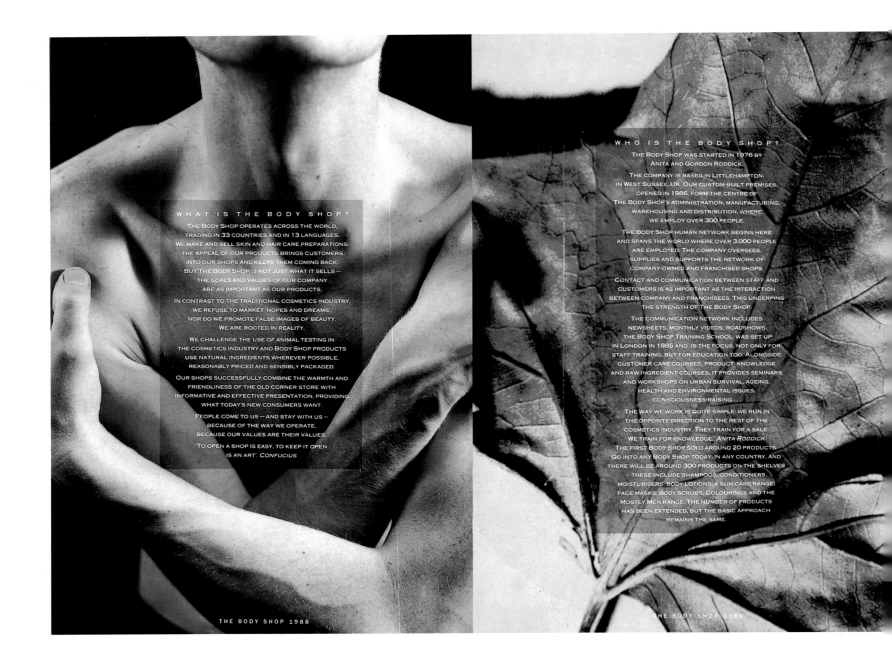

WHAT IS THE BODY SHOP?

THE BODY SHOP OPERATES ACROSS THE WORLD,
TRADING IN 33 COUNTRIES AND IN 13 LANGUAGES.
WE MAKE AND SELL SKIN AND HAIR CARE PREPARATIONS:
THE APPEAL OF OUR PRODUCTS BRINGS CUSTOMERS
INTO OUR SHOPS AND KEEPS THEM COMING BACK.
BUT THE BODY SHOP IS NOT JUST WHAT IT SELLS —
THE GOALS AND VALUES OF OUR COMPANY
ARE AS IMPORTANT AS OUR PRODUCTS.

IN CONTRAST TO THE TRADITIONAL COSMETICS INDUSTRY,
WE REFUSE TO MARKET 'HOPES AND DREAMS',
NOR DO WE PROMOTE FALSE IMAGES OF BEAUTY.
WE ARE ROOTED IN REALITY.

WE CHALLENGE THE USE OF ANIMAL TESTING IN
THE COSMETICS INDUSTRY AND BODY SHOP PRODUCTS
USE NATURAL INGREDIENTS WHEREVER POSSIBLE,
REASONABLY PRICED AND SENSIBLY PACKAGED.

OUR SHOPS SUCCESSFULLY COMBINE THE WARMTH AND
FRIENDLINESS OF THE OLD CORNER STORE WITH
INFORMATIVE AND EFFECTIVE PRESENTATION, PROVIDING
WHAT TODAY'S NEW CONSUMERS WANT.

PEOPLE COME TO US — AND STAY WITH US —
BECAUSE OF THE WAY WE OPERATE,
BECAUSE OUR VALUES ARE THEIR VALUES.

'TO OPEN A SHOP IS EASY, TO KEEP IT OPEN
IS AN ART'. CONFUCIUS

THE BODY SHOP 1988

WHO IS THE BODY SHOP?

THE BODY SHOP WAS STARTED IN 1976 BY
ANITA AND GORDON RODDICK.

THE COMPANY IS BASED IN LITTLEHAMPTON,
IN WEST SUSSEX, UK. OUR CUSTOM-BUILT PREMISES,
OPENED IN 1986, FORM THE CENTRE OF
THE BODY SHOP'S ADMINISTRATION, MANUFACTURING,
WAREHOUSING AND DISTRIBUTION, WHERE
WE EMPLOY OVER 300 PEOPLE.

THE BODY SHOP HUMAN NETWORK BEGINS HERE
AND SPANS THE WORLD WHERE OVER 3,000 PEOPLE
ARE EMPLOYED. THE COMPANY OVERSEES,
SUPPLIES AND SUPPORTS THE NETWORK OF
COMPANY-OWNED AND FRANCHISED SHOPS.

CONTACT AND COMMUNICATION BETWEEN STAFF AND
CUSTOMERS IS AS IMPORTANT AS THE INTERACTION
BETWEEN COMPANY AND FRANCHISEES. THIS UNDERPINS
THE STRENGTH OF THE BODY SHOP.

THE COMMUNICATION NETWORK INCLUDES
NEWSHEETS, MONTHLY VIDEOS, ROADSHOWS.
THE BODY SHOP TRAINING SCHOOL WAS SET UP
IN LONDON IN 1985 AND IS THE FOCUS, NOT ONLY FOR
STAFF TRAINING, BUT FOR EDUCATION TOO. ALONGSIDE
CUSTOMER CARE COURSES, PRODUCT KNOWLEDGE
AND RAW INGREDIENT COURSES, IT PROVIDES SEMINARS
AND WORKSHOPS ON URBAN SURVIVAL, AGEING,
HEALTH AND ENVIRONMENTAL ISSUES,
CONSCIOUSNESS-RAISING . . .

THE WAY WE WORK IS QUITE SIMPLE: WE RUN IN
THE OPPOSITE DIRECTION TO THE REST OF THE
COSMETICS INDUSTRY. THEY TRAIN FOR A SALE.
WE TRAIN FOR KNOWLEDGE.' ANITA RODDICK
THE FIRST BODY SHOP SOLD AROUND 20 PRODUCTS.
GO INTO ANY BODY SHOP TODAY, IN ANY COUNTRY, AND
THERE WILL BE AROUND 300 PRODUCTS ON THE SHELVES
— THESE INCLUDE SHAMPOOS, CONDITIONERS,
MOISTURISERS, BODY LOTIONS, A SUN CARE RANGE,
FACE MASKS, BODY SCRUBS, COLOURINGS AND THE
MOSTLY MEN RANGE. THE NUMBER OF PRODUCTS
HAS BEEN EXTENDED, BUT THE BASIC APPROACH
REMAINS THE SAME.

THE BODY SHOP 1988

THE BODY SHOP

BODY SHOP
International PLC

THE STUDIO SOUGHT TO DEVELOP inspired working collaborations, and for this project client and designer seemed well suited. Brody was at odds with the design industry and The Body Shop had established itself as an anti-cosmetics industry retailer selling cosmetics.

During his time at *The Face* and *Arena* Brody worked with the then politically-motivated listings magazine, *City Limits*, and put his cards on the table by redesigning the Labour Party magazine *New Socialist*. He was seen as a prime candidate to create modern designs for clients and organisations that were essentially anti-design, highly critical of consumerism in general, wanting nonetheless to target a wider audience.

The Body Shop had quickly expanded from a small chain to a multinational franchising operation. The company had recently been floated on the Stock Exchange, yet it was still run in the spirit of a family business, dealing with real issues in the marketplace.

Business for The Body Shop was in fact a crusade and it recognised the importance of highlighting environmental issues at every opportunity. Editorially, the brochure was structured as a cross between a magazine and product catalogue, with interviews, propaganda, sound-bite stories, shop displays and anti-cosmetic beauty tips. The photography was commissioned from associates of *Touch* and *Arena*.

The 1987/88 Annual Report and brochure was the first to be printed on recycled stock, hoping that this example would persuade other companies to abandon their wasteful habit of using virgin gloss paper. It was also an opportunity to create an aesthetic tailored to the materials, using earth colours, coarse-grain photographs, bold typography and line drawings.

With *Touch* Brody had already tested the printability of recycled paper with a set of posters published the previous April. Contact with a sympathetic printers had since been established; many had previously been against using recycled

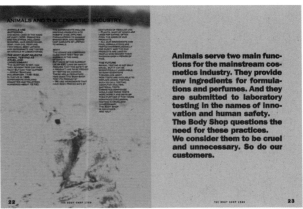

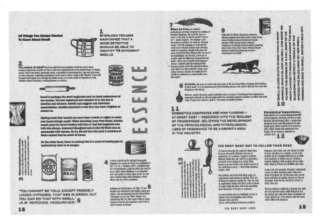

stock because it tended to clog up printing machine rollers
and tear too easily. Thus the machines had to be run slowly,
and less speed meant less profit.

**406–411. Opening concertina, front cover and pages from
The Body Shop brochure, London and Littlehampton 1987**
The Body Shop commissioned a design agency to source the availability
of every recycled paper stock in Britain. We were shown samples of
some beautifully textured and organically-coloured 'recycleds' but it
turned out that in most cases you had to buy it by the ton, usually having
to order supplies way in advance. We were nonetheless able to source
four varieties which were used for different spreads in the brochure, the
coarse grain of the sugar paper working well with the out-of-focus photography. Later, working with Greenpeace, we discovered that there was only
one recycled paper readily available in the country that was not de-inked
using a chlorine-based process.

BODY SHOP CO-ORDINATOR: SUE JACKSON; EDITOR: JON WOZENCROFT; DESIGNED WITH IAN
SWIFT AND LIZ GIBBONS; PHOTOGRAPHY BY PANNI CHARRINGTON, JÜRGEN TELLER, RICHARD
CROFT AND IAN McKINNELL

RALPH GIBSON: TROPISM
March 11 – April 16

VERDI YAHOODA: WINDOW DRESSING
March 4 – April 9

Left:
412. *Ralph Gibson: Tropism*, **The Photographers' Gallery, London 1987**

Above right:
413. *Behold the Man*, **The Photographers' Gallery, 1988**

414. *Roy DeCarava & D–Max*, **The Photographers' Gallery, 1987**

415. *Industrial Image*, **The Photographers' Gallery, 1987**

THE PHOTOGRAPHERS' GALLERY
5+8 GREAT NEWPORT STREET, LONDON WC2. TUESDAY TO SATURDAY 11-7

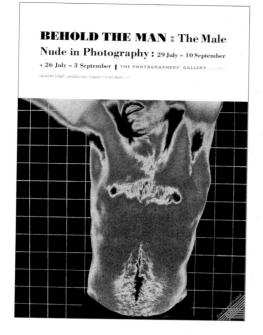

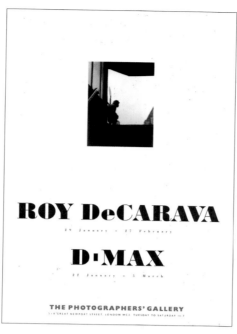

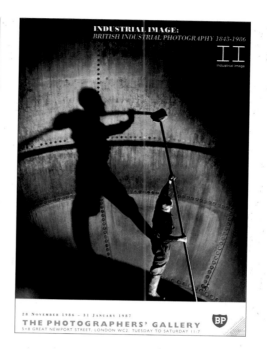

Right:

416. *Mari Mahr: Isolated Incidents,* **The Photographers' Gallery, 1989**
Brody and the studio continued the central philosophy of white space, simple use of image and clear structure into this period of redesign, having produced exhibition posters for the Photographers' Gallery over the previous four years.

Right and below:

417. Brochure cover, *In Our Time: The World as Seen by Magnum Photographers*

418–421. Promotional posters for *In Our Time: The World as Seen by Magnum Photographers,* **The Hayward Gallery, 1990**
Forbidden to crop the Magnum photographs, this series of posters, displayed on the London Underground and on bus shelters, achieved maximum impact by contrasting monochrome with varying colour detail.

DESIGNED WITH SIMON STAINES

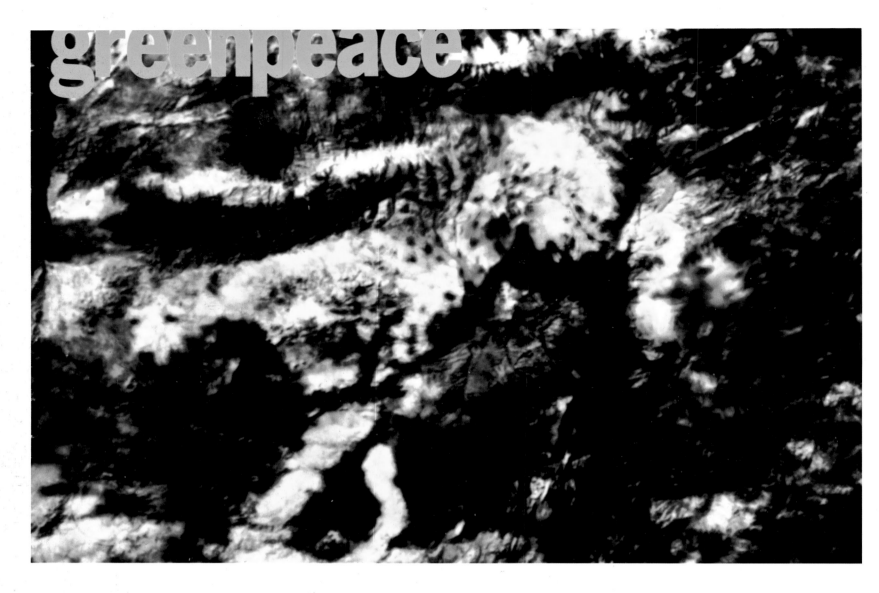

greenpeace

422. Cover for *Breakthrough*, Various Artists, Greenpeace/Melodiya Records, London and Moscow 1988
The printers in Moscow had a field day trying to decipher the mark-up and the construction of the LP's front cover. The photo of the Siberian tiger was not cut to white to leave a 30mm white border at the top of the cover, but faded away with an airbrush effect; the "Greenpeace" type (originally printed with a fluorescent ink) remained uncropped, and most mysteriously of all, the word "Breakthrough" appeared from nowhere in *Gill Kayo*. The image is shown here as applied (correctly) to the cover of the brochure which was produced in England and then shipped to the USSR to be inserted in to the LP sleeve. The main problem was to work with Cyrillic text,

adapting its line-length to fit the editorial space. *Helvetica Cyrillic* was the only sans-serif typeface then available, and in keeping with the physical translation process the headlines were made distinctive by distorting them through a half-tone screen and then copying them on the fax machine.
Despite the bizarre juxtaposition to serious environmental information, the Russian friends of Greenpeace insisted that the record and booklet included promo photographs of all the groups and artists involved, for these were what the Russian public would most want to see. We designed the gatefold section of the LP in the style of a football match programme.

DESIGN WITH JON WOZENCROFT, TONY COOPER
AND ANDY GAMMON

BREAKTHROUGH WAS A CHARITY PROJECT, a variant of "Live Aid" for the Soviet Union's Green activists which would be used as a catalyst to setting up Greenpeace USSR. Thanks to an arrangement made with the Soviet state record company, *Melodiya*, Western Rock groups were to have their music officially released in the USSR for the first time, an event that Greenpeace would use to draw attention to the serious environmental condition of the country. At the time, this was a revolutionary step.

For this project, Greenpeace did not want images of whales, polar bears or baby seals, but something less comforting. Brody and the studio decided upon an image of a Siberian tiger, an endangered species but nonetheless a predator of man, superimposed on to a Landsat photograph of the Russian steppes by merging two polacolor slides. The image was used for the cover of the compilation record featuring Western Rock stars and for an accompanying booklet that highlighted the dangers of nuclear power, deforestation, industrial pollution, the hole in the ozone layer. On the back cover was a satellite photo of the slash-and-burn damage done to a section of the Amazonian rainforest.

Soon afterwards, Brody became involved with the setting up of Greenpeace Japan, but this soon fell apart. Greenpeace USSR worked because commercial marketing had been exploited as a politically-active tool. Greenpeace Japan refused to entertain such capitalist strategies; as a result, its membership only numbered 1200.

ORF 1

ORF 2

"Time is an essential factor in the pictorial field. Even partial actions take place in time and can be rounded out later into totality and equilibrium."
Paul Klee, *Notebooks Volume 1: The Thinking Eye*,
Lund Humphries 1961.

TELEVISION GRAPHICS, LIKE CORPORATE DESIGNS, are often typified by two extremes – sober systems built around traditional logos which announce themselves like mediæval fanfares, and flying three-dimensional logos with fast changing typestyles appropriated from glossy magazines. Television executives rarely create the context for innovative graphic design to be brought to the fore. Most modern television uses the American system as its model. Exceptions are hard to find. In the UK, Channel 4's logo has become a modern classic, and BBC2 has commissioned an inventive set of animated sequences for its programme 'idents'; elsewhere, the new logo for London's ITV franchisee, Carlton, is a pastiche of the London Underground's signage system and so backward-looking that it looked overexposed and out-of-date the first time it was broadcast. Familiarity was the prime consideration.

Rarely does a designer get the chance to determine a visual identity across the whole spectrum of a radio and television network because of the number of vested interests that have to be satisfied. When Brody received a commission from Gerd Bacher at the Austrian state broadcasting company Österreichischer Rundfunk (ORF) in 1991, it was an oppor-

**423, 424. Logos for ORF 1
and ORF 2, Vienna 1992**
Typographic simplicity, the colour wheel
system, a modular block.

tunity to take both TV graphics and the traditional notion of corporate identity a step further by creating a completely integrated design philosophy.

Brody had to take into account the success of the ORF's existing graphic identity over the previous 25 years, and the changes in broadcasting structures and viewing habits that would keep the main graphic applications contemporary for only a limited period, estimated to be five to seven years. The growing competition from cable TV channels shifts the emphasis towards a more commercial imperative.

He set up a modular structure based around a colour wheel – an idea that Paul Klee had also focused on during his teaching at the Bauhaus, "the rainbow seen as a ring" – adapted and remodelled as a satellite system retaining the existing central ORF identity, the eye, at its core. The name and image was kept to its original colour scheme of black, white, red and grey, but could be combined with other individual colours in the circle to represent specific departments or programme areas, representing *localised* concerns.

Working with Simon Staines from the London studio, Brody set up a simple visual network with a sense of purity and clarity. The intention was to enable ORF to use their new identity just as one speaks a language. Decoration for its own sake was avoided at all costs and replaced by a focus on the necessary, involving certain strict do's and don'ts as with any form of grammar. The elements of typography, colour, shape and the eye fit together in different ways depending on what is being said and where it is being applied. "The central idea is one of graphic structure and relationships. It is vitally important to realise that within this apparently strict system is the space for a greater creative freedom. A modular system of shapes was the only possible way to relate all the diverse elements of ORF's activities. Within clearly set out boundaries, the possibility is there to push creative communication further because, by using a clear and solid language, it is possible to say anything necessary without the traditional problem of needing to somehow afterwards inject an identity."

The ORF identity makes a clear break with the concept of corporate identity created in the 1950s in favour of a far more organic approach on all levels from the first contact between client and designer to the final implementation and day-to-day usage of the identity.

Brody insisted upon an independent third-party company, which had absolutely no involvement with ORF's daily machinations, to organise and manage the design project. Run by Hubert Schillhuber and Oliver Kartak in Vienna, Design for Media and Communication (DMC) became the company that directed the redesign and print production. Wolfgang Lorenz was Brody's main contact at ORF.

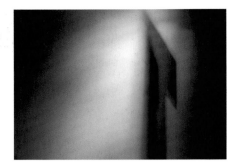

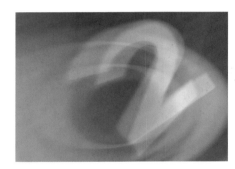

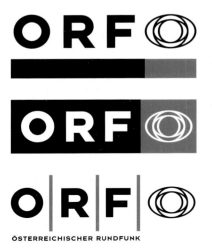

425. Signations for ORF 1 and ORF 2, 1992
Light was projected and then filmed before processing and editing the footage on a Quantel Harry. The soft outlines of the flowing images blend to the hard graphic of the main identity. Abstraction leads to confirmation, like a journey by train where the natural landscape is suddenly no more than a blur seen through a carriage window, and, on arrival, the station's architecture beckons like a new cathedral.

Left:
426–428. Proposed logos for ORF, 1992
These three initial ideas included a linear version of the standard ORF Eye logo, but the station's directors decided that this element represented too significant a feature of ORF's tradition and identity – the old eye should not undergo an operation.

Opposite:
429, 430. Penultimate signation frames for ORF 1 and ORF 2, 1992

431–437. Radio logos for ORF, 1992
Shape, colour and simplicity formed the basis of these main radio logos. Some stations have their own regional identity that had to be reflected by the design (see over).

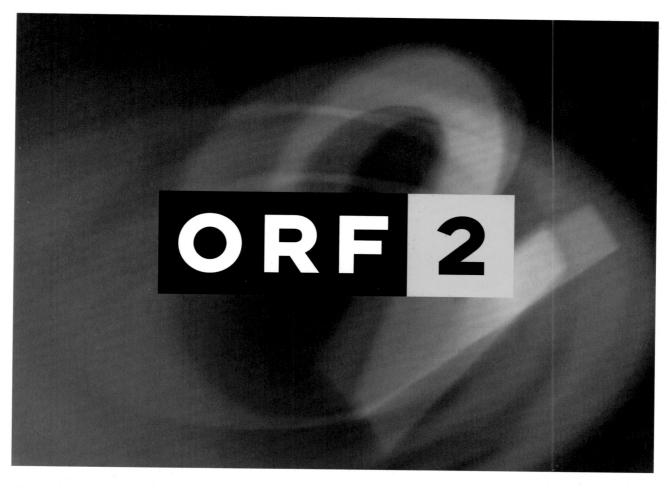

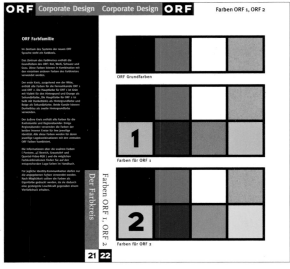

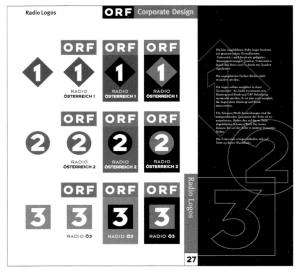

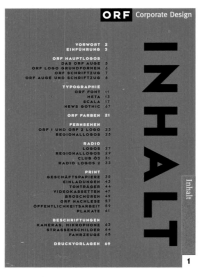

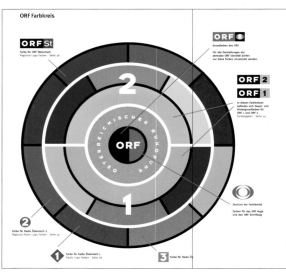

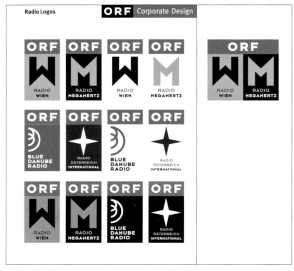

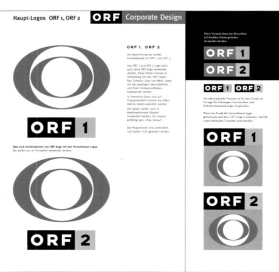

438. The ORF Manual, 1992

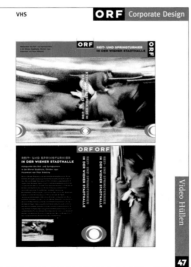

Opposite and above:
439–456. Pages from the ORF Manual, 1992
The guidelines for the in-house use of the ORF design are strict and specific. Dominant features are the central importance of the colour wheel, the use of black holding bars for information, and the split eye that wraps around the spine when applied to merchandise like books or records.

463–465. Pre-trailer signations, ORF 1992
Indicating the time and date of a programme whose trailer is about to follow, these signations work on the contrast between shifting focus and depth of field.

Below:
466. Advertising break signation, ORF 1992
467. ORF Text Express, 1992
Part of a new design for ORF's teletext service.

A central typeface in three weights was designed by Brody to be used for titles, headlines and introductions in print and to support the ORF eye on screen. *Meta*, a modern gothic, and *Scala*, a modern Dutch serif by Martin Majoor, were used for text or to subtitle the *ORF Font*.

On screen, the type and the eye logo had to be immobile in order to avoid graphic tricks and clichés, in particular the tendency to over-communicate the use of computers in the language the computers are being used to transmit. The ORF logo was applied as a hard-edged graphic form that could be contrasted against an essentially soft-focused image or a fast animation sequence.

Brody concentrated on developing an emotive and dynamic visual language using the movement and *transition* space between different images as they came on screen. Television relies on the impact of the image and overlooks the possibilities of this third connection.

In a discussion paper Brody sent to ORF's designers, he proposed, "Question: is TRANSFORMATION emotional? Transition is the key, telling us how to react and respond to what is coming and what is gone. What we are missing from all TV channel graphics is emotion, feeling, dialogue, depth. We must develop a language which is at the heart of television, go to the root before we can rebuild, and not just paint over the cracks. So we should investigate the emotion of pattern, of motion, of light."

457–462. Split-channel Information card, Programme announcement, Viewer information service, End-of-day caption card, Programme trailer, Clockface, ORF 1992
The programme announcement uses a Blue Box moving background; the end-of-day card brings in *Meta* for the information; the clock was never used.

DIGITAL GRAPHICS
TEAM AT ORF:

MARKUS HANSER
HELMUT STADLMANN
PETER PUTZ
RUPERT PUTZ
MICHAEL HUBER
BARBARA LAZAR
NORBERT WUCHTE
HELMUT STIEDL
MICHAEL SÜSSMAYER
HELMUT MARK

IN LONDON:
PAULA NESSICK

468. *ZIB*, ORF main news broadcast, 1992

The programme *Zeit Im Bild* – "News in Pictures" – is split into three sections: main news, culture and sport, followed by the weather report. The *ZIB* main title echoes the station identity, with an opening signation where the earth rises. The studio and news-readers are framed by TV monitors that underline the link with the world at large.

Reports and later programme items are headlined through semi-transparent blocks using *News Gothic*; on-screen credits are brought up with a soft-shadow surround.

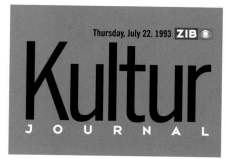

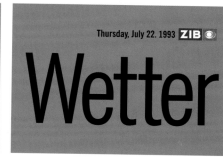

469, 470. *Kunststücke*, ORF, 1992

Devised with Helmut Stadlmann, Kunststücke is a weekly cultural programme, changing its main signation every week which is designed by students at Vienna's School of Applied Arts. Each signation experiments with the idea of revealing the main title and using it in an unusual context, made even more surreal by its juxtaposition with an unrelated sound. Kunststücke is granted exemption from ORF's standard graphic rules and uses a split-screen effect that holds still as well as moving images. *FF Kipp* is the typeface seen here.

471. *Teleskop*, ORF, 1992

For this news magazine show, *Helvetica Bold Ultra Compressed* and video footage are combined on a large studio video projection.

Premiere

PremiereKino

PremiereSport

PremiereKinder

PremiereDokumentation

PremierePresse

PremiereTechnik

PREMIERE IS A PAY TV CHANNEL based in Hamburg. It produces a certain number of its own programmes, generally shown in the Clear Window, the part of the broadcast which is not coded, but mainly it shows films. The audience can only watch them having subscribed to the channel – they then receive a decoder which unscrambles the signal. Unlike *Canal Plus* in France, the audio part of the broadcast is not coded, only the visual part.

The main problem that was faced in producing the design was to differentiate Premiere from all the other channels. At least 20 are currently available, and there are many homes on cable in Germany.

The norm in Germany is to use computer animation and produce "flying logos", in spite of the very systematic approach to the structural element of design in the country. In order to make this structure entertaining to a TV audience, surprisingly cheap devices have been used which may be interpreted as kitsch by any outsider. Although there is a high level of technology available, it is usually used to produce clichéd effects.

Brody's criteria for Premiere was therefore to question all television convention and produce something unexpected. As Premiere carries no advertising, the income being derived only from subscriptions, an unusually high emphasis is placed on the main station ident. This is seen many times each day and must be kept both entertaining and simple, yet strong enough to remain enduring.

Early on, Brody decided that the basis for the design was to be the station broadcast structure itself. Flying logos and three-dimensional animation were rejected as it was felt that the television audience was tired of these effects, and that television had become, alongside most daily culture, over-

designed. The look of television design in the future will be far simpler and more informational in its basis.

Type was finally selected as the main design element for the channel in order to clarify the channel structure and information for the audience. It established a clear contrast between channel announcements and actual programmes, giving the channel itself a strong personality. It suggested a sense of effiency and organisation without the feeling that the channel had to shout out its own identity. The system of pure type was also used because it provided a strong contrast with all images, allowing a sense of purity to the station content. The design does not compete with programme material, it supports it.

Brody decided not to design a symbol-as-logo for the channel. Instead, the same typeface family was used for the name as is used for all information, with one device, a capital P, specially drawn for the initial. In this way, the channel identity is maintained through all design. The Premiere logo and system is also viewed as a branding structure that extends itself to all related print material.

The typeface used is *Franklin Gothic*. This was selected because it is a "warm" typeface with personality, unlike *Univers* or *Helvetica*. It also avoided certain design statements made by fonts like *Futura* and *Avant Garde*. *Franklin Gothic* was chosen for its modernity and simplicity, plus the flexibility afforded by its large family of weights and cuts. As the design structure was based on pure information, this informational typography had to be given more personality, achieved by the use of a colour coding system.

Colour choice became paramount. Different programming areas were designated their own colour systems – cinema information is purple, documentaries, beige and green. The type used is generally set tightly spaced, again to extend the design from being only pure information.

In Germany, most channels use white or coloured screen backgrounds. It was decided for Premiere that all information would appear on a black screen. This maintains the unique channel identity while emphasising colours. Two-dimensional movement was used for the titles. All movement is slow and graceful, with soft fades, contrasted by the use of fast and hard cuts. The visual rhythm is emphasised by the sound-track, sound and colour both having an unusually high prominence on Premiere.

The television graphics deliberately avoid many screen clichés. Borders are never used, neither are computerised wipes or fades such as Encore effects. Vertical type and logos are avoided, as are gradated backgrounds.

The underlying principle behind the design for Premiere is one of a return to Modernism, a new look at the philosophy that is still basic to modern society. The nineties will see a rejection of the over-design of the eighties, a dissatisfaction with short-lived styles and trends. Premiere's design is solid and reliable, simple and universal.

Television graphics for Premiere, Hamburg 1991–94

Opposite:
472. Main Logo and Colour system

Right:
473. Heute Premiere
To specify trans-mission times.

Below:
474. Montag
A trailer announcing programmes on another day of the week.

475. Programme caption card

476. Clock & caption "Coming next".

477. Information system for film trailers

478. Premiere signation

Overleaf:
479. 0137
A now-defunct daily interview show.

480. TvTv
A look at the world of television.

481. Premiere Kinder

482. Football graphics
Derived from a specially drawn set of information symbols.

483. ShowBiz 94
A self-produced news magazine.

484. Premiere cartoon

485. Tacheles
A political chat-show. *Tacheles* means "talking" in Turkish.

486. Airplay
A weekly music show.

487. Programme Vorschau
A regular programme review showing trailers.

488. Kino
Opening signation appearing before films.

489. Extra
Trailer announcing short experimental broadcasts.

490. Premiere Special
Shown before live events.

491. Premiere Sport

492. Megamax
A crazy sports show.

493. Kino 94

DESIGNED WITH HUBERT SCHILLHUBER, PATRICIA POELK, THORSTEN BUCH, IAN THOMSON, SIMON STAINES, CORNEL WINDLIN

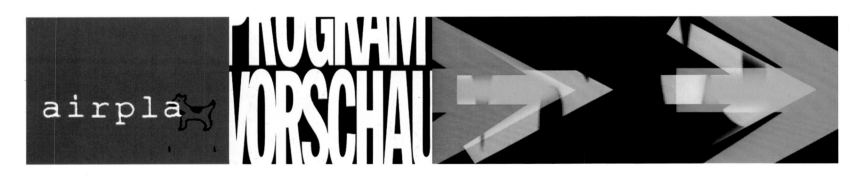

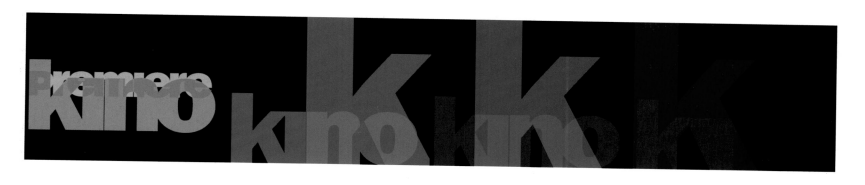

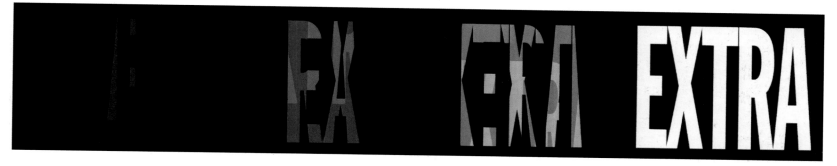

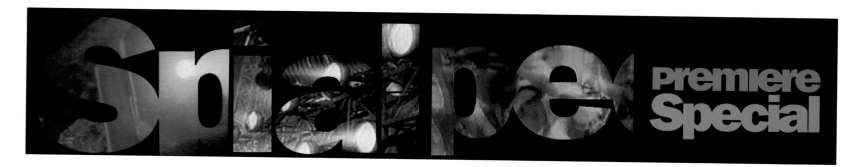

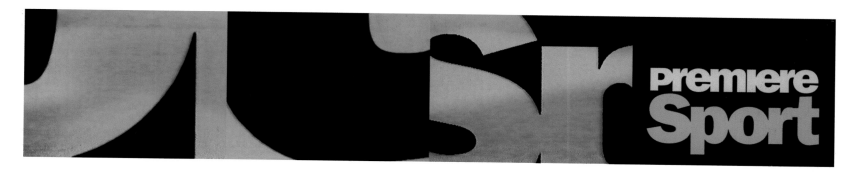

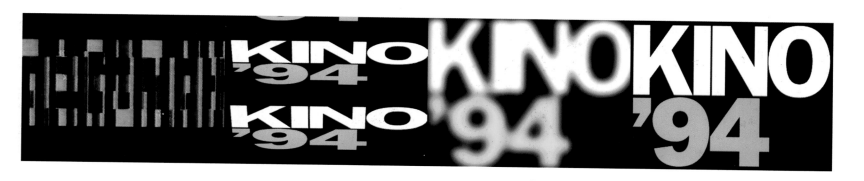

493–508. Signage system and rough ideas for Korakuen, Japan 1992
Korakuen is an entertainment complex in Tokyo, a traditional funfair that is in the process of redeveloping its attractions to include new technologies such as virtual reality. Divided up into four areas – one of which, Geopolis, is underground – Korakuen is a caricatured Science Fiction. Brody was commissioned through I&S and collaborated with Propeller Art Works in Tokyo to create a new signage system, involving the creation of a new typeface and information design that integrates the different sites that make up the centre's attractions. Brody wanted the park's language to be as crazy as possible. A Japanese version of the font is under development by Propeller Art Works.

Exemplified by Disney World in Orlando, Florida, the theme park is the marriage of utopia and leisure, a controlled climate with a political, economic and (above all) linguistic motive. Their development would be impossible without the complicit language of film and TV. The sites are anti-geographical, a place where the effects of multiculturalism, urban displacement and deprivation can go unquestioned. A place where children can be children having been stripped of their childhood. The theme park swaps individual expression for collective gratification.

The new set of social conditions – crime, family breakdown, fears for the future – provide the context for a new architecture of deception. Simulations of historical nirvanas can rest alongside junior Gulf War games. Complex surveillance systems back up toyfully-uniformed staff. Theme parks capitalise on the removal of the democratic public forum, giving a software spin-off to an increasingly closed-down urban environment.

The theme park has become a metaphor (as viral as virtual reality) that infiltrates every area of contemporary life. Inner cities become tourist stopovers, the countryside a set from some TV serial. With the latest advances in "cosmetic psycho-pharmacology" and the success in the USA of the mood-enhancing drug, Prozac, the inner workings of the human brain will be increasingly theme-parked by doctors and psychiatrists, who will be able to manipulate our neurotransmitters to fix our mental state as if it were Legoland.

geopolis

Towerland

Coasterland

Parachuteland

KORAKUEN

aBcDEFGHIVKLMNOPQRSTUVWXY×ZBSD
EFGHIJKLMNOPQRSTUVWXYZ1234567890
ABCDEFGHIJKLMNOPQRSTUVWXYZabc
defghijklmnoprstuvwxyz1234567
ABCDEFGHIJKLMNOPQRSTUVWXYZabc
defghijklmnopqrstuvwxyz12345678
ECghCdEfghijklmnoprstuvwxyz

Opposite:
510–515. Logos for Men's Bigi, Japan 1988–90
Applied to the company's stationery, the main logo
takes a mock American corporate style, reflecting
the stature of the Bigi Group in Japan's retail environment (see p.69). The secondary logos, some
of which can be seen opposite, were applied at
various stages to the Men's Bigi shops' products,
clothing and print materials.

516. Proposed MA1 jacket for Men's Bigi, 1989

517, 518. Carrier bags for Men's Bigi, 1988–89
The symbols used for the carrier bags indicate the
emergence of global and environmental consciousness in Japan. The design is based on the concept
of altered activity – hence the handles placed in
odd positions, suggesting a lack of balance that
has to be righted by the individual as well as corporations. The logos were all hand-drawn, the symbols taken from an old dingbat catalogue and
adapted on the photocopier. The smaller symbols
were also used on the labels of Men's Bigi clothing.
Metallic silver was used as the second colour for
the carrier bags.

DESIGNED WITH IAN SWIFT

519. Men's Bigi frisbee, 1990
The first and last example of a direct ecological message applied to Men's Bigi merchandise.

520–523. Logos and advert for Men's Bigi, 1990
Produced for the Parco exhibition catalogue and adapting the frisbee graphic, the advert is shown second from the left. Cornel Windlin, Yuki Miyake and Ian Swift were all involved in the design of the logos, based around an eco-logical theme.

524, 525. Logo and symbol for Global Force, Men's Bigi 1990
The missing links. Following a graphic style that constantly referred to industrial imagery, these designs indicate a rougher, more blatant approach. The name Global Force evolved out of the many different names suggested for a new Men's Bigi collection – the project, however, was rejected by the directors of the Bigi Group.

Nintendo – or GameBoy – is a portable screen gem. Already 95% of all boys under the age of 15 in the USA own one, causing teachers to bemoan their lack of attentiveness in class and inability to concentrate. Last Christmas, Sega was top of the "must have" list. The products do not come cheap. GameBoy sells at around £70 and comes with 2 games included, but others have to be bought as cartridges that cost around £30 each, though, such is the fanaticism for the new and the unseen among peer groups, cartridges are imported from Japan that retail at over £90 each. *Tetris*, which comes free, involves a set of five rectangular shapes. They fall down the screen and have to be positioned neatly against each other to form lines: and as more lines are knocked off the screen, the speed of the game increases.

"On Boxing Day I did *Tetris* for about ten hours non-stop. It's really addictive. I lost track of time completely and was amazed to see that it was four in the morning when I finished. When I got up to have a wash I started hallucinating, seeing the shapes. When I looked into the mirror, I looked weird, big bags under me eyes. It was like half a tab of crap acid. The really strange thing is, though, the next day I started seeing life itself in terms of *Tetris*, like on a philosophical level. It was very strange, the effect lasted for several days."
Mike Bottomley, *New Musical Express*, 1 February 1992.

"In the world of marketing, a product is not just a piece of chicken or a pint of soda, but a set of associations, a mystique. Advertising doesn't just communicate these intangible qualities, it creates them, and hence advertising itself becomes part of what you're selling. In global advertising, that means you're selling similar associations, similar dreams... For those who favour global marketing, this is the realisation of an age-old dream: one world, united by common tastes and a common propensity to consume. But those who deplore global marketing may see something different: one small industry, Madison Avenue, homogenising the world and destroying precious cultural diversity in the process. Both sides would agree however that globalisation is here to stay."
Paul Solman, 'Going Global', Transcript of a report broadcast on the *MacNeil/Lehrer Newshour* 29 Sept. 1987, from *Global TV*, ed.Cynthia Schneider & Brian Wallis, The MIT Press 1988.

GLOBAL FORCE CAME ABOUT as a result of Brody's desire to promote social issues and multicultural activity in a commercial setting. Based on the experience of working with The Body Shop and Greenpeace in London, HdKdW in Berlin and following the outcome of the work for Men's Bigi and Greenpeace in Japan, Global Force was planned to be a multimedia production company based in Tokyo and London, involving all those who had been centrally involved in setting up the *Graphic Language* exhibition at Parco.

The central idea was to create an alternative to the corporate tendency that viewed globalism as no more than a fashionable update of colonial exploitation. By combining the example of the cultural interventions made by World Music with the promise of digital technology to create an international visual language, Global Force intended to create a forum that would not be bound to notions of ethnicity and exoticism. The idea was to develop a cross-continental dialogue on the beneficial possibilities of digital communication by establishing two agencies at opposite ends of the globe to organise special events, publications and broadcasts with the active participation of larger companies not directly driven by an immediate profit margin.

If this sounds like an idealistic replay of many of the West's existing cultural institutes, then it was. We wanted to modernise the potential of such performance-based organisations, and at the same time challenge the true potential of corporate funding to see just to what extent large companies would put their money where their mouths professed to be.

Global Force sought to be as commercially confrontational as the recent Benetton ad. campaign has sought to be, yet the primary use of the advertising medium was immediately rejected as being too ephemeral whatever the message.

Brody created these designs. I wrote various texts. Fwa Richards and Grant Gilbert worked in London, liaising with Junko Wong and the embryonic company, Planet Plan, based around the Men's Bigi core team of Yuri Funatsugawa and Yuji Imanishi – but it was not to be... yet.

526. MA1 jacket, Global Force, London and Tokyo 1990
Designed to coincide with the opening of the *Graphic Language* exhibition at Parco, the "American airforce" jacket was produced by Yuji Imanishi and Yuri Funatsugawa. The back is shown here.

Below:
527–529. Graphics and symbols for Global Force, 1990
These three elements were used as details on the jacket sleeves.

530–535. Logos for Global Force, 1990
Alongside the graphics developed for Men's Bigi, these logos demonstrate the immediate effect of the Mac on Brody's designs. The type was specially created for Global Force, made into a full character set, but never published. Contrasting an original and organic geometric style with rounded edges (enabled by FreeHand), the logos suggest a mock sportswear language, offset by the use of positive/negative and mirror effects that signal a linkage, an apex and centrepoint.

536. Life Rescue Jacket, Parco, Tokyo 1988
Using hand-drawn type and symbols, the jacket was designed for staff to wear during an emergency.

537. MA1 jacket, Quattro, Tokyo 1989
Another Parco-owned store, the Quattro complex also includes a concert space.

DESIGNED WITH IAN SWIFT

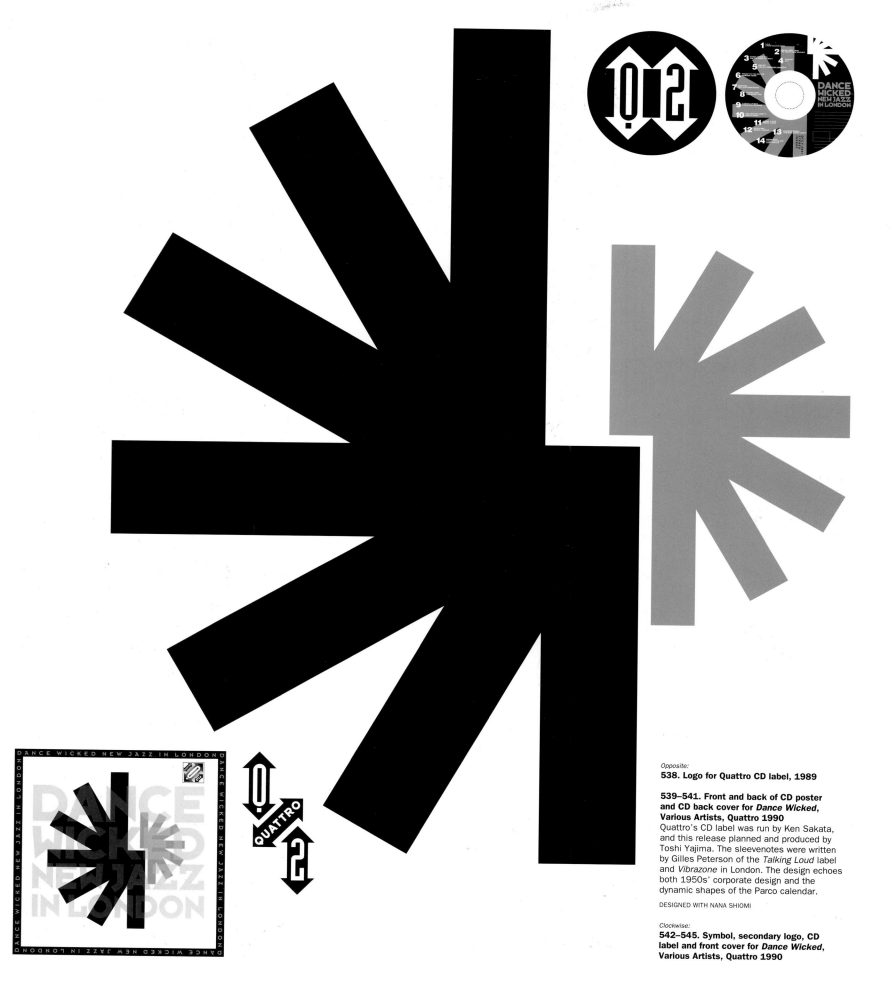

Opposite:
538. Logo for Quattro CD label, 1989

539–541. Front and back of CD poster and CD back cover for *Dance Wicked*, Various Artists, Quattro 1990
Quattro's CD label was run by Ken Sakata, and this release planned and produced by Toshi Yajima. The sleevenotes were written by Gilles Peterson of the *Talking Loud* label and *Vibrazone* in London. The design echoes both 1950s' corporate design and the dynamic shapes of the Parco calendar.

DESIGNED WITH NANA SHIOMI

Clockwise:
542–545. Symbol, secondary logo, CD label and front cover for *Dance Wicked*, Various Artists, Quattro 1990

SUPER BAZAR

SUPER BAZAR

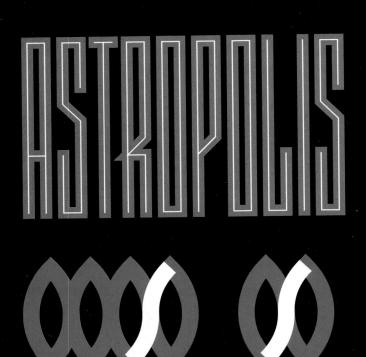

ASTROPOLIS

Japanese logos, 1988–92

546. Superbazar, 1990
The logo for a shopping campaign
at Parco's Quattro store.
547. Astropolis, 1991
The logo for the cover of a book
by Taruho Inagaki.
548. Saylor, 1989
A creative agency based in Tokyo.

Opposite:
549. Movin, 1989
A shop logo, designed with Ian Swift.
550. Varié, 1989
A clothing company.
**551. Creative
Intelligence Agency, 1988**
Owned by Si Chen, CIA is the architect
Nigel Coates' agency in Tokyo.
**552. Sarawak
Campaign Committee, 1992**
A pressure group trying to stop Japan's
heavy involvement in the destruction of
South East Asian rainforests. Designed
with John Critchley.
553–555. Saylor, 1989
Three variations on the central logo.
**556. 10th Anniversary
Laserdisc Original, 1989**
Four variations for the agency, J Wave.
557. Atoll Pacifica, 1989
A club; designed with Tony Cooper.

"When all is said and done, why bother to think 'deeply' when you're not *paid* to think deeply?"
Dick Hebdige, *Hiding in the Light*, Routledge 1988.

We have come to accept that products, packaging and their success are dependent upon (and interdependent with) advertising and marketing strategies. Specific and implicit messages are encoded in popular iconography using images and symbols. Items such as the Coke bottle

design, Marlboro packet, the Porsche car, are to our societies as religious madonnas and the crucifix were to a previous age, *articles of faith*.

At the same time, they are so familiar that we feel secure in our control over these forces and can readily decide that a consumer product is not the same as a religious icon. For one thing, there is no suggestion of suffering in the image, only in the inability to live up to it. However, if we really do perceive products to have assumed many of the ritualistic functions that were previously the domain of the church,

then we totally underestimate the impact of this realisation and what it implies.

The motives may be clear enough – to sell, generate profit, to create a sense of affluence and quality of living. It is far better after all to belong to the Pepsi generation, clear of the trouble spots, than have to boil polluted water.

The iconography appearing on the containers of everyday products is drawn from an image bank, a common storehouse of visual rhetoric which is streamlined into a persuasive language we think we understand, have access to,

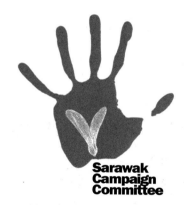

558. Slate, 1988
A publishing company. The blurred type
is achieved by repeated photocopying.
559. Hugh Hastings, 1988
A PR agency.
560. Orange, 1993
The digital repro house who worked on
the image and film processing for this
book. The logo uses Erik Spiekermann's
Meta typeface.

Opposite:
561. Axis, 1989
A London modelmakers.
562. Bandits, 1988
Jean-Baptiste Mondino's video production
company.
563. The *Viennale*, 1992
Logo for the Vienna Film Festival, using
Tobias Frere Jones' *Garage Gothic*; designed
with Simon Staines and Oliver Kartak.
564. Philips Compact Disc, 1992
Music sponsorship logo.
565. Plein Sud, 1989
French fashion company; designed
with Tony Cooper.
566. Dome, 1991
A record shop in Vienna.
567. Freezer, 1987
Italian fashion company, produced
for Attila & Co.
568. Red Hot Again, 1992
An AIDS campaign logo.
569. Massimo Rubini, 1987
Italian fashion company.
570. UFA, 1992
A German media production group;
designed with Johannes Erler in
collaboration with Buro X.
571. Daily Blue, 1987
Italian fashion company.
572. Barooni, 1987
Dutch record label; designed with
Jon Wozencroft.

and have control over – and to a certain extent we do, otherwise the system could not operate. Nevertheless, concealed within the contract are a series of assumptions, notably the one that says "this is only a material good".

Heavily promoted items become an unavoidable part of our daily diet; because this mental food is invisibly consumed, it is easily dismissed on that level as being inconsequential – taste, but lacking the sharpness of sensation. Products, labels, colours, logos and their advertisements are loaded with symbols that are not

dead or passive implements, but active energies. These energies make them magnetic. They resonate. Their magnetism is what attracts us to them, and at the point of contact we overlook the fact that most products are assiduously composed items where very little, if anything, is left to chance. We think we are partaking in a simple transaction – the product is for sale, I choose to buy it (or not) – when in fact we have become involved in a sculpted process we generally prefer to ignore. At the same time, the symbolism used for many prod-

ucts is seldom investigated by manufacturers and advertisers in terms of its original meaning, but in terms of its referential relationship to other symbols of market success.

The creation, promotion and consolidation of products is a new form of narrative, but it effects the opposite of empowerment. We do not feel the energy of the speaker, circled around a camp fire. Instead, fulfilment is no more than a fractal moment in a corporate chaos held together by money invested into more money. Inanition, gratification, bulimia.

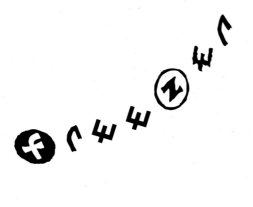

573. La Baus Fundicio, 1993
Spanish performance group La Fura dels
Baus created a foundation to support other
events and publishing activities.
574. TOTH, 1988
A US design agency – the logo was intended
to be used both horizontally and vertically,
and printed white ink on white paper.

Opposite:
575, 576. Andy Catlin, 1991
Two logos for a London-based photographer.
577, 578. Katherine Hamnett, 1988
Two proposed ideas for a subsidiary clothing
range.
579. Die Wöche, 1993
The Pegasus logo was used as the masthead
for this German weekly newspaper.

580, 581. Ezee Possee, 1990
Two logos for a London dance music group.
582, 583. Vanity, 1989
Two logos for a one-off issue by an Italian
magazine. Six were sent, all were used.
584. Minimal Compact, 1985
Brussels-based group.
585, 586. Shield, 1992
The female and male emblems for Nick
Coleman, a London fashion company;
designed with John Critchley.

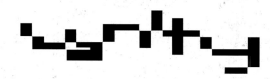

Below;
587. Barracuda, Armand Basi, Barcelona 1990
The catalogue for the Barracuda range took the form of concertinad tourist postcards, printed by a Spanish postcard printer.

For the Barracuda collection, the fashion company
Armand Basi outlined a direction that combined the
diverse themes of underwater life and space travel
with flower forms and colour schemes alluding to a
tropical paradise. These elements were redrawn as
mechanical objects.

LEGEND

588. *Legend*, **Armand Basi, 1991**
The *Legend* collection is an emotive visual retelling of the disparate and often baffling parts that are brought together in mythology. Over time, these icons become so familiar that it is often forgotten that every myth is a carefully constructed story whose combination of the obscure and the everyday seeks to reveal a third dimension.

Here, a visual surrealism reminiscent of William Burroughs takes a jaguar, the serpent, skulls that evoke the Mexican Day of the Dead as filmed by Buñuel, and joins these directly ritualistic motifs to the chevron pattern of a New York taxi cab and the hard-edged outline of a computer game invader. The various icons were treated as if they could be members of an exclusive nightclub – hence the number 1, held within the distorted shape of a sheriff's badge.

**589. Advert for *Legend*,
Armand Basi 1991**
The formation echoes a game of space
invaders. The *Legend* logotype (below
and opposite) uses the "go faster"
graphics of a Grand Prix circuit. One
of the proposals for *Legend* was the
production of a computer game.

ARMAND BASI is a couture house based in Barcelona which produces high-fashion garments for the international market. Chu Uroz, designer of the men's collection *Hombre*, and Noemi Campano, designer of the women's collection *Mujer*, contacted the Brody Studio looking to develop an original graphic language to incorporate into their fabrics. They wanted to investigate the possibilities of using more complex graphic forms within the limitations of the knitwear machines that Armand Basi was using to produce its fashionwear.

Originally trained as an industrial designer, Uroz was less interested in fashion and more engaged by the possibilities of textiles and weaving, with an emphasis on the surface of fabrics. He explored a number of techniques of applying images to fabric such as acid-etching two interwoven materials of differing resistance, and experimenting with rubber printing and embroidery in a bid to come up with new surface treatments.

Struggling to pinpoint the feeling he was trying to get across, Uroz would arrive at the studio with a collection of elements that he felt might form the basis of a new collection. Uroz, Brody and John Critchley would then grapple and play with this apparently random set of disjointed objects in an exploratory session that had no fixed points, no rules or preconceptions, searching for the key to the special language Uroz was reaching for. His anarchistic energy and his ability to mesh wildly disassociated sources fused with the studio's lateral approach to design.

Brody and Critchley worked on four collections with Uroz and Campano. The first, *Barracuda*, reflected Barcelona's geographical position as a sea port for which the studio created a series of mechanical fish. Uroz contrasted this reference to his hometown with the idea of paradise, trying to allude to summertime and the tropical colour of Hawaii in a new way.

Legend mixed the tales of metamorphosis common to South American folklore with contemporary video games – this crash of differences being extended to draw on such seemingly disparate items as New York taxi cabs and Aztec icons associated with the Mexican Day of the Dead.

Having just visited Japan, for the third collection, *Psycho*, Uroz wanted to reflect the crazy, schizophrenic environment of Tokyo by combining images of superheroes, the graphic style of porno magazines and comics with Pachinko games, the Japanese equivalent of pinball.

The final range that Uroz and the studio worked on, *Deluxe*, was a point of departure from the original aims. Instead of concentrating on strong graphics, Uroz was keen to pursue what he described as "dirty design", focusing on the idea of an "undesigned splash of oil and grease" which he particularly wanted Brody and Critchley to create on the Macintosh as a way of building artificially created textures.

590. *Deluxe*, **Armand Basi, 1992**
The title is ironic. Oil and other urban pollutants were used to break down the expectation of luxury in *haute couture*.

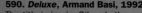

Deluxe

591. *Psycho*, **Armand Basi, 1992**
Originally entitled *Fever*, then *Psycho Golf*, the Japanese superhero as toy robot "transformer" saves the earth which is played out in the style of a Pachinko house.

DIGITALOGUE

[ABCDEFGHIJKLMNOPQRSTUVWXYZabcdefghijklmnopqrstuvwxyz1234567890]

[Language] 2 Binary Universe

Our world and our perceptions of it are not shaped by the artist, nor by political vision: the power and speed of technology dictate the patterns of the present. Concurrent with the now rapid implementation of digital systems after years of definition and refinement comes the "double bind" – the fundamental loss of direction that comes from the realisation that whichever way one chooses, nothing looks like being resolved. Short-term crisis management, the common current option prescribed by the soundbite culture of television news, fails to smother the long-term implications for a planet and for a species whose fundamental difficulties are always deferred to a perpetual tomorrow.

To cover up their incompetence, leaders resort to a deepening of the conflicts that revolve around society's vices (divide and rule), since any appeal to vision and transformation would swiftly bring about their own demise. Deep down, everybody knows that falsification is disruption for the future, but the forces of retrenchment are so fervent, when any alternatives *are* voiced in the mass media they are quickly burned away by the "purifying flames" of the marketplace.

Since the dawn of the Industrial Revolution, technology has been looked upon as a cure and a salvation. Our Western societies have followed a policy of non-stop invention as a reaction to the unforeseen effects of previous inventions. Technology can only be the answer to a problem if the problem is properly assessed before a new technology can twist it into yet another shape. This is impossible when everything is in a constant state of flux. In other words, the situation is beyond being a paradox and is closer to paralysis. Back to the double bind.

Therefore, we can only assess the effects in terms of their alluvial condition, surfing on the flood waters, unable to stop the big wave as it thunders on ahead. Once "eradicated", one disease or social malaise is quickly replaced by the appearance of another. Technology is 'great' when it works for us but it is 'evil' when it works against us. Having put our faith in its powers of transformation, as the end of the millennium approaches we suddenly look around (in spite of numerous warnings) and find that human capabilities are being overtaken by machines. Roman civilisation with its emphasis on law and order posed the question, *Quis custodiet ipsos custodies?*, "Who guards the guards?"; today we have to ask, "Who programmes the programmers?"

Technology fixes progress to the amplified complexity of its problems. Technology promotes a medical view of change that has to be curative, but we seem no longer able to differentiate the relative powers and drawbacks of an invention. "IT'S NEW" is the only straightforward message we receive, and because every invention or refinement is immediately justified as a "solution to a problem", marketing methods lull us into believing that each item is unique and performs a predetermined function. This is the Victorian view of progress, but it is still central to the social vision of technology in spite of the increased awareness of the ecological damage that has resulted. The two sides of this double bind spiral in and out of focus and an everyday schizophrenia has emerged, directly related to the binary code's effect on language.

The 'One–Zero' system will soon become the kitchen that supplies all our food, most of it the regurgitated produce of another time and place. This makes it even more crucial that we surmount "the chaos of mere appetite, narrow sectional interest and the tyranny of received ideas."[1]

CIVILISATION REPRESENTS NOTHING MORE than man's continual struggle against the forces of nature, declared Freud. We have reached an apogee and the point where this relationship flips. Both mental and physical environments are generally perceived to be not only out of control, but beyond our control. The perfect analogy (especially as far as Britain is concerned) is with the weather. Everybody is always remarking upon it, complaining about adverse conditions, but the individual can do nothing about it. Come rain or shine, the weather is the weather. In a volatile climate like Iceland's, the saying goes, "If you don't like it, wait for ten minutes and it'll change." Mentally we are currently living through a tornado, clinging on to robust objects only to see them fly off into the wind, clutching something else before that too is uprooted and scattered.

As conventional forms become distressed and dissolved by technological changes, when the quality of communication seems to be entirely legislated by the class differentials imposed by technological capabilities, then people readily rally round constructs to which 'value' can be visibly attached. In this context, nationalism and intolerance can be paraded as a virtue. More pervasively, and to an unprecedented extent, money has become an overbearing yoke on our world. If the compact computer is being proclaimed for its ability to enhance the means of communication, then, so far, the main beneficiaries of this have been financial institutions.

The invention of the digital process has enhanced the status of money in our societies, money being seen as the only means of setting any 'clear' limits. The consolidation of the power of money, budgets, cashflow charts, inflation rates, exhange mechanisms, and so on, also serves to sanction economic prerogatives whenever previous technologies or skills are dismantled and scrapped "to lay the way for new investment". Money governs, and "the root of all evil" is turned upside down. "The spiritual dimension comes with deciding what one does with the wealth," said Margaret Thatcher. Different nations and cultures might once have looked to their artists, their composers, their explorers to define their stature. They now assess their standing relative to the dollar, the deutschmark and the yen.

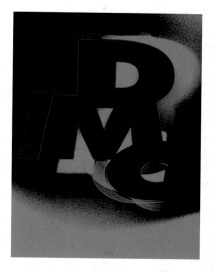

592. Poster for Digitalogue, Tokyo 1993
593. Logo for DMC, Vienna 1992

Digitalogue is a CD–ROM publisher. DMC is the company Brody runs with Schillhuber and Kartak to design for television. Computer and televisual media are on the point of converging into a desktop hybrid. The concept of an interactive, multimedia future – like virtual reality – has already been heavily marketed, yet the communicative power it will enable is less reliant on heavy financial investment, merging as it does many existing formats, upgrading the role of video and the camcorder. The element of familiarity will make it more accessible, therefore its impact and effects will be more unpredictable.

The process of merging various media into the miniature, domestic workstation is a technological translation of *Gesamtkunstwerk*, the concept of "total art work" developed by German artists and composers in the late 19th and early 20th centuries to appeal to all the senses. This determination was remodelled by propagandists during the Second World War. The switching between the "positive" and "negative" outcomes of this concept can be sourced to the original meaning of the word 'double' – from the Latin *duplu-s*, meaning "twice as much", itself a hybrid of *du-o*, "two", and -*plus*, which comes from the root *ple-*, "to fill".

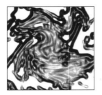

**594. Background image for
Armand Basi, Barcelona 1992**

In the 1820s Charles Babbage brought digital perception into focus by proposing a calculating machine that could register and analyse different codes on a strip of perforated card: in effect, the first scanner. His "Analytical Engine" was never completed because it was deemed impossible to manufacture the precision metal parts it required, and the idea was generally forgotten until his writings were rediscovered in 1937. The first IBM computer, the Automatic Sequence Controlled Calculator (known as Harvard Mark 1) completed in 1944, was controlled by instructions coded onto punched paper tape. The machine was enormous: 15m long and 2.4m high.

In 1847, hoping to capture the "laws of thought" of a human brain, George Boole devised an algebraic system that unified the principles of logic with those of mathematics. He extended the distinction "true/false" into an operating principle of "and/or" (addition, negation and multiplication) that could be formularised into the arithmetical values of "1" and "0", "on" and "off". He wished to create a binary code whereby "all truths of the reason would be reduced to a kind of calculation", creating the basis for electronic computer switching theory.

In 1937, Claude Shannon proved that automatic circuits of communication obeyed the principles of Boolean algebra. Beyond this, in England during the 1930s, Alan Turing researched into "thinking machines" that then were used as the basis for cracking the German High Command's 'Enigma' code in 1940; this opened the door to the first digital computer and gave form to the theory of artificial intelligence. All of this was kept top secret. Winston Churchill referred to "the geese who laid the golden eggs and never cackled". Founded on the triumphs of the Ultra intelligence work, the genesis and military development of digital technology was so closely guarded that any acknowledgment of the existence of Turing's ground-breaking work at the Government Code and Cypher School at Bletchley Park was officially denied until the mid 1970s.

Secrecy is still the rule. Censorship is making a comeback whilst privacy is disappearing. Language needs mystery, not custody.

The conformity brought on by financial re-regulation is inherently destructive. Once the defensive reflex to "batten down the hatches" is institutionalised, the lack of daylight becomes so normal a condition that any direct exposure to strong light is blinding (like the intensity of an interrogator's lamp), so we shy away and keep to our corner. People are unable to give their best if the general climate is one of insecurity. It has been proved that social interactions are better natured when the sun is shining, and that a medical condition can be brought on by the long nights of winter, Seasonally Affected Disorder or SAD for short. There is nothing one can do about the weather – except to avoid CFCs, aerosols, old fridges, and wear sunscreens. It's another double bind.

In "deregulated" Europe, if you exchange £100, currency to currency through each member state, you will end up back home with £66 having bought nothing. How is your financial set-up? Bearing such shields as "share dividends", "base rates" and "market forces", those in power have tried to nail the population to their bank statements. But money in itself is never going to hold back the necessity for fundamental changes, it will only delay and exacerbate them. Prices (and therefore values and allegiances) change so quickly on international money markets that dealers themselves are consistently outperformed by the infrastructure set up to serve their interests. Since the status quo is precariously preserved by richer nations who are able to invest money into money to make capital far in excess of the world's GNP from raw materials and manufacturing, any poorly-timed judgment or sequence of computerised mistakes will be catastrophic.

So much has been invested into the "holding power" of money that the capacity for any alternative is itself limited. Imminent breakdown is a more accurate representation of the world's hyped up and sandbagged financial system, thus the maintenance and impression of stability requires constant tricks of illusion. Since the electronic exchange network has so far successfully made invisible resources concrete (they are not resources as such because they do not exist; they are only potentials, ie. virtual), it is generally assumed that the digital revolution is in full swing (this is far from the truth). Everyone is urged to become "computer literate".

This suits those already in power. As people struggle to make the transition, the structures for the next wave of information distribution can be grafted onto the remnants of the old, which are purchased on the cheap. "Computer literacy" – where it is selectively made available – insists only upon the ventriloquial ability to perform the machine's language, which is not the same thing as understanding it.

We can already see the signs of political processes being gridlocked by economic mismanagement at the very point that the economic has become the only issue. "There is no escape from economic reality," warned one UK Government minister during the 1992 ERM crisis. "We need Picasso to explain this surreal situation," said a BBC reporter as exchange rates went haywire.[2] Too bad for the common people. Politicians and executives have made such a mess of handling the effects of new technology that society itself is going haywire. To safeguard the situation, huge investments are also having to be made into security and surveillance systems that attempt to freeze-frame social structures, public space and patterns of behaviour that have already been smashed to pieces. Problems, anxieties, paranoias... everything filters down from the top, except the money.

This provides ample opportunities for the manipulation and control of communication. In the Free Market, communication is dead expensive. Pen and paper are no longer enough. Free speech and access to mainstream broadcasting is extremely rare for those without access to camera crews, editing facilities and publicity budgets. In the present and more sophist world of posture politics and marketing, the effect is to corrupt the common language. The performance of communication is seen to be more important than its content. The platform is paramount – encompassing every aspect of the process, from format and outlet to star and stylist – all of which distracts and detaches us from what is (or is not) being said. Here the tornado appears as a fast-rewind sequence of stylistic changes, with the computer screen at the epicentre. Hence the next major factor that federates the schizophrenic, binary universe as it now stands: the technology divide between those who can pay to plug in, scan, store, and reconfigure, and those who have not got the money.

The political *canard* that "there are two opposing camps" has reduced itself down through continual retrenchment to a deadlock situation ruled by two basic distinctions, abundance and poverty. Both conditions are underscored by feelings of emptiness and disempowerment, however appeased the former might be by short-term material comforts.

THE WAY FORWARD is being located around a homeopathic strategy of confronting like with like. In homeopathic medicine, a disease is treated by administering a minute dose of a drug which produces the same symptoms in a healthy person, attempting to build up the body's immunity to the infection. Extrapolating this method of treatment, there is the potential that the increased access to computer and televisual technology – multimedia – will foster an enhanced awareness of media processes. In *Wired* magazine, Michael Crichton has proclaimed his belief that in ten years, the mass media will become extinct, like a dinosaur, "vanished, without a trace".[3] A subsequent issue of *Wired* threw down the question, "Is Advertising Finally Dead?", suggesting that home computers would empower users with the ability to exert more control on the content and their exposure to advertisements. Let's hope.

"Contrary to what critical sociology has long believed (with good reason unfortunately), standardisation, uniformity, the manipulation of consensus and the errors of totalitarianism are not the only possible outcome of the advent of generalised communication, the mass media and reproduction. Alongside these possibilities – which are objects of political choice – there opens an alternative possible outcome. The advent of the media enhances the inconstancy and superficiality of experience. In doing so, it runs counter to the generalisation of domination, in so far as it allows a 'weakening' of the very notion of reality, and thus a weakening of its persuasive force... experience can again acquire the characteristics of oscillation, disorientation and play."
Gianni Vattimo, *The Transparent Society*, Polity Press 1992.

For most of this century, broadcasting monopolies have been of great service to anyone wanting to manipulate and consolidate ideologies. In the coming years, "narrowcasting" will compete with traditional strangleholds and show up different truths. Potentially, this is a real threat to major concerns, but much groundwork has already been laid in intercepting this threat. The use of camcorder news footage, relocated in

595. **Poster for** *Fuse* **exhibition, FontShop International 1994**
Freeform language challenges the reductive process of digital conversion. Set against the decades of research and development that went into refining digital systems, Freeform is a purposeful leap into the unknown, where chance, intuition and danger play a key role, but with a different underlying motive, using language as a form of transfusion and transfiguration.

Two essential features in any linguistic form have to co-exist, always uneasily – expression, and categorisation, the need to quantify. The sequence of discoveries that led to the power of digital technology connects with this second function, which effectively bonded memory (storage) with property (materialism).

drama series, assimilating the look of the alternative, cheaper process into the corporate language, is one tactic. Overall, the perceptual effect will be to stretch the shape of our experience in two directions at the same time: mass media (broadcasting, manufactured reality), set alongside low-level and localised "niche" activities (narrowcasting, evidently personal opinion), which gives openings both to innovation and fundamentalism but serves, in general, to create a mediocre shadow of the main item – narrow broadcasting.

IN AN ATTEMPT TO MAKE SENSE of the hybrid offshoots of new technologies, multiculturalism, mass and vigilante media, Postmodernism is a category and a genre that tries to stem the chaos, but unleashes even more chaos and bafflement. It is a symptom of the search for a consensus where none exists, a look for root causes when the cord that linked us back to them has been broken. The term describes a condition diagnosed by the philosopher Jean-François Lyotard who recognised that "the loss of the grand narratives" such as the Christian doctrine, liberalism, childhood, the family and their spiralling fragmentation would create a psychic disorder in our lives. As soon as chaos had been given a name, this element of prophecy has by and large been consumed by columnists and culture-mongers who engaged in a feeding frenzy over the entrails of the old *and* the new order, matched by advocates of "Back to Basics" policies who try to pilot the present by pretending about the past.

The arrival of Postmodernism has been translated into an autopsy said to have revealed the failure of Modernism, which obscures the possibility that the former is simply the latter in its next phase, distorted by information technologies – Hypermodernism. What certainly differentiates the two is the Modernist belief in the possibility for improvement. However, its legacy – the inability to view towerblock housing as a short-term postwar measure, thus the social cost – will not be forgiven, and its successes, principally aesthetic, psychological and linguistic (such as the development of montage) have been hijacked and distorted by the mass media.

Technology gives man the illusion of omnipotence at the same time as it erodes his autonomy. Technology meets the demands of the child within us, but the child can also be a monster. Postmodernism, by aligning montage to historical pastiche (the present versus a plastic view of the past), is not so much a development as a suspended animation of its predecessor. Critical to the montage of Modernists is the space between two separate objects or ideas, their contrast revealing an intuitive world beyond spoken language. Typical of Postmodern connections is the overdecoration of every item involved so that nothing has the chance to be what it is, which creates the opposite effect – closure. This makes the genre an entirely suitable depiction of the current situation. It serves as a way of papering over the cracks with stylistically centred techniques so that the cracks themselves can then be celebrated as being of aesthetic interest. While we surf on the flood waters, will the dam hold fast?

Complicit with Postmodern theory, there is a great demand to fill media slots with whatever is going. Driven by narrow agendas, the combination of all this chaos with media expansion fuels a Theory Industry which has caused an air traffic control pile-up in almost every outlet. In the Theory Industry, who can say that any ideas have any other motive than personal celebrity anymore?

The experience of Jean Baudrillard has been a vivid example of this. According to Baudrillard, the Modernist era has lapsed into a state of utter confusion – "Everything is sexual. Everything is political. Everything is aesthetic. Simultaneously." Writing as a Marxist academic before the term Postmodern was even coined, his writings were slowly taken up as vivid versions of the state of things, with terms like "hyperreality", "simulation" and "the ecstacy of communication" quickly gaining currency during the mid-80s. For Baudrillard, the years leading up to the end of the century represent a progressively intensive temperature increase, as if the thermostat with which we calibrate our sense of reality has gone into automated overdrive.

The bulk of his writing – and the written responses to it – signal how the application, the balance, and the understanding of the double (expressed in male–female, the play within the play, the paradox that the French call *mise en abyme*) has effectively been flattened out, reprocessed, and installed as a mechanised loop by the communications revolution. Extending McLuhan's argument, the bridge between right and left brain is sentinelled by TV, advertising, and their technologies so that magical illusion is amalgamated with special effects. Intuition and the imagination is desiccated and invited to compete, or be barred from competition. In the transitional period between the laying down of digital networks and the direct application of artificial intelligence to human physical functions, clarity of thought cannot match One–Zero accuracy. Baudrillard argues that the effect of new technology has been to impose a "double spiral" on human perceptions; he plays with this idea, describing his writing techniques as *Fatal Strategies* because, "Just as the world drives to a delirious state of things, we must drive (slowly) to a delirious point of view." This, he suggests, is the only way to deal with a climate in which "everything co-exists in total indifference".

At the beginning of 1991, he caused controversy by publishing *The Gulf War Will Not Happen*, later adapted to *The Gulf War Never Happened*.[4] Baudrillard's propositions were not intended to be "right" or "wrong". The Gulf War *did* happen, and succeeded in marking out the gulf between technology and its screen image, fixed in language and disengaged activity by euphemisms like "surgical strike". Remote control war was met with a remote control reaction. But the message to any potential aggressor was immediate – we have the technology. As was the message to viewers at home – soon you too will have it, provided you stay tuned.

All the new technology that has been religiously developed on behalf of the military for the last 50 years has started to crash land on consumer markets. Since we have the habit of seeing technology both as progress and destruction, will we have any hope of finding any space between two extremes? The implications of the coming nanotechnology – molecular manufacturing that will create supercomputers with processing speeds measured in billionths of a second – will raise fundamental questions about the limits to growth, which we have scarcely begun to address realistically. By the time the shift from digital processing to neural networking and genetic engineering has taken place, what state will we be in?

Will we keep trying to escape, everyone an individual astronaut in their privatised space station, searching for different environments because we cannot wake up to the one we have? The artificial world may well be our oyster. What will it look like? How much will it cost? Any answers to these

596. Contact, *Touch*, London 1990/94
Contact is a recording made by John Duncan and Andrew McKenzie constructed entirely from the sounds technology utters. The impact of a dense wave of radio, fax, TV, road traffic, and domestic appliances creates a sonic confusion that shocks you into the feeling that the senses are separated, but clamouring for the same meeting point. This electromagnetic flux is reflected by Brody's image for the re-released CD.

597. CD–ROM cover for
***Yellows*, Photography by**
Akira Gomi, Digitalogue,
Japan 1993
Sound travels as a waveform, not as a collection of tiny-squared particles; in nature, curves are not formed from a series of right angles. The dual and complementary forces that govern human experience cannot be formularised into a binary system without compounding the broad generalisations of the binary. One of its highlighted future applications will be to articulate and effortlessly change the shape of our fantasies. This will give us the impression we are in control.

dilemmas, luckily for us, MUST include a process whereby the change-through-technology to which we have become accustomed is itself questioned.

This can only take place on a personal level. No company is likely to sponsor these deep conversations with our own mental faculties, and as Steiner stresses in *The Language Animal*, not only are we controlled by laws of pattern of which we are largely unconscious, "our skull is like an echo chamber" making the process of deep self-enquiry frightening and unnatural. "It requires a fairly strenuous act of extrapolation to see our primary linguistic dimension, to step momentarily outside our own essential skin."

"Ninety-nine percent of all important evolutionary trends are invisible. Ninety-nine percent are either unapprehended or uncomprehended by society."
R. Buckminster Fuller, *Utopia or Oblivion*, Allen Lane 1969

BEFORE ANY AGE OF IMPROVEMENT, as was proclaimed for the Victorian industrial era, there has to be an age of repair. Maybe this will enable us to enact a series of non-violent revolutions that effectively ambush the technological ambush that lies in wait for us.

The present response to our condition, in keeping with Baudrillard, binary logic, MTV and homeopathy, is epitomised by the Biosphere 2 experiment – the idea that the best way to deal with the greenhouse effect is to live in a greenhouse, in this case an artificial climate in the Arizona desert, three acres of New Age sterility sealed by glass, its nearest town called Oracle. Cut off from the 'real world' for two years, but subject to the continual gaze of sightseers, the eight all-Americans were only able to connect with the rest of the world telectron-

ically. Visiting reporters could interview the Biospherians through closed-circuit TV. "I got the impression that they watch a lot of TV…" wrote one such enquirer, Michael Sorkin; "Biosphere is resonant architecturally because it represents our already daily life *in extremis*."[5]

Other reporters were more interested in whether or not, and if so with whom the eight bionauts had had sex, bringing to mind Yevgeny Zamyatin's *We*, written back in 1920. In this precursor of *Brave New World* and *1984*, "D–503" keeps a diary of his life in a glass-enclosed city, The One State, whose Benefactor appoints Sexual Days upon which the inhabitants can obtain one hour of privacy in exchange for a strictly rationed "pink ticket". This fiction, on its publication an attack against Stalinism, will soon be virtual fact in the world of computerised sex, known as "Teledildonics". Biosphere's descent into an ecological theme park has since resulted in the mass resignation of its scientific management committee.[6]

There is a way out of all this, the same as always, back to the human sphere. The digital system takes the flowing forms of analogue processes and sends all information as a concentrated burst of two polar opposites. The finished article is accepted as a given. We need to create a new language for this mode of communication, not take it manufactured. Digital technology should be taken as a template and used a springboard to develop new forms of communication, based on humanism not mechanisation.

1. Alain Finkielkraut, *The Undoing of Thought*, The Claridge Press 1988. **2.** BBC2 *Newsnight*, 24 Sept. 1992. **3.** *Wired*, Sept./Oct. 1993 and Feb. 1994. As McLuhan advised, "Any situation you go into deeply enough reverses." **4.** Baudrillard first published the article in French *Libération* (later translated and published in the *Guardian*, Feb. 1991). *La Guerre du Golfe n'a pas eu lieu* was published by Gallimard, Paris 1991. **5.** *I.D.* magazine, Sept/Oct 1993. **6.** The *Guardian*, 4 April 1994.

BIBLIOGRAPHY + ACKNOWLEDGMENTS

In addition to the works mentioned in the text, the following titles, listed in alphabetical order, were building blocks to this book. All are published in Britain, except where indicated.

The Alphabet – A Key to the History of Mankind,
    David Diringer, Hutchinson's 1948
Against Interpretation, Susan Sontag, André Deutsch 1987
The Art of War, Sun Tzu, Shambhala 1991
The Book Before Printing, David Diringer, Dover Publications 1982
The Codebreakers, David Khan, Sphere Books 1973
Critique of Cynical Reason, Peter Sloterdijk, Verso 1988
Crowds and Power, Elias Canetti, Peregrine 1962
Electric Language: A Philosophical Study of Word Processing,
    Michael Heim, Yale University Press 1987
The Film Sense, S. Eisenstein, Faber & Faber 1944
The Gutenberg Galaxy, Marshall McLuhan, Routledge 1962
Illuminations, Walter Benjamin, Harcourt Brace & World (NY) 1968
Invisible Cities, Italo Calvino, Picador 1972
La Jetée, Chris Marker, Zone 1993
The Media Lab, Stuart Brand, Penguin 1987
The Medieval Machine, Jean Gimpel, Victor Gollancz Ltd. 1976
Not I, Samuel Beckett, Faber & Faber 1973
The Postmodern Explained to Children, Jean-François Lyotard,
    Turnaround 1992
Pure War, P. Virilio & S. Lotringer, Semiotext[e] (NY) 1983
On Difficulty, George Steiner, OUP 1978
Orality & Literacy – The Technologizing of the Word,
    Walter J. Ong, Methuen & Co. Ltd. 1982
Steps to an Ecology of Mind, Gregory Bateson, Ballantine (NY) 1972
The Third Mind, William S. Burroughs & Brion Gysin, John Calder 1979
Alan Turing: The Enigma of Intelligence, Andrew Hodges, Counterpoint 1985
Unbounding the Future – The Nanotechnology Revolution,
    K. Eric Drexler & Chris Peterson with Gayle Pergamit, Quill (NY) 1991
War and Cinema, Paul Virilio, Verso 1989
War in the Age of Intelligent Machines, Manuel de Landa, Zone 1992

Magazines: *International Design*, *New Scientist* and *Wired*

We would like to thank all those at the Neville Brody Studio: Fwa Richards, Simon Staines, John Critchley, Giles Dunn, Simon Emery, Ian Wright and Linda Sinfield; and all those who have worked with us in the past: Dawn Clenton, Tony Cooper, Jon Crossland, David Davies, Pat Glover, Mark Mattock, Yuki Miyake, Nana Shiomi, Tim Soar, Ian Swift and Cornel Windlin. Thanks to all who have supported us over the past six years: Mark Adams; Ron Arad; David Berlow; Phil Bicker; Jean-François Bizot; Roger Black; Lo Breier; Julian Broad; Maureen, Maurice, Kay, Lea and Trevor Brody; Noemi Campano; Ed Cleary; Gunther Coenen; Mike Collins; Dave Crow; Hubert Schillhuber, Oliver Kartak and all at DMC in Vienna; Robin Derrick; Elisabeth Djian; Dorothy and Ian; Paul Elliman; Naomi Enami; Erik and Joan Spiekermann, Beth, Jürgen, Karen, Andreas and all at FSI in Berlin; Anthony Fawcett and Jane Withers; Catherine Gaitte; Malcolm Garrett; Grant Gilbert; Akira Gomi; Alan Greenberg; Jo Hagen; Garth Hall; Janice Hart; Russell Haswell; Paul Hefting; Shizuo Ishii; Harald Jähner; Stuart Jensen; Tobias Frere Jones; Tibor Kalman; Laurence King; Rudi Klausnitzer; Martin Kohlbauer; Peter Kruder; Debbie and Stephen at Kudos Productions; Manfred Langlotz; Olivier Maupas; Jean-Baptiste Mondino; Yannick Morisot; Garry Mouat; Gerd Bacher and all at ORF; Mik Faherty and Ian Greatorex at Orange; all at Parco Co. Ltd. and Planet Plan in Tokyo; Gustav Peichl, Markus Peichl; Paul Rambali; David Rosen; all at the Schauspielhaus in Hamburg; Neil Spencer; Swim; Fellipe Taborda; Jürgen Teller; Alastair Thain; .Too Corporation in Tokyo; Mike Harding, Andrew McKenzie and Panni Charrington at *Touch*; James Truman; Chu Uroz; Nick Logan and all at Wagadon; Bruce, Colin and Graham of Wire; Malcolm and Junko Wong; the Wozencroft family; thanks to everyone who has helped in one way or another with the realisation of this book, a list too numerous to include here. Lyric reproduction of "40 Versions" by kind permission of Carlin Music Corporation. Finally, thanks to Clarissa Cairns, Chris Ferguson and Thomas Neurath at Thames and Hudson.

TECHNICAL

This book was created on an Apple Macintosh Quadra 840AV with a 1Gb internal hard disk and 64Mb RAM, using a Hitachi 21-inch colour monitor, 1gb Wave external hard disk, Apple 300 CD-ROM, 44Mb SyQuest and 128Mb D2 Optical drives. The final pages were created in Quark XPress 3.2, importing Aldus FreeHand and Adobe Photoshop documents. Typefaces used are *FF Blur Bold* and *Light* for headings, *Franklin Gothic Book* and *Italic* in 8.25/10.25 point for main text, incorporating 7/8 point *Franklin Gothic Demi* and *Book* for captions. The book is a 100% digital production from studio to printing press.

The text for the book was planned out on paper, written on a Macintosh Powerbook Duo 8/120 with Duo MiniDock and 14-inch Apple Colour Monitor using QuarkXpress 3.1 and 3.2, printed out and checked on an Apple LaserWriter NT before being cut and pasted into the master Quark documents stored on the Quadra 840AV.

Two additional Quadra 840AVs with the same storage and processing power were used by Orange to prepare the files for film output. The Quadras were linked to Eizo F760i–W 24-bit 21-inch colour monitors, D2 600Mb and 128Mb Optical drives, and 88Mb SyQuests. Quark XPress, Aldus FreeHand, Adobe Photoshop and Adobe Illustrator were used to hand-trap, retouch, enhance, spread and choke the master documents which were then proofed on an Iris SmartJet 4012, calibrated to wet-proof output with Orange's own colour tables.

The film was output on a Scitex Dolev 800 A1 plus ImageSetter, imposed 8-up using Geometric screening (part of Scitex's Class Screening technology) and Kodak Scanner 2000 SHN film.

The Neville Brody Studio uses the following computer equipment: Macintosh Quadra 900, 200Mb HD with 64mb RAM, Sony 19-inch colour monitor, SyQuest and DAC Datapack Optical drives; two Macintosh IICI's, both 80Mb HD with 8Mb RAM, one using an 18-inch black-and-white Radius monitor, the other an Apple 13-inch colour monitor, both using Radius Rocket accelerators and SyQuest drives; Macintosh II (the studio's original colour machine), upgraded from its original 4/40 capacity to 240Mb HD with 8Mb RAM, 13-inch Apple colour monitor, Radius Rocket accelerator and Radius monitor card. For administrative work, the studio uses a Macintosh II 8/40 with Radius Rocket, Powerbook 170 4/40, and a Macintosh SE 2/20. Brody owns a Powerbook Duo 230 8/120 for overseas work, etc.

There are two colour scanners at the studio, a Microtek Scanmaker 2 and an Agfa–Gevaert Focus Colour Plus. The original black-and-white Apple Scanner still works. Two Apple LaserWriter II's are networked to each computer – a Canon BJC 820 A3 Colour Jet Printer is also used. The multifunctional Canon Laser Copier Scanner NP 9030 is unfortunately beyond repair and only one photocopier is left, an A3 black-and-white Canon NP 1215. A Konica 500 fax machine and modem link complete the set up. The PMT machine, an Agfa–Gevaert Repromaster 310, for the moment stands idle.

For the past five years, the studio has worked mainly with Quark XPress, Aldus FreeHand and Adobe Photoshop software applications. Altsys Fontographer and Letraset FontStudio are used for font design, and Macromind Director for animation and presentations. LetraStudio, ImageStudio and MacPaint have been used at various times in the past. Macwrite and Word are needed rarely these days. Other key software used by the studio has included Adobe Type Manager, Digital Darkroom, Pixel Paint, Ready Set Go, Norton Utilities, Studio 8, DiskDoubler, CopyDoubler, Silver Lining, Cachet, JAG, Crystal Quest, Monkey Island, Spectre, Maelstrom, Tetris, Tristan, Suitcase, SAM Intercept, Adobe Premiere, KidPix, Adobe Dimensions, Sound Extractor and Excel.

Of the thousands of fonts available, aside from self-designed typefaces, the studio has focused the great majority of its work on these few families – *Franklin*, *Akzidenz*, *Helvetica*, *Meta*, *Bodoni*, and *Garamond*.

The first computer the studio bought in 1988, a black-and-white Macintosh SE 2/20, is currently under repair.